CATALYST™
PRIME

NOBLE™

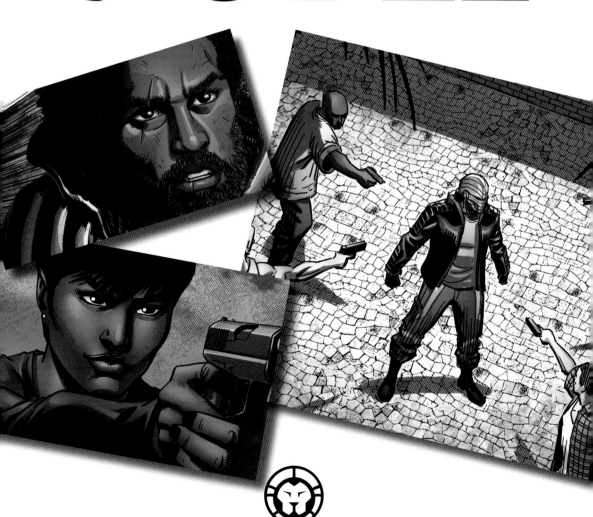

LION™
FORGE

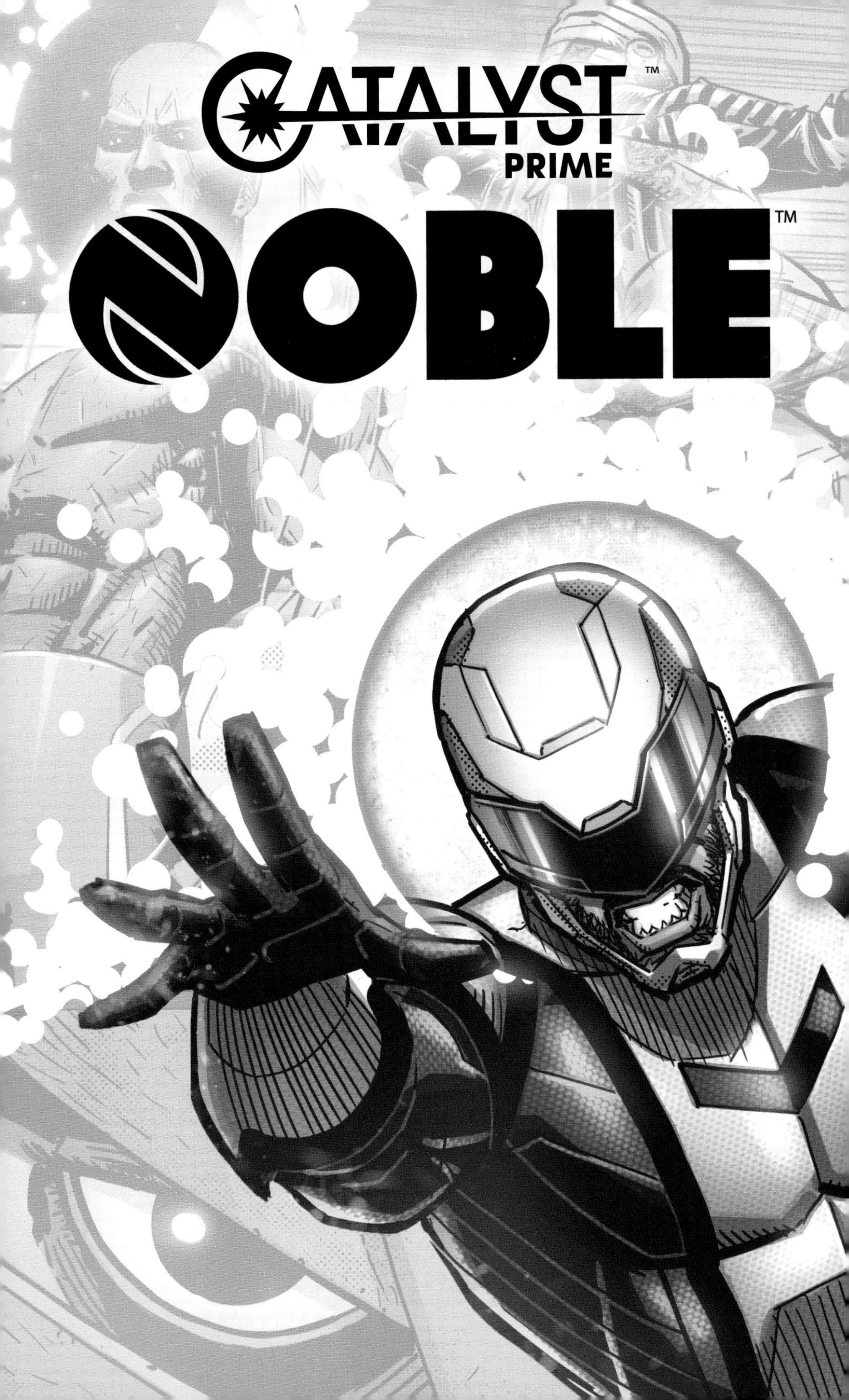
CATALYST™
PRIME
NOBLE™

"GOD SHOTS"

Written by BRANDON THOMAS
Illustrated by ROGER ROBINSON,
JAMAL IGLE, and ROBIN RIGGS
Lettered by SAIDA TEMOFONTE
Colored by JUAN FERNANDEZ and SOTOCOLOR

"THE EVENT"

Written by PRIEST and JOSEPH PHILLIP ILLIDGE
Illustrated by MARCO TURINI and WILL ROSADO
Lettered by ANDWORLD DESIGN
Colored by JESSICA KHOLINNE

JOSEPH ILLIDGE - Senior Editor

DESIREE RODRIGUEZ - Editorial Assistant

Cover by
ROGER ROBINSON and JUAN FERNANDEZ
Cover Design by
SMOLHAUS DESIGN and ASSOCIATES
Interior design by
ANDWORLD DESIGN

LION FORGE

Publisher's Cataloging-In-Publication Data

(Prepared by The Donohue Group, Inc.)

Names: Illidge, Joseph P., editor. | Rodriguez, Desiree, editor. | AndWorld Design (Firm), designer, letterer.

Title: Noble. Vol. 1 / Joseph Illidge - Senior Editor, Desiree Rodriguez - Editorial Assistant, interior design by AndWorld Design.

Other Titles: Catalyst Prime

Description: [St. Louis, Missouri] : The Lion Forge, LLC, 2017. | "Portions of this book were previously published in Noble, Vol. 1, Issues 1-4 and FCBD 2017 Catalyst Prime: The Event." | Summary: "Astronaut David Powell helped save the Earth from an approaching asteroid. In the resulting explosion, David gained superhuman telekinetic powers but lost his memories. Now back on Earth, David is on the run from the Foresight Corporation, using his new powers to stay alive long enough to regain his memories, family, and identity."-- Provided by publisher.

Identifiers: ISBN 978-1-941302-36-1 | ISBN 978-1-5493-0146-9 (ebook)

Subjects: LCSH: Astronauts--Comic books, strips, etc. | Amnesia--Comic books, strips, etc. | Psychokinesis--Comic books, strips, etc. | Identity (Psychology)--Comic books, strips, etc. | LCGFT: Graphic novels.

Classification: LCC PN6728 .N63 2017 (print) | LCC PN6728 (ebook) | DDC 741.5973--dc23

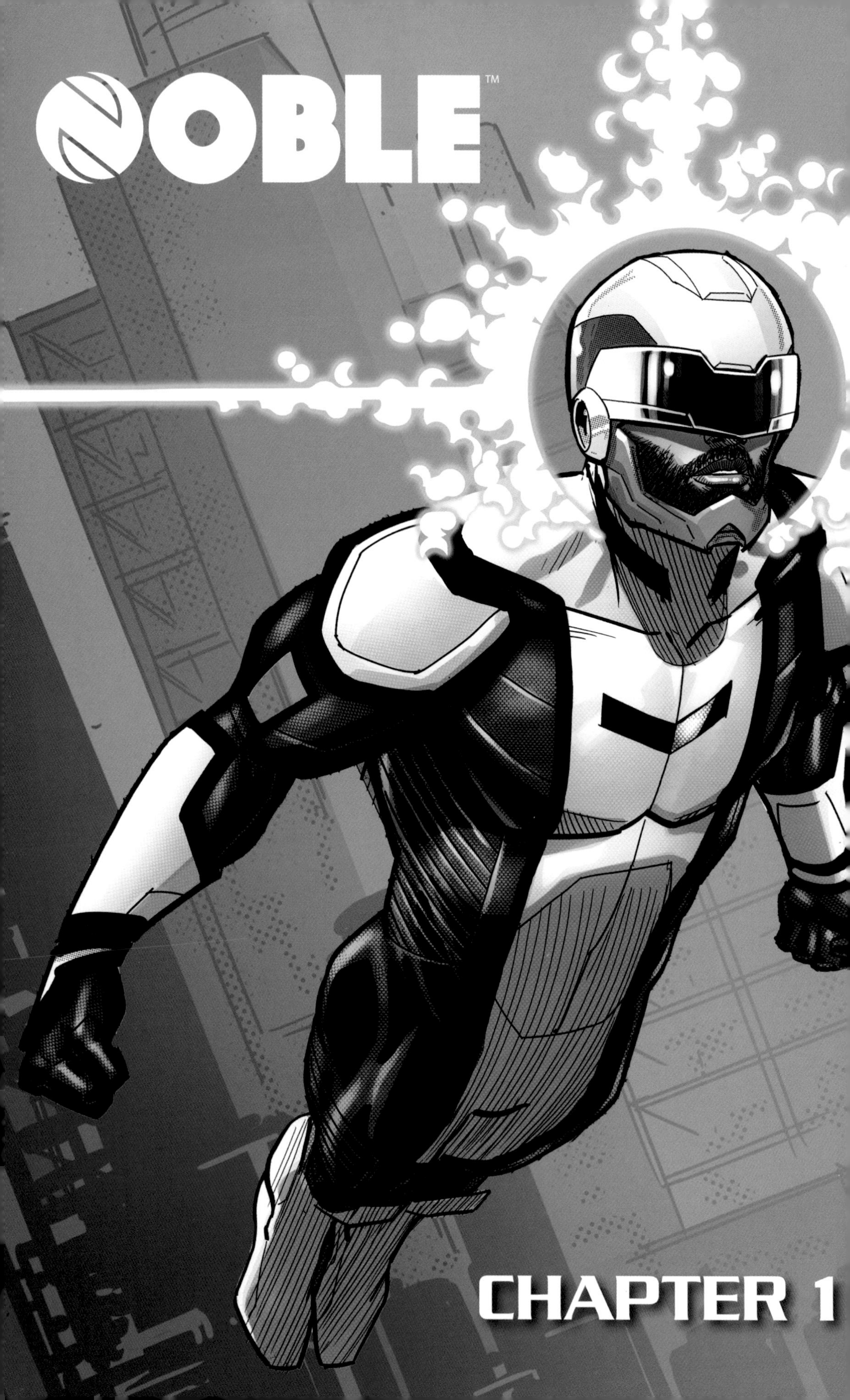
NOBLE™
CHAPTER 1

ASTRID ALLEN-POWELL
FORESIGHT INDUSTRIES AEROSPACE INITIATIVE
(HOUSTON, TEXAS)

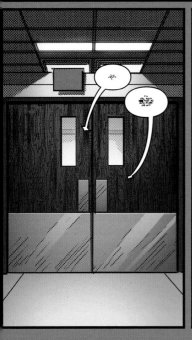

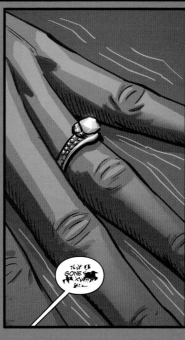

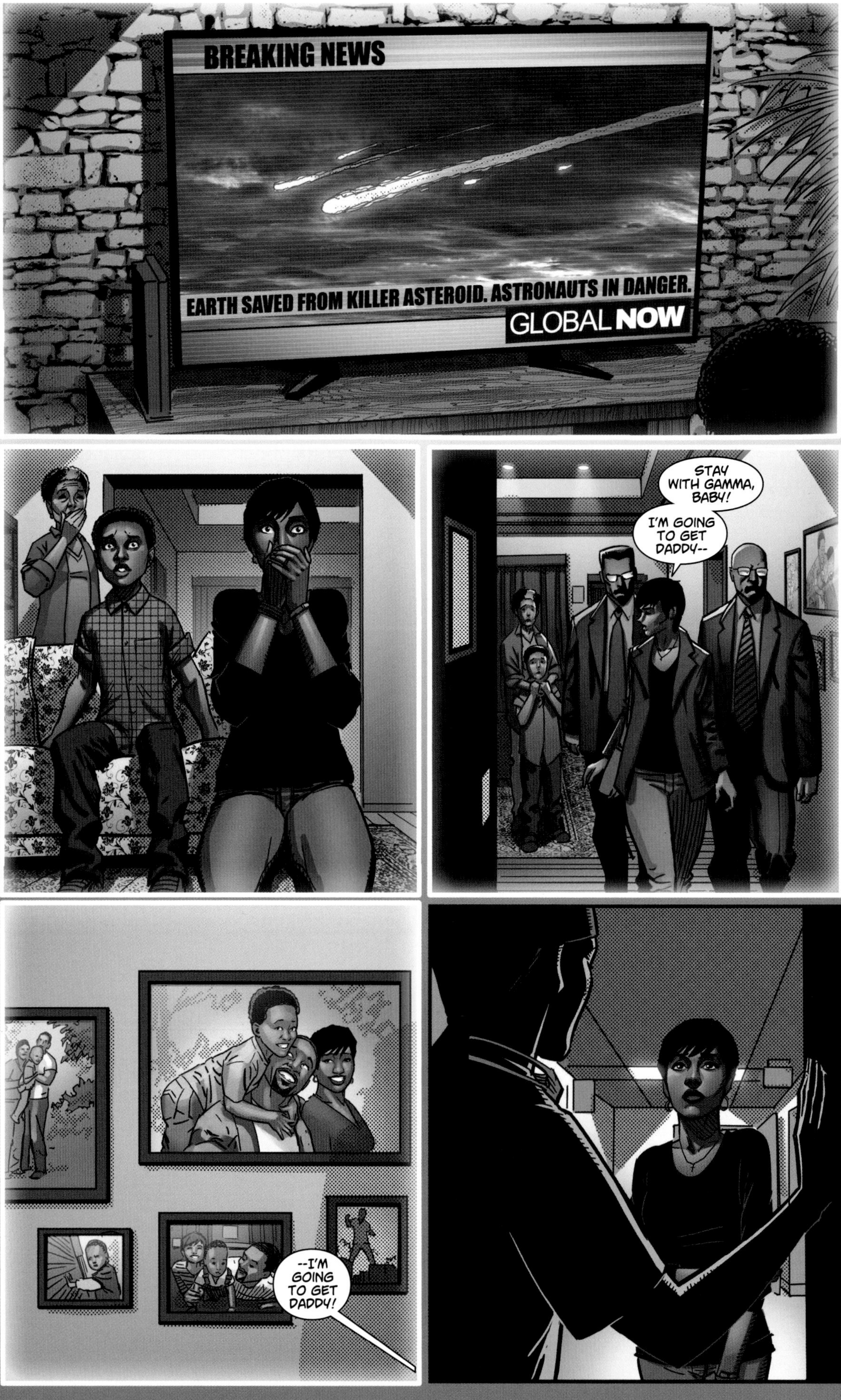
BREAKING NEWS
EARTH SAVED FROM KILLER ASTEROID. ASTRONAUTS IN DANGER.
GLOBAL NOW
STAY WITH GAMMA, BABY!
I'M GOING TO GET DADDY--
--I'M GOING TO GET DADDY!

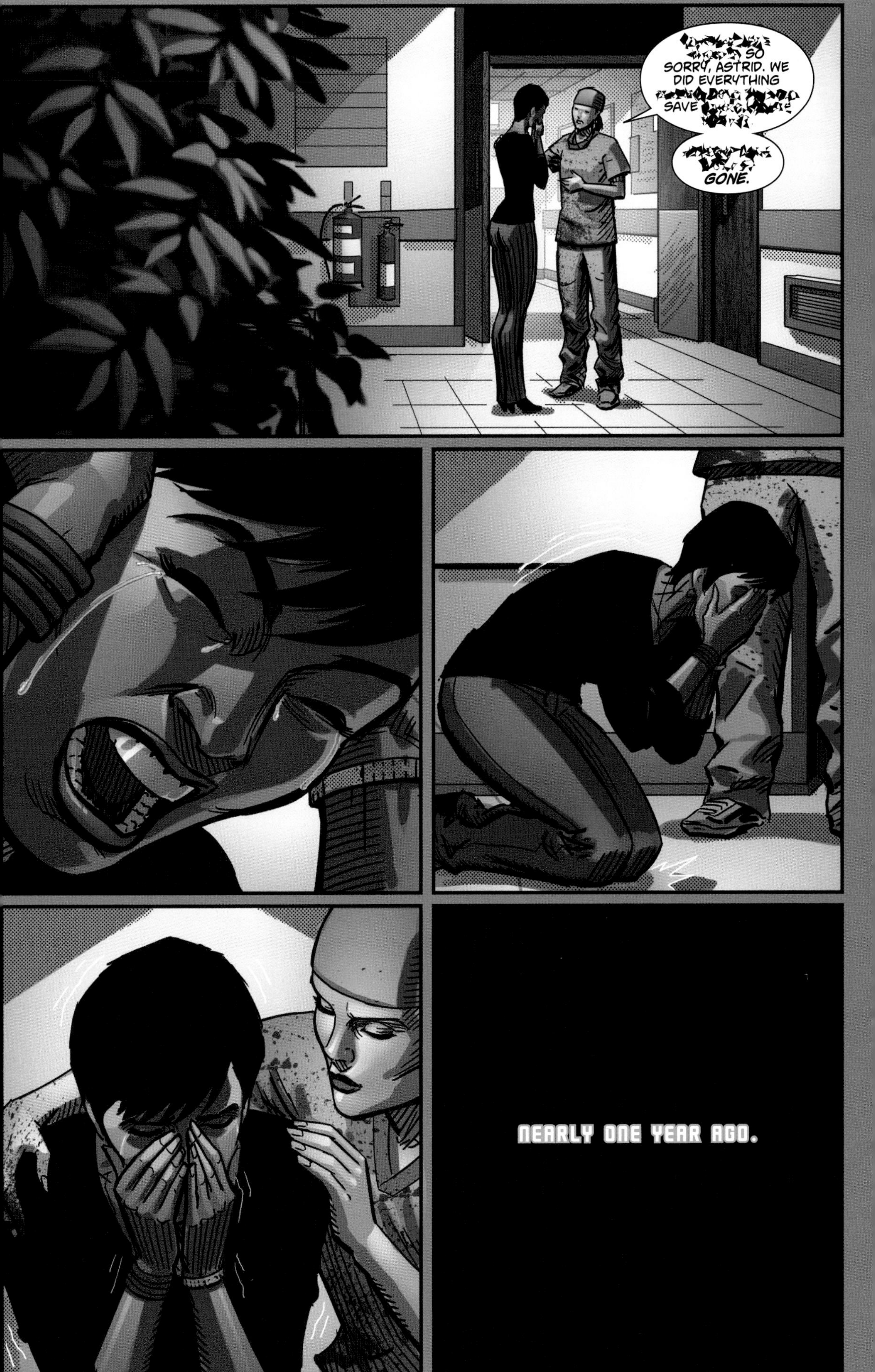
SO SORRY, ASTRID. WE DID EVERYTHING
SAVE
GONE.
NEARLY ONE YEAR AGO.

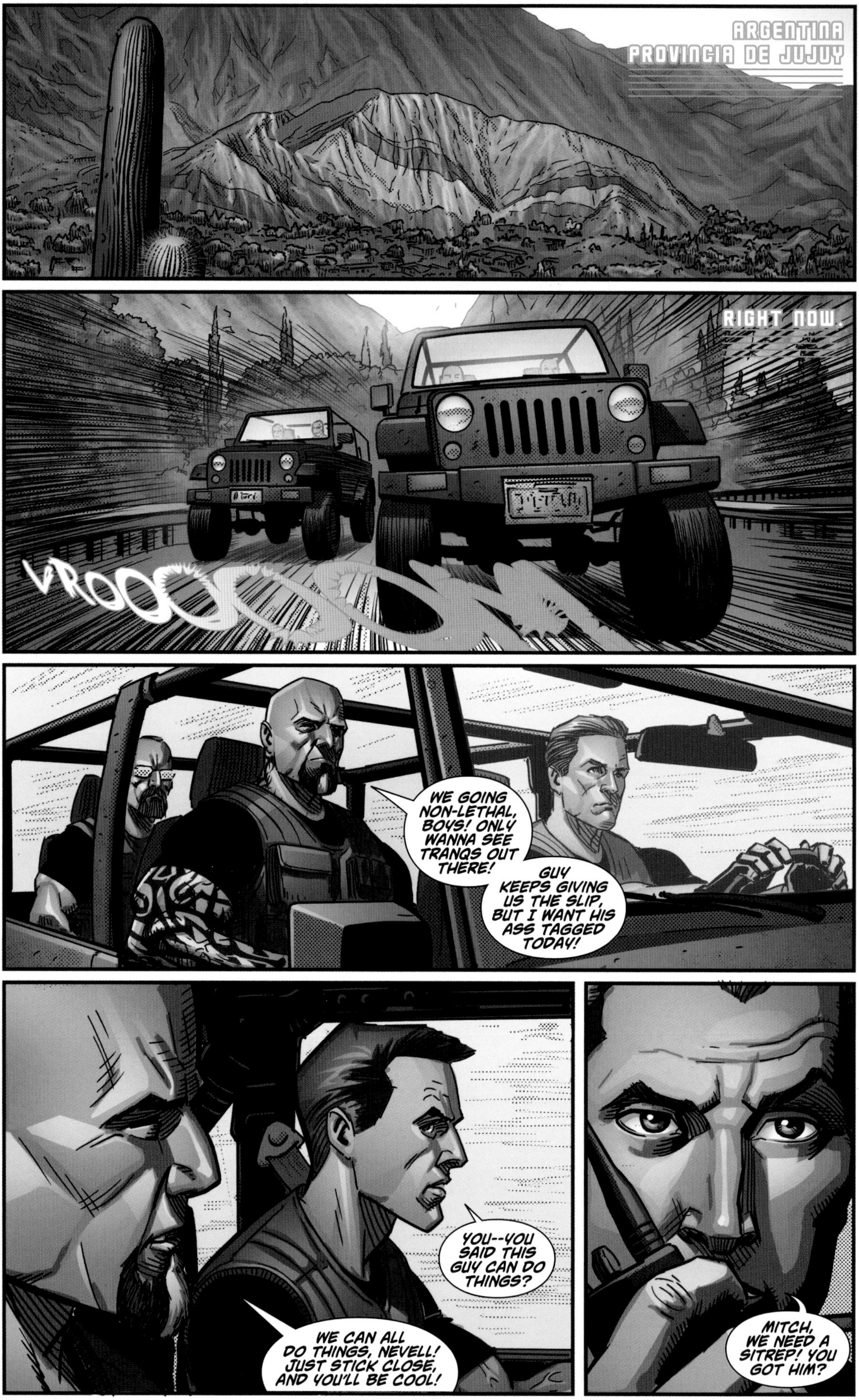
ARGENTINA
PROVINCIA DE JUJUY
RIGHT NOW.
VROOOOOOM
WE GOING NON-LETHAL, BOYS! ONLY WANNA SEE TRANQS OUT THERE!
GUY KEEPS GIVING US THE SLIP, BUT I WANT HIS ASS TAGGED TODAY!
YOU--YOU SAID THIS GUY CAN DO THINGS?
WE CAN ALL DO THINGS, NEVELL! JUST STICK CLOSE, AND YOU'LL BE COOL!
MITCH, WE NEED A SITREP! YOU GOT HIM?

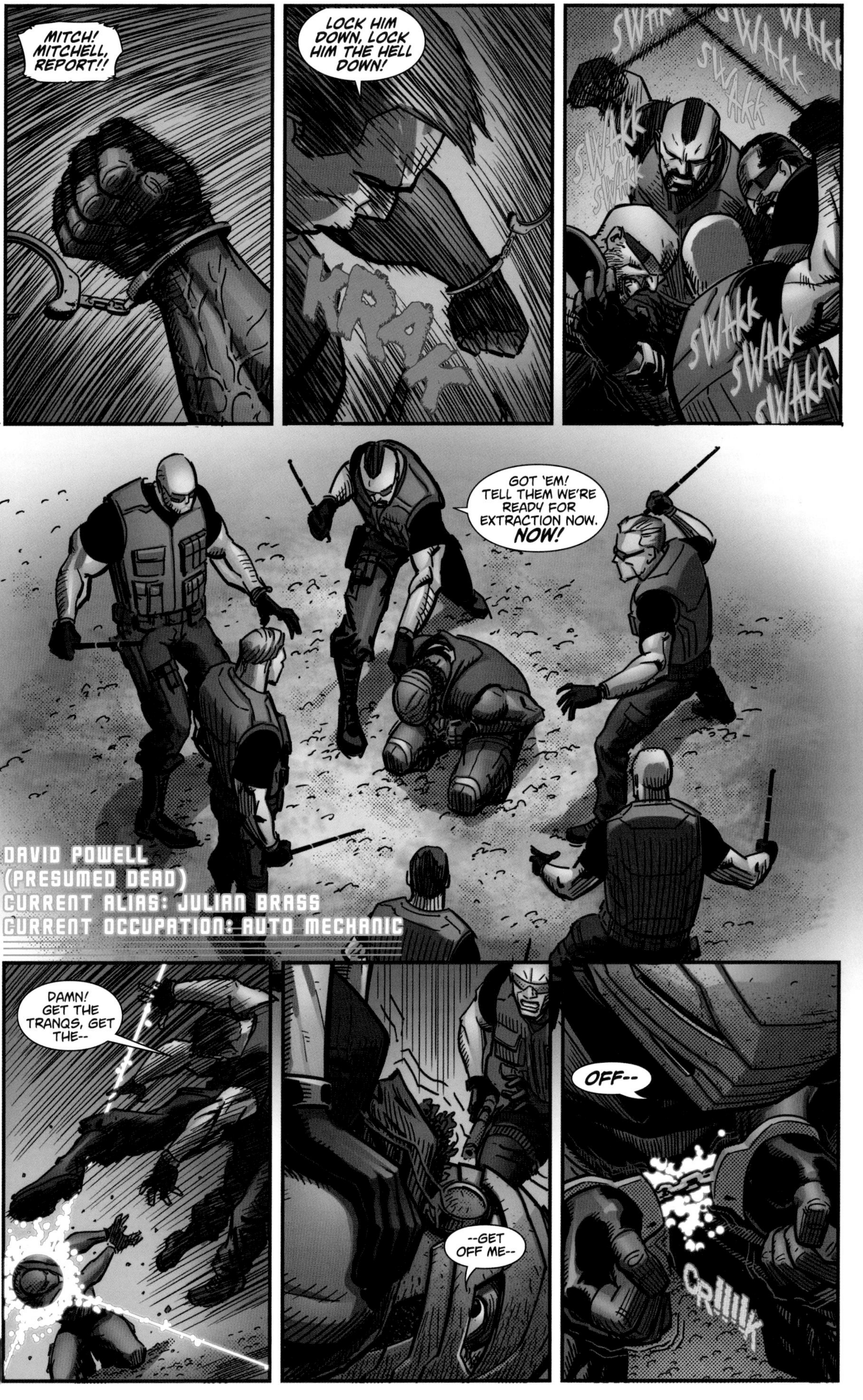

MITCH! MITCHELL, REPORT!!
LOCK HIM DOWN, LOCK HIM THE HELL DOWN!
KRAK
SWAKK SWAKK SWAKK
SWAKK SWAKK SWAKK
GOT 'EM! TELL THEM WE'RE READY FOR EXTRACTION NOW. NOW!
DAVID POWELL
(PRESUMED DEAD)
CURRENT ALIAS: JULIAN BRASS
CURRENT OCCUPATION: AUTO MECHANIC
DAMN! GET THE TRANQS, GET THE--
--GET OFF ME--
OFF--
CR!!!!K

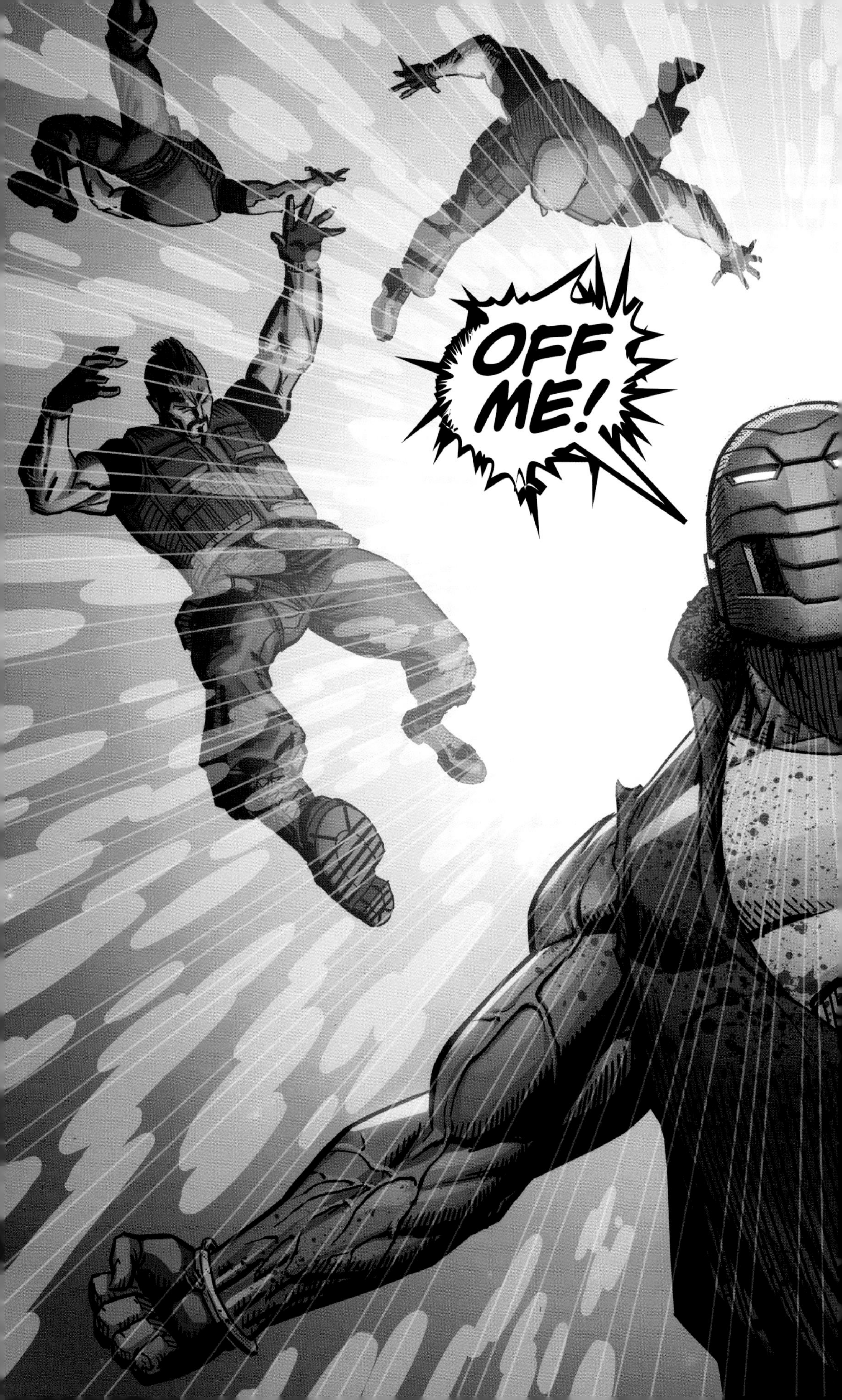
OFF ME!

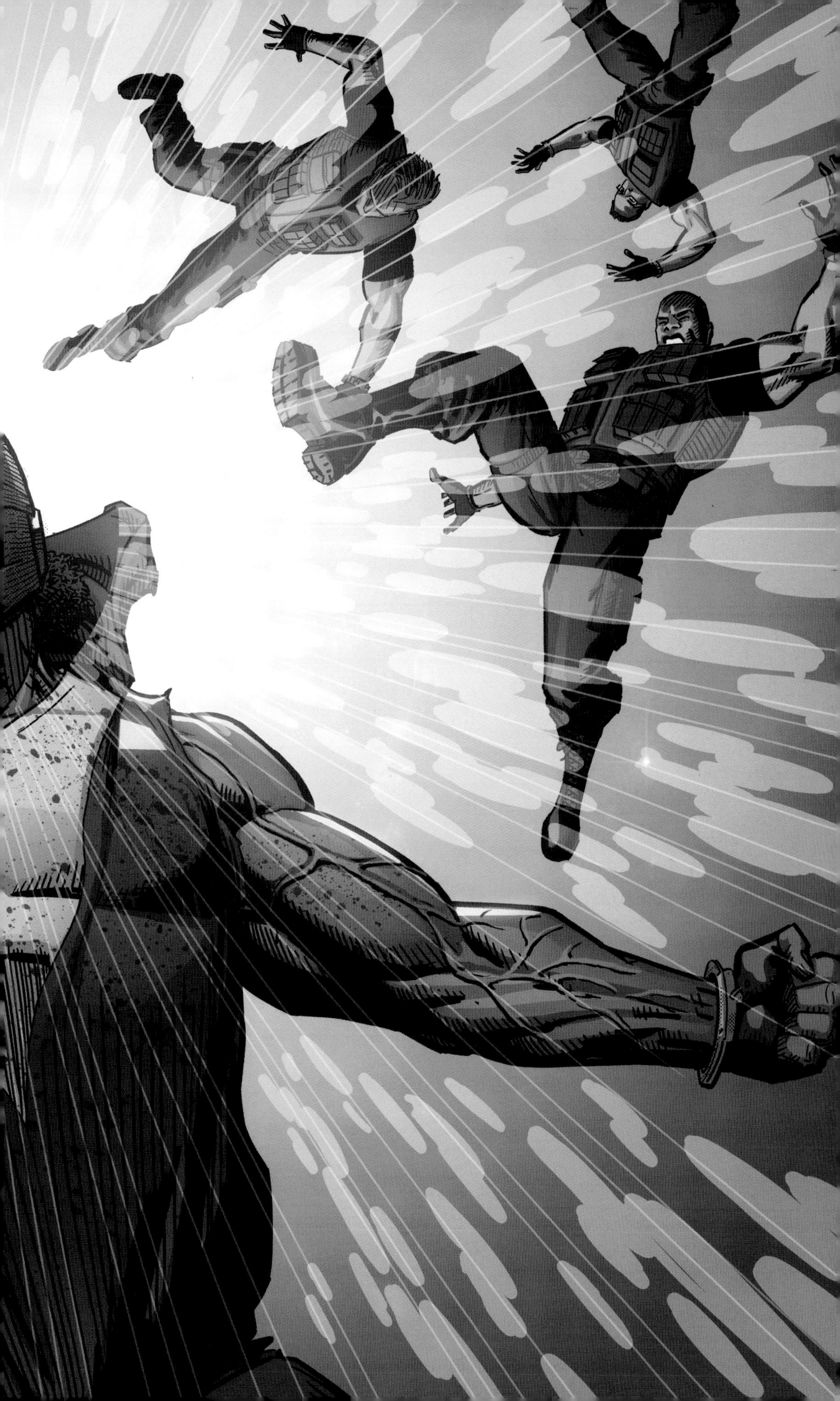

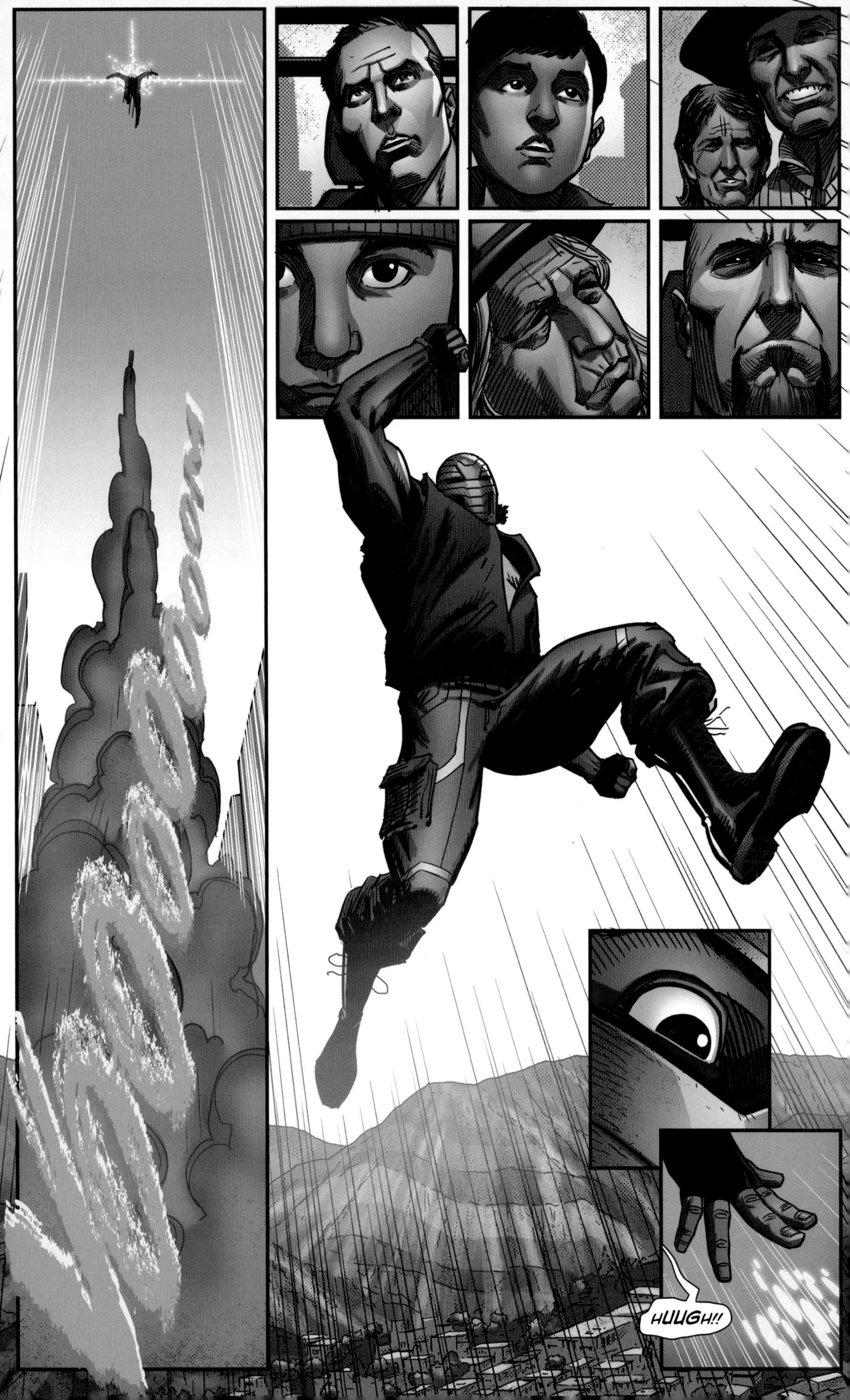
HUUGH!!

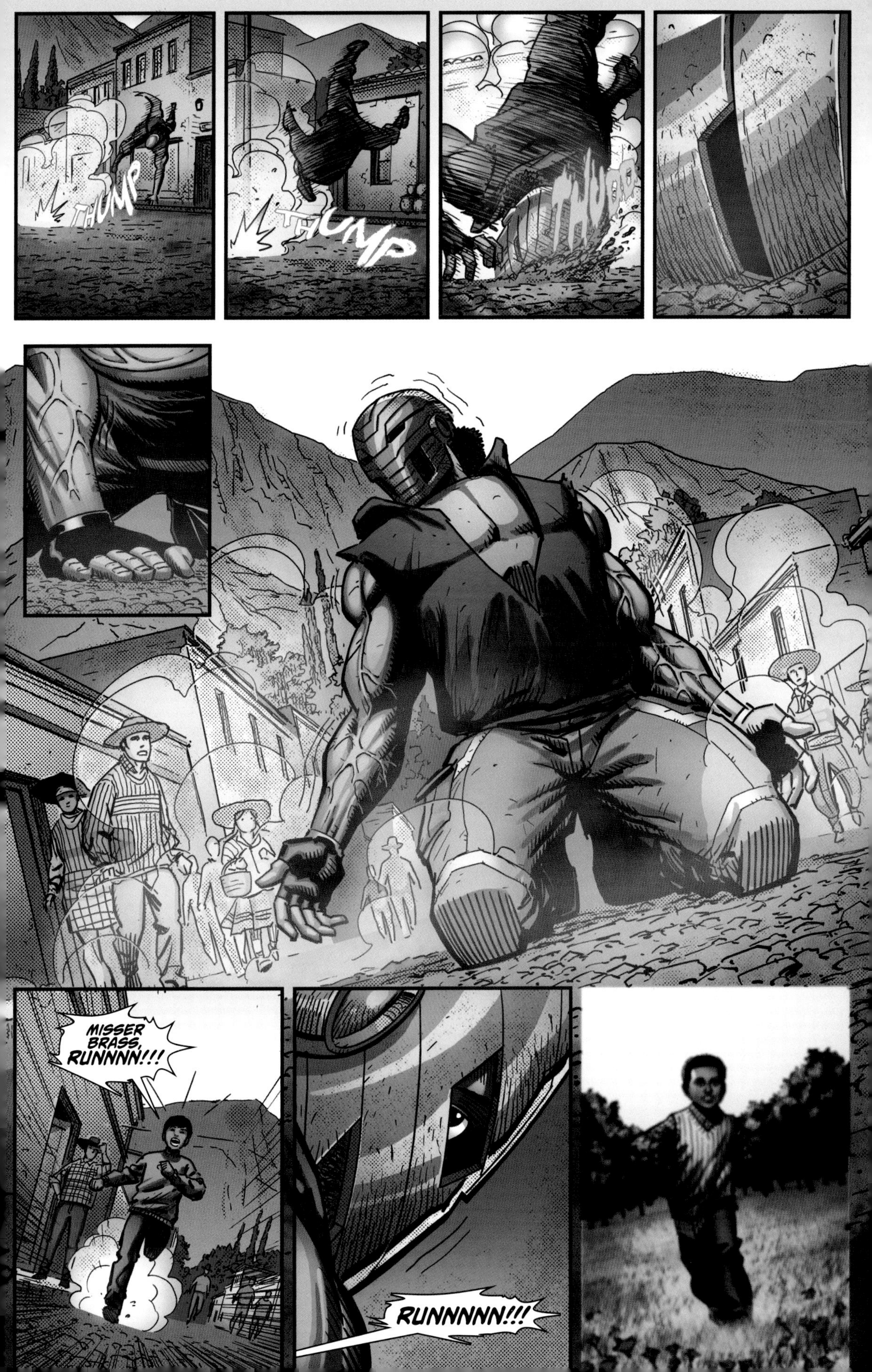
THUMP
THUMP
THUDD
MISSER BRASS, RUNNNN!!!
RUNNNNN!!!

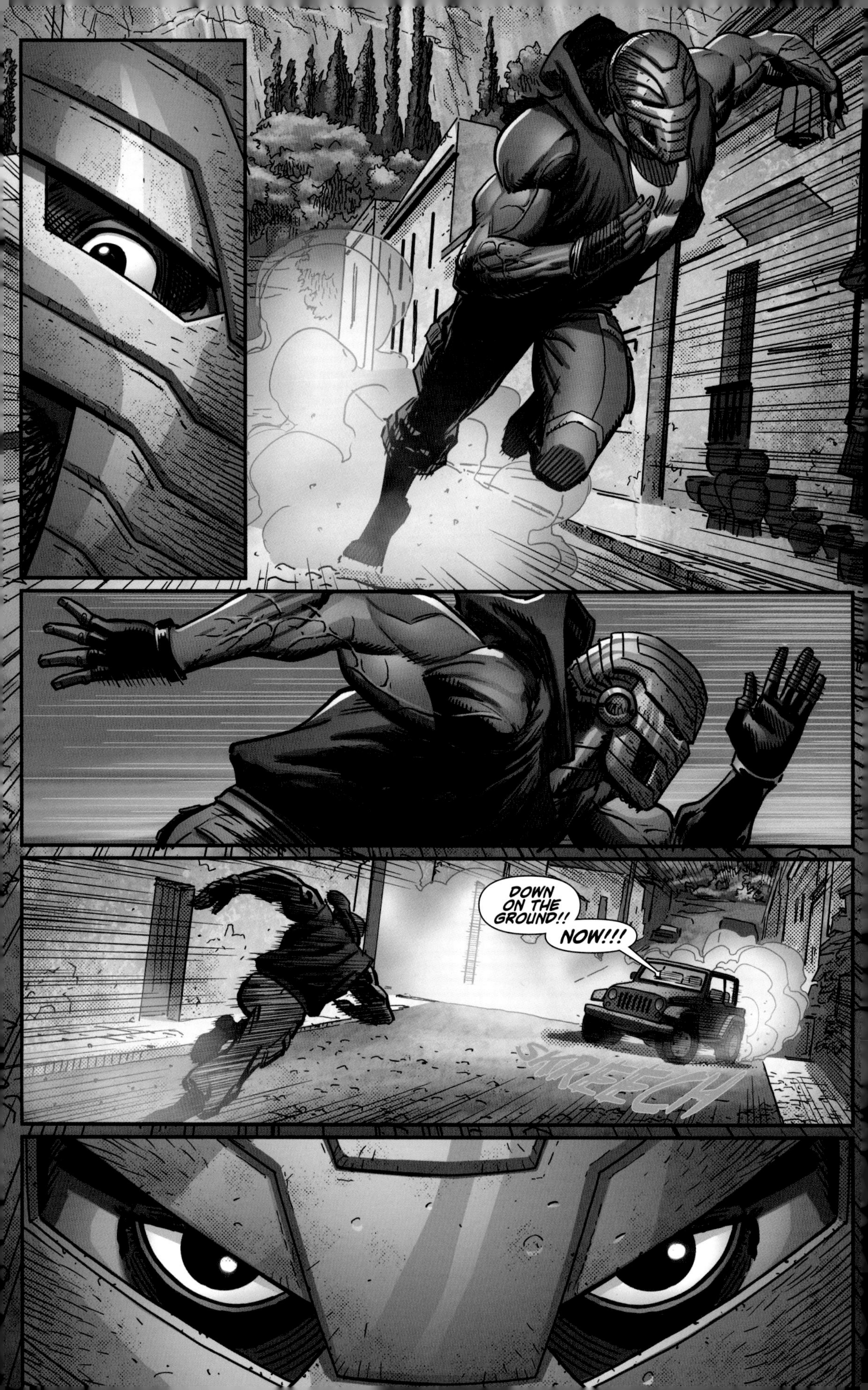
DOWN ON THE GROUND!!
NOW!!!
SKREEECH

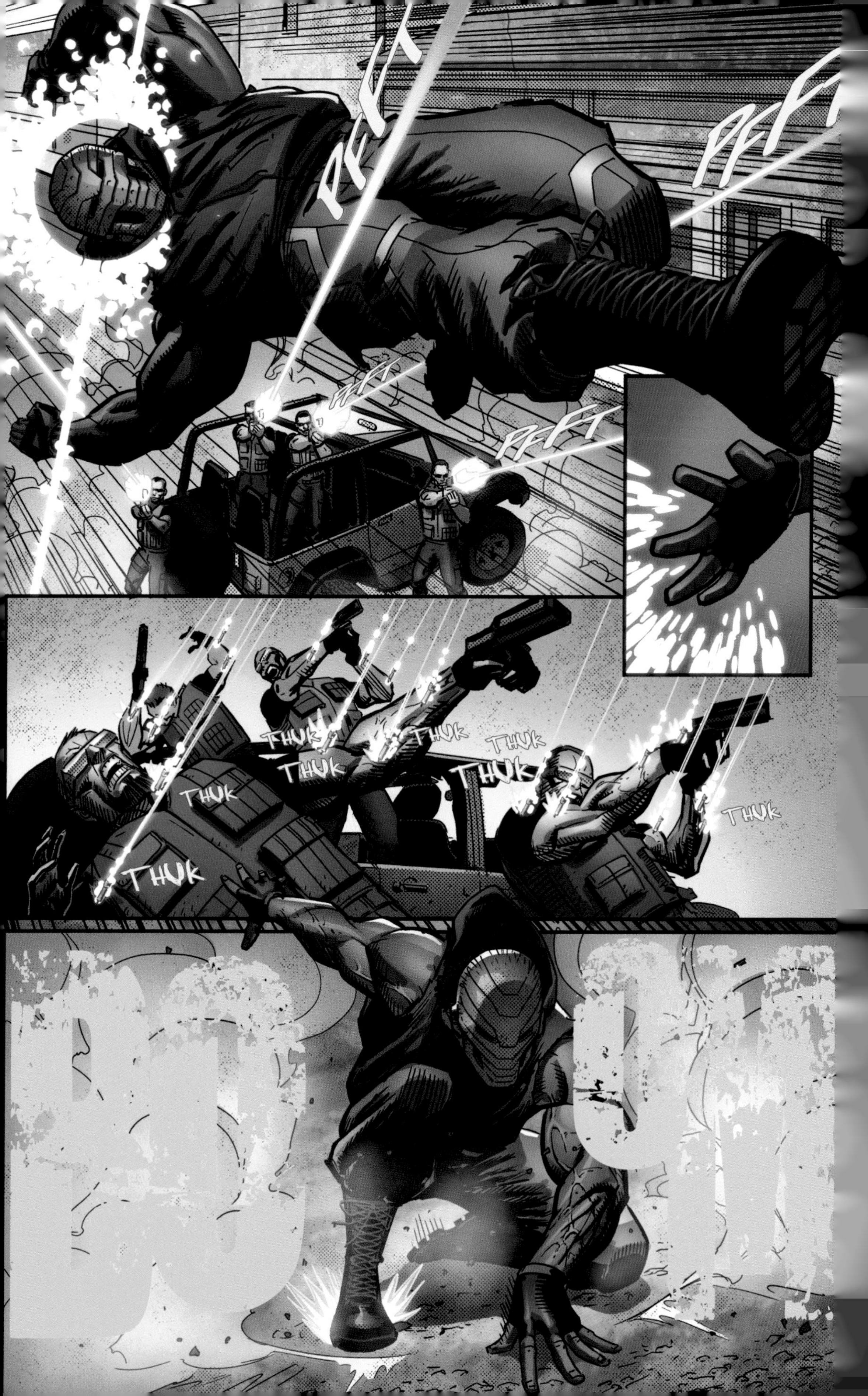
PFFT
PFFT
PFFT
PFFT
THUK
THUK
THUK
THUK
THUK
THUK
THUK
THUK

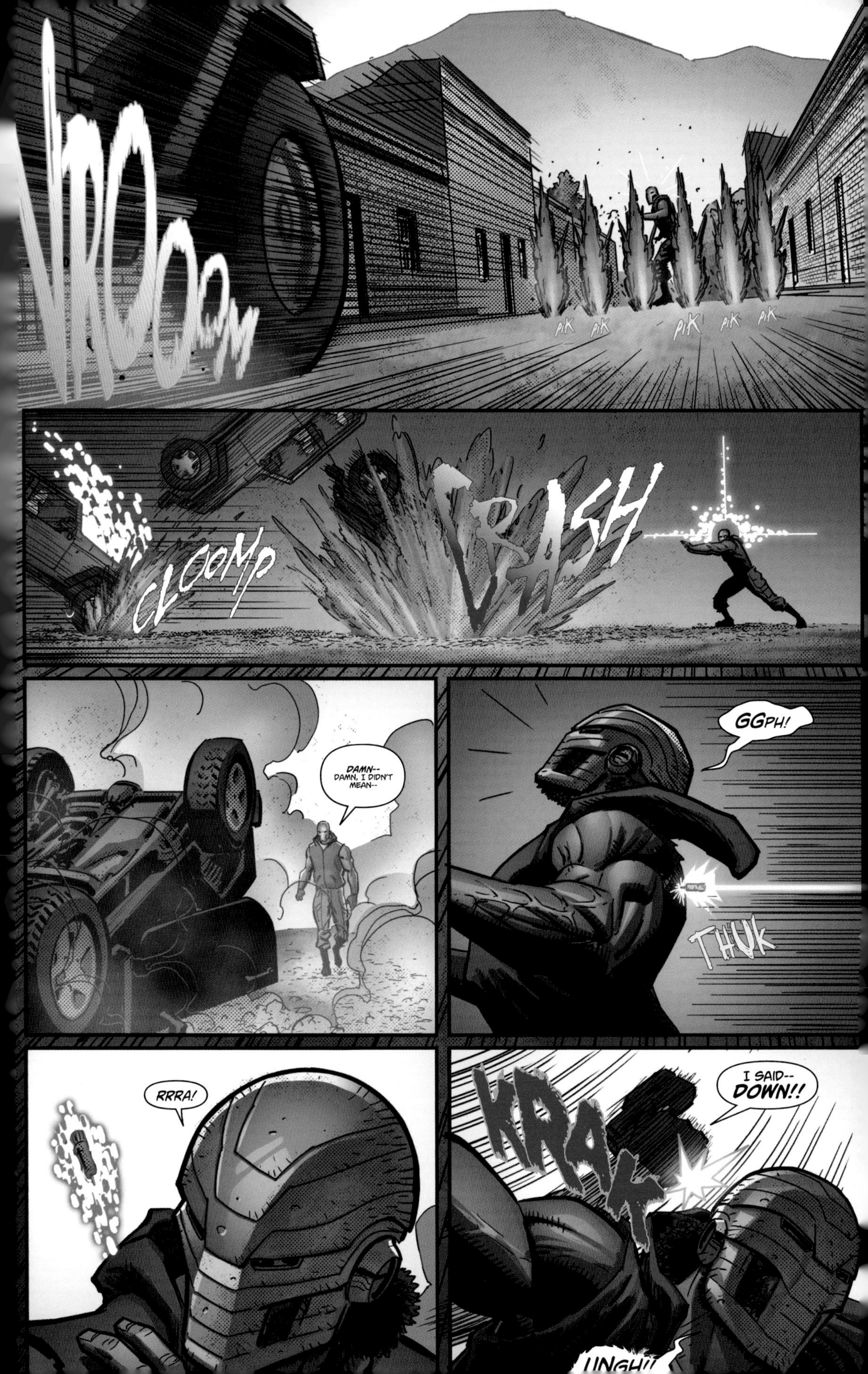
VROOOOOM
PiK
PiK
PiK
PiK
PiK
CLOOMP
CRASH
DAMN-- DAMN, I DIDN'T MEAN--
GGPH!
THUK
RRRA!
KRAK
I SAID-- DOWN!!
UNGH!!

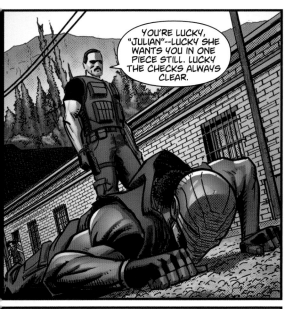

YOU'RE LUCKY, "JULIAN"--LUCKY SHE WANTS YOU IN ONE PIECE STILL. LUCKY THE CHECKS ALWAYS CLEAR.

FOR WHAT'S IT'S WORTH, MAN? I GOT A WIFE, THREE KIDS, AND TWO GOLDENS AT HOME THAT OWE IT ALL TO YOU AND YOUR CREW--

--SO THANK YOU. I REALLY MEAN THAT.

PFFT

GUUH!

KLUDD

UNNFF!

GUNNFF!!!

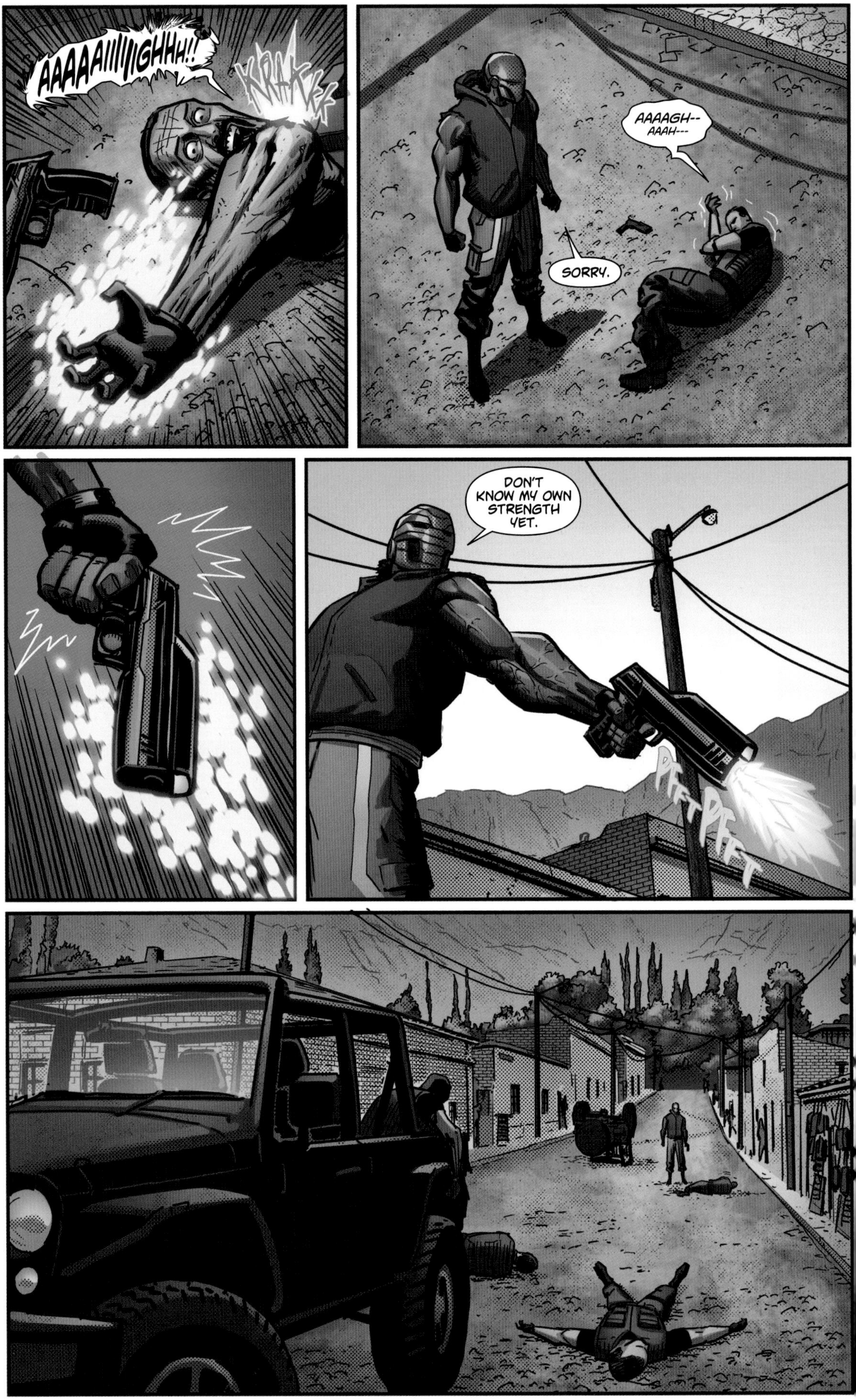
AAAAAIIIIIIGHHH!!
KRAKK
AAAAGH--
AAAH---
SORRY.
DON'T KNOW MY OWN STRENGTH YET.
PFFT PFFT PFFT

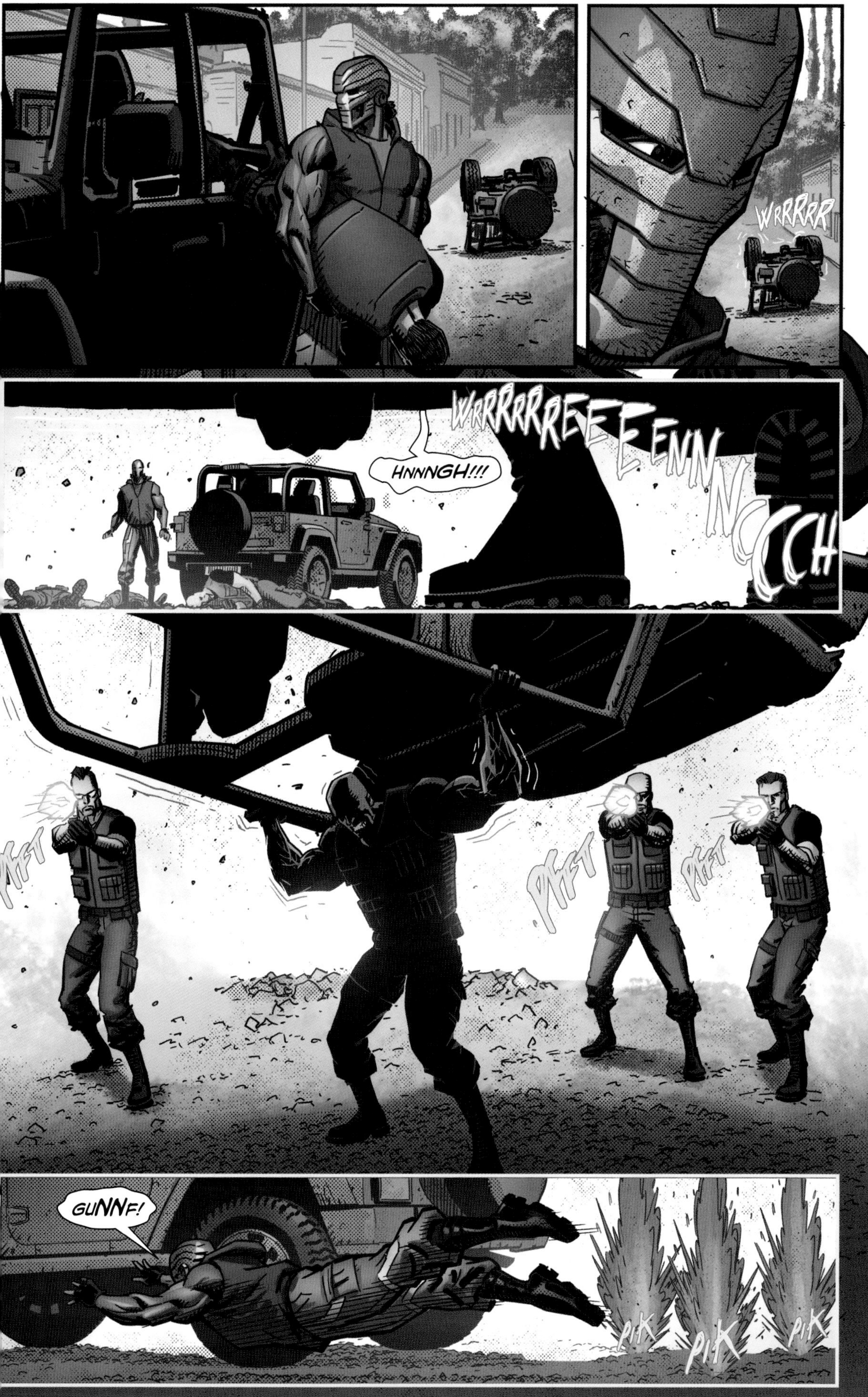
WRRRRR
HNNNGH!!!
WRRRRRREEEENNNCCCH
PFFFT
PFFFT
PFFFT
GUNNF!
PIK
PIK
PIK

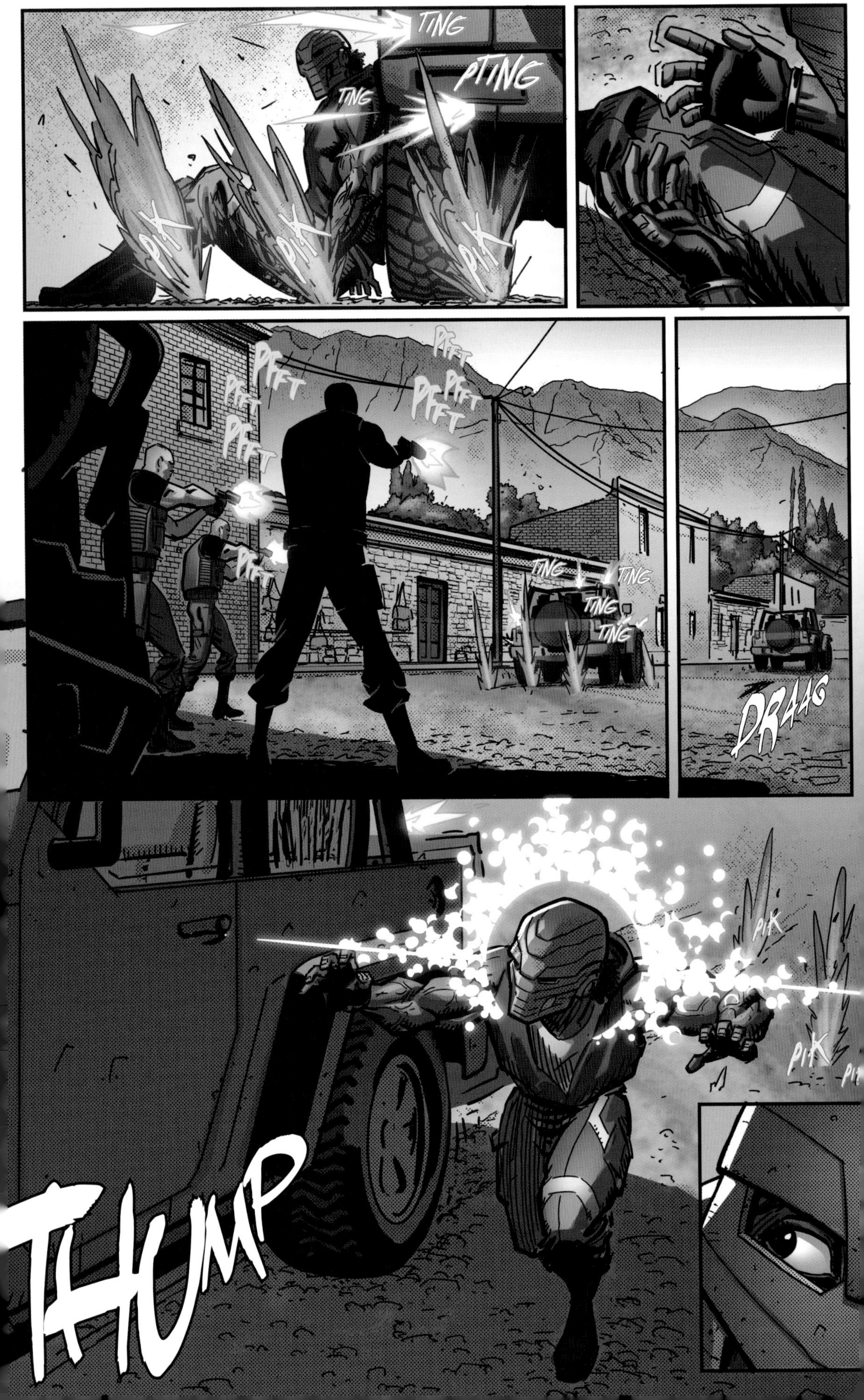
TING
PTING
TING
PIK
PIK
PIK
PFFT
PFFT
PFFT
PFFT
PFFT
PFFT
PFFT
PFFT
TING
TING
TING
TING
DRAAG
PIK
PIK
PIK
THUMP

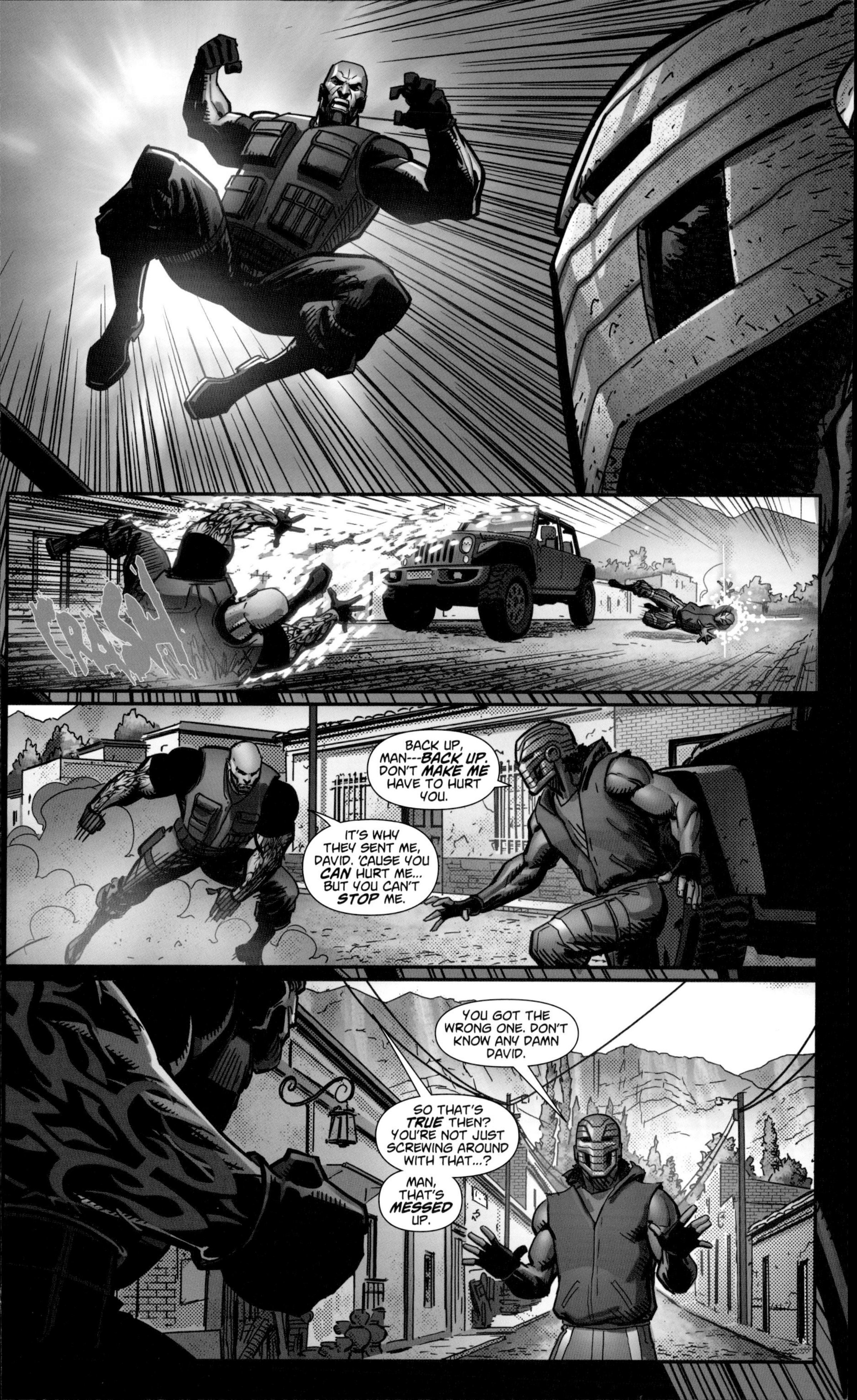
CRASH
BACK UP, MAN---BACK UP. DON'T MAKE ME HAVE TO HURT YOU.
IT'S WHY THEY SENT ME, DAVID. 'CAUSE YOU CAN HURT ME... BUT YOU CAN'T STOP ME.
YOU GOT THE WRONG ONE. DON'T KNOW ANY DAMN DAVID.
SO THAT'S TRUE THEN? YOU'RE NOT JUST SCREWING AROUND WITH THAT...?
MAN, THAT'S MESSED UP.

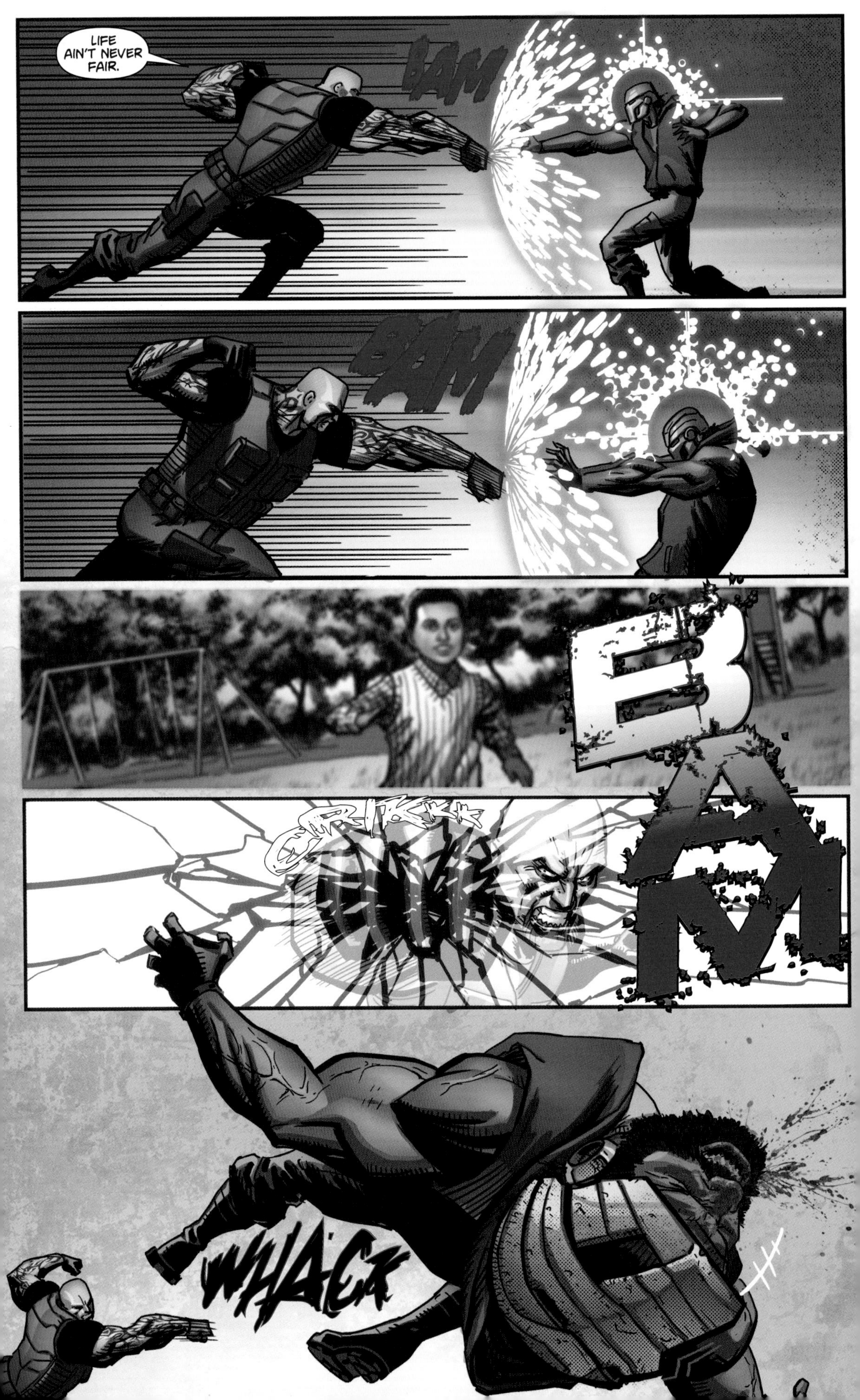
LIFE AIN'T NEVER FAIR.
BAM
BAM
BAM
CRIKKK
WHACK

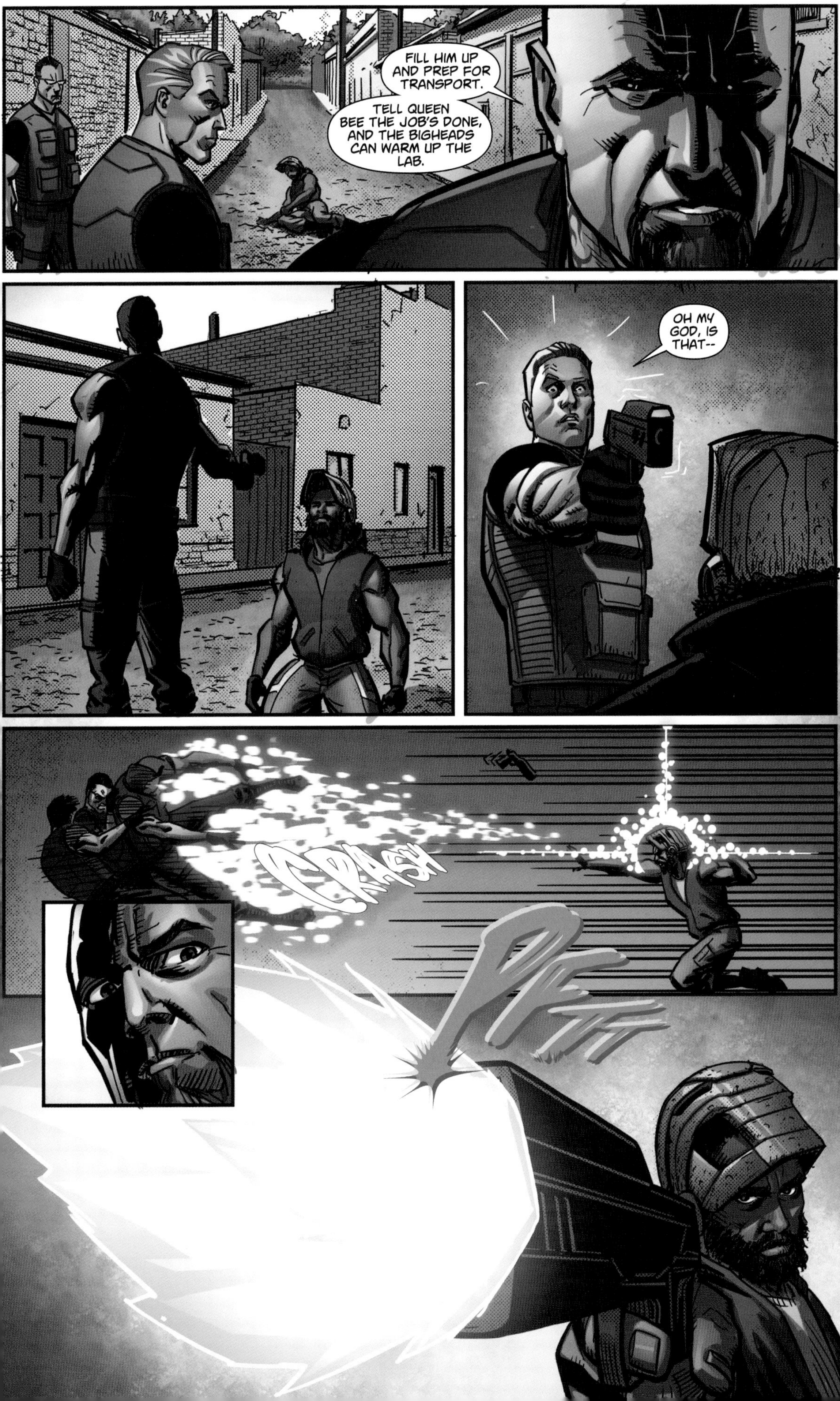
FILL HIM UP AND PREP FOR TRANSPORT.
TELL QUEEN BEE THE JOB'S DONE, AND THE BIGHEADS CAN WARM UP THE LAB.
OH MY GOD, IS THAT--
CRASH

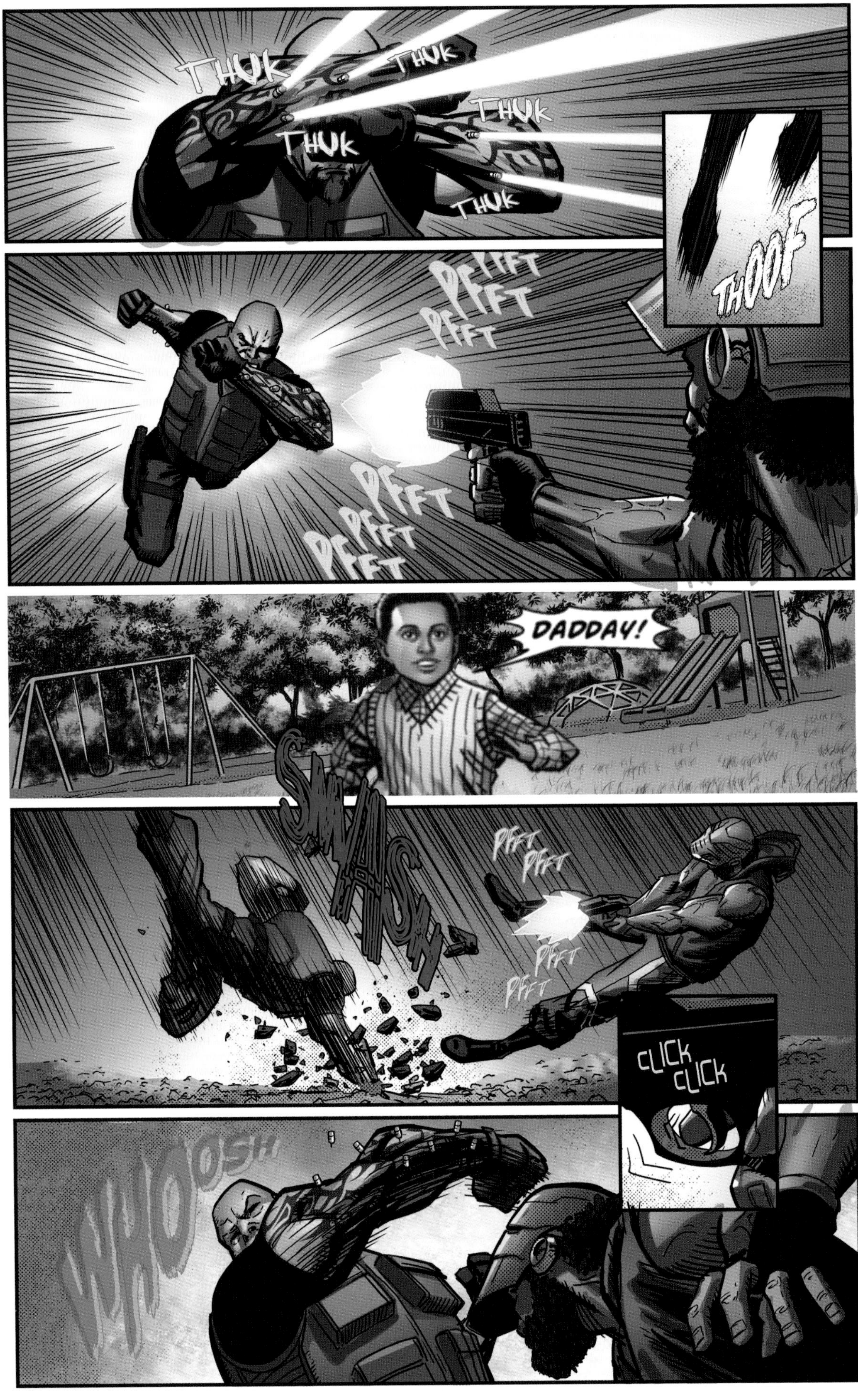
THUK
THUK
THUK
THUK
THUK
THOOF
PFFFT
PFFFT
PFFFT
PFFFT
PFFFT
PFFFT
DADDAY!
SMASH
PFFT
PFFT
PFFT
PFFT
CLICK
CLICK
WHOOOSH

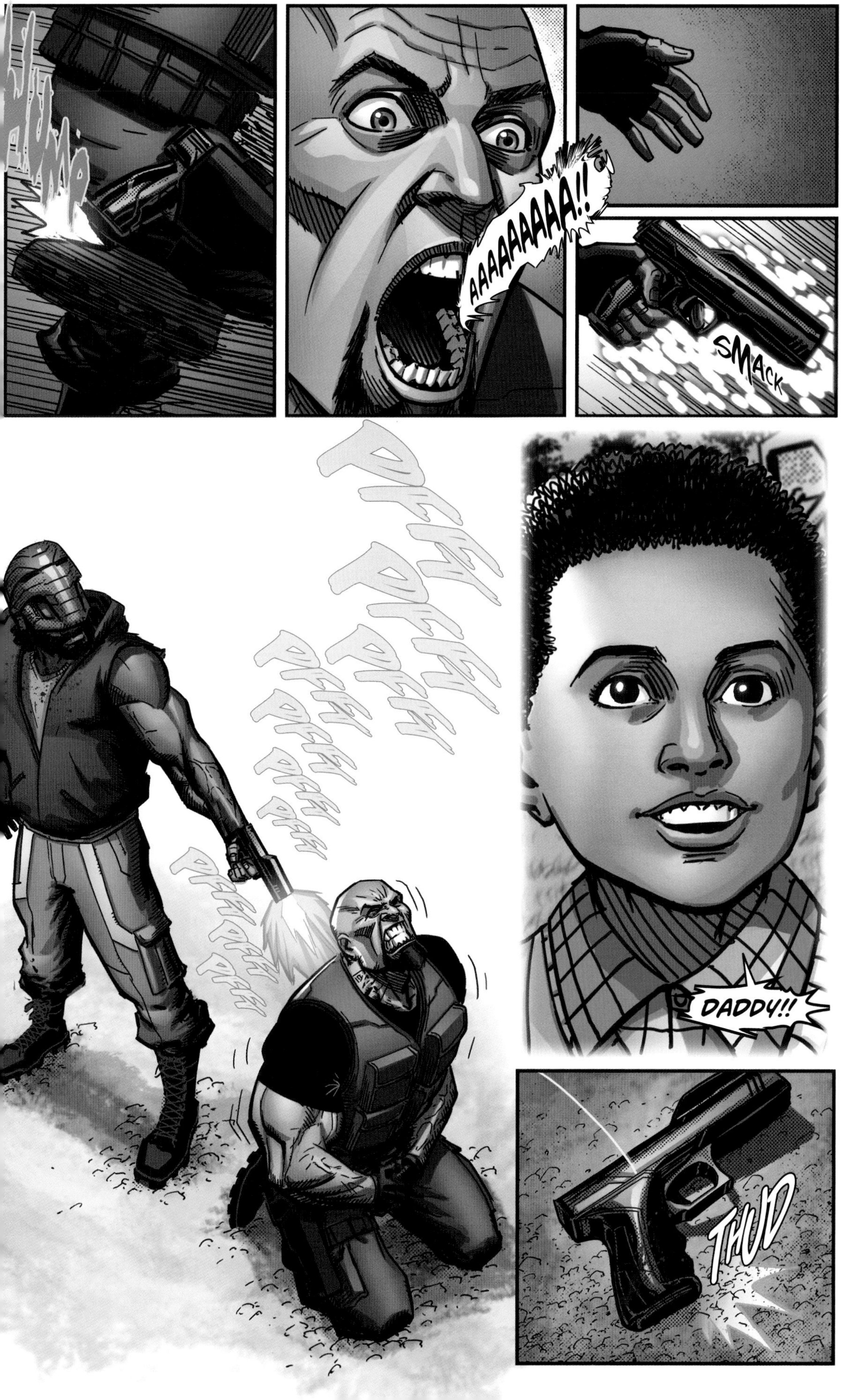
AAAAAAAA!!
SMACK
DADDY!!
THUD

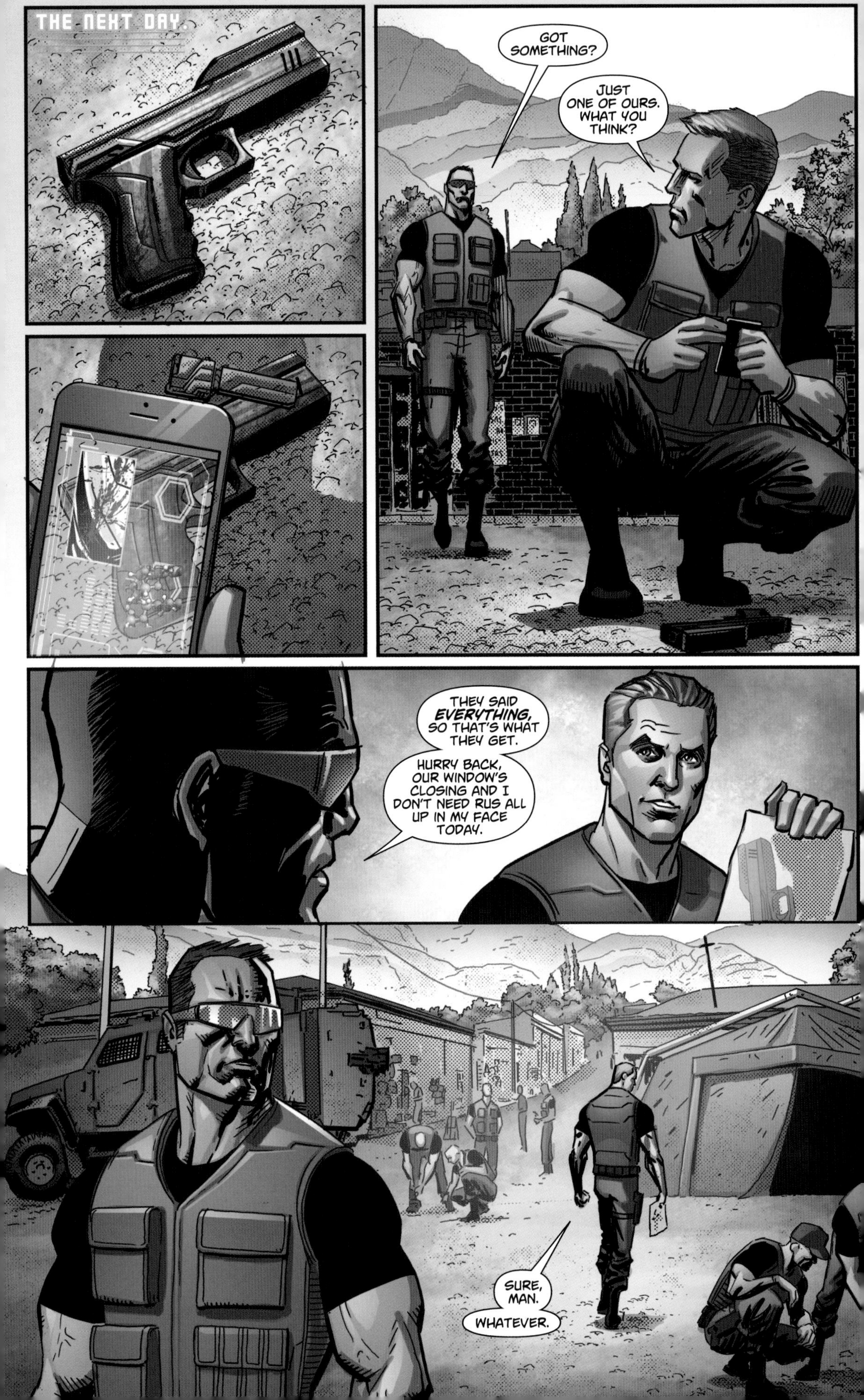
THE NEXT DAY.
GOT SOMETHING?
JUST ONE OF OURS. WHAT YOU THINK?
THEY SAID EVERYTHING, SO THAT'S WHAT THEY GET.
HURRY BACK, OUR WINDOW'S CLOSING AND I DON'T NEED RUS ALL UP IN MY FACE TODAY.
SURE, MAN.
WHATEVER.

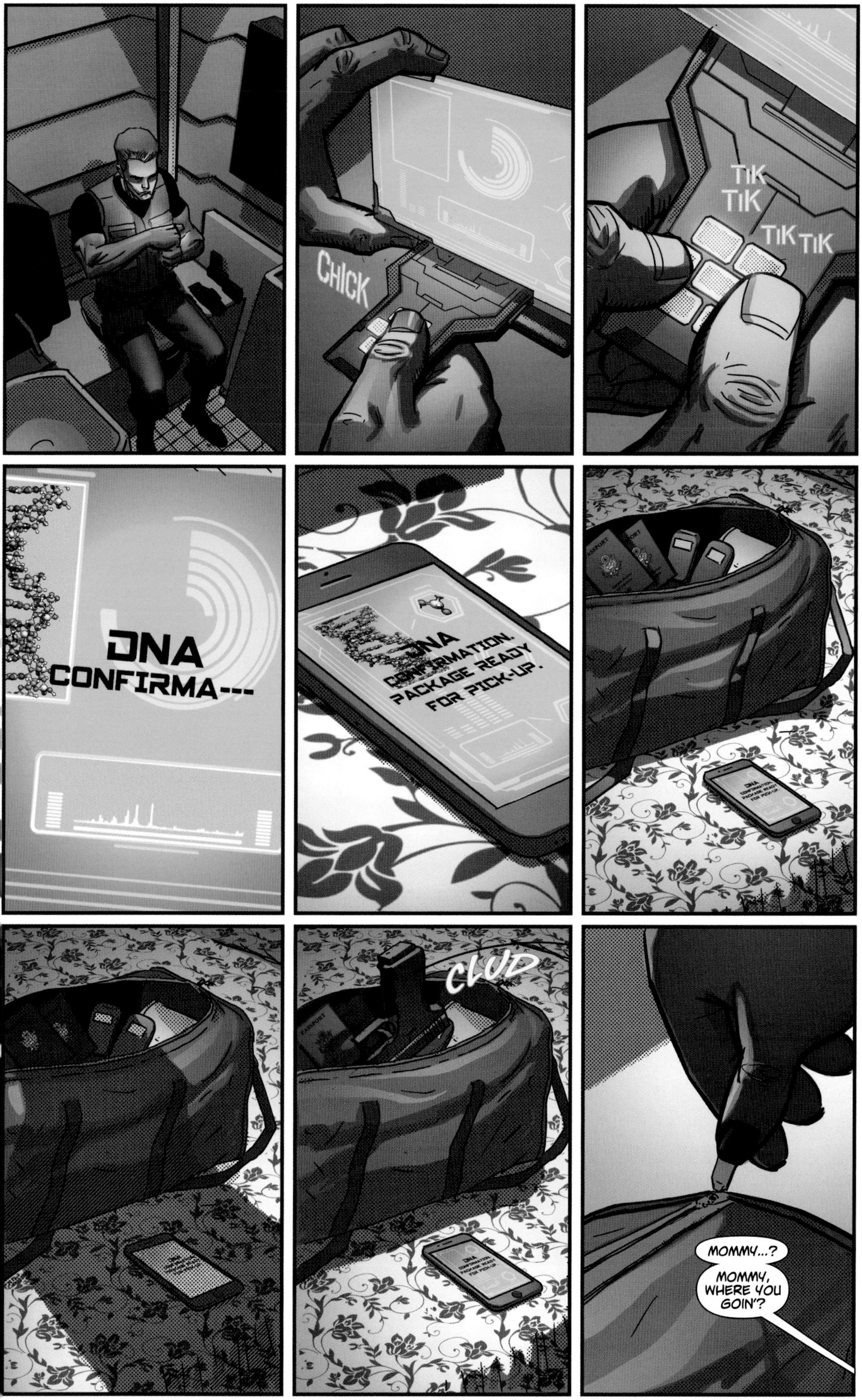
CHICK
TIK
TIK
TIK TIK
DNA
CONFIRMA---
DNA
CONFIRMATION.
PACKAGE READY
FOR PICK-UP.
CLUD
MOMMY...?
MOMMY, WHERE YOU GOIN'?

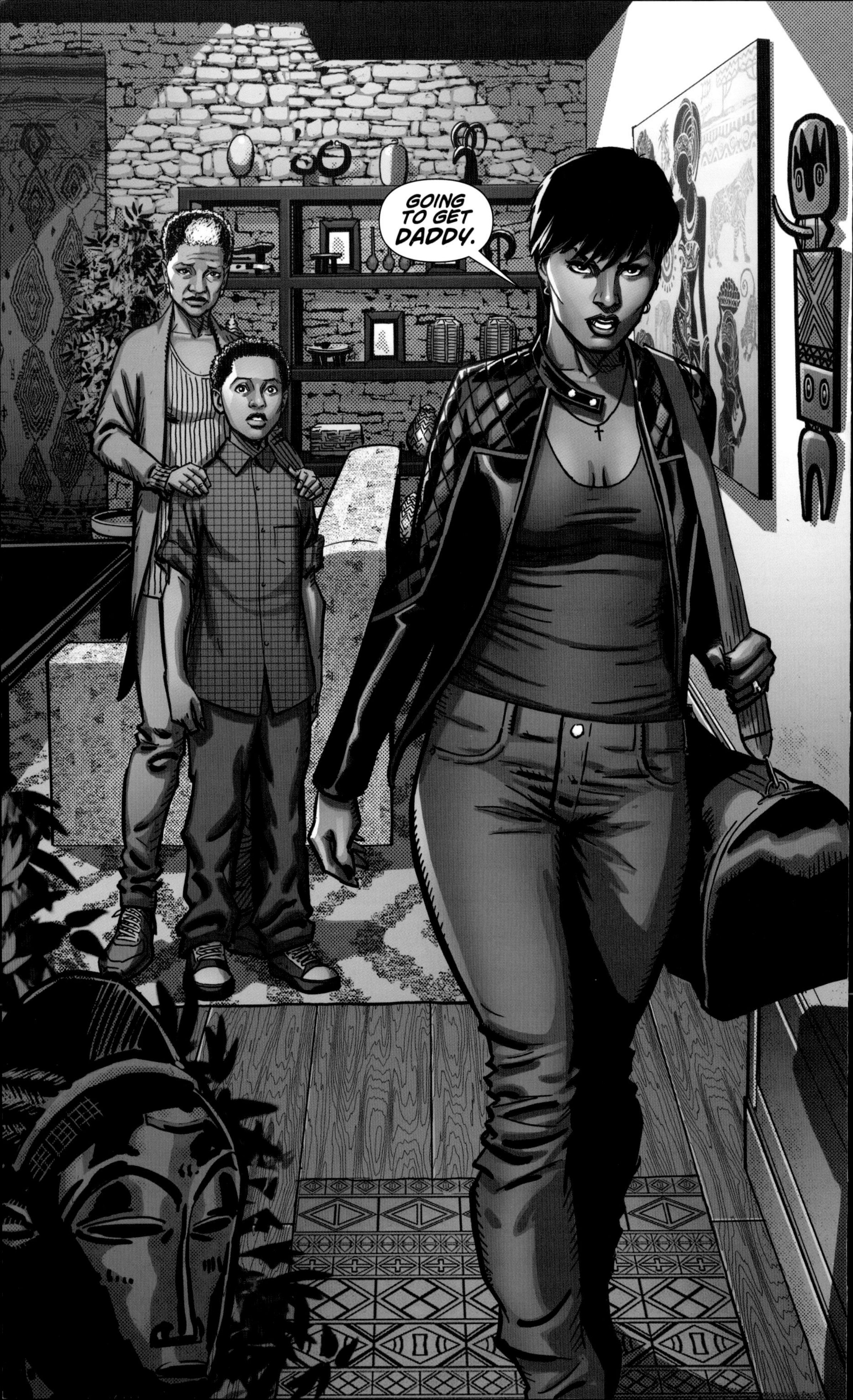
GOING TO GET DADDY.

THREAT LEVEL: SCARLET

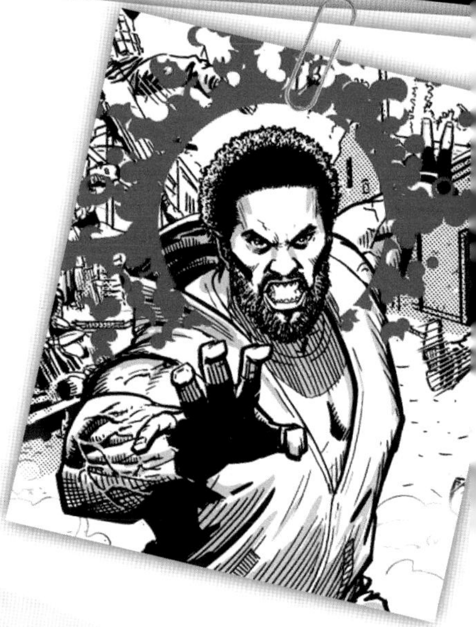

NOBLE

FILE NUMBER: CPU-001N - ALPHA

REAL NAME: David Powell

LEGAL STATUS: American citizen; officially deceased, as of May 6, 2017

KNOWN ALIASES: Julian Brass, Michael Burnett

PRIORITY LEVEL: Ultraviolet, for exclusive and sole review by Chief Executive Officer Lorena Payan

ENHANCED ABILITIES: Superhuman capacity for mental brainwave projection, facilitating relocation of matter, organic and inorganic. Application of abilities has been observed on objects, as well as the subject's own physical mass.

POWER LEVEL: As of this writing, subject's abilities range between a 5 and 7 on the Bingham Measurement Scale. Since the powers are growing with every encounter, this rating is subject to change.

THREAT LEVEL: Scarlet

NEXT STEPS: Thorough testing of subject's limits of abilities and psychological resiliency, in the wake of a fractured memory state. Activation of next-level EWOWs (Enhanced Weapons of War) is imminent.

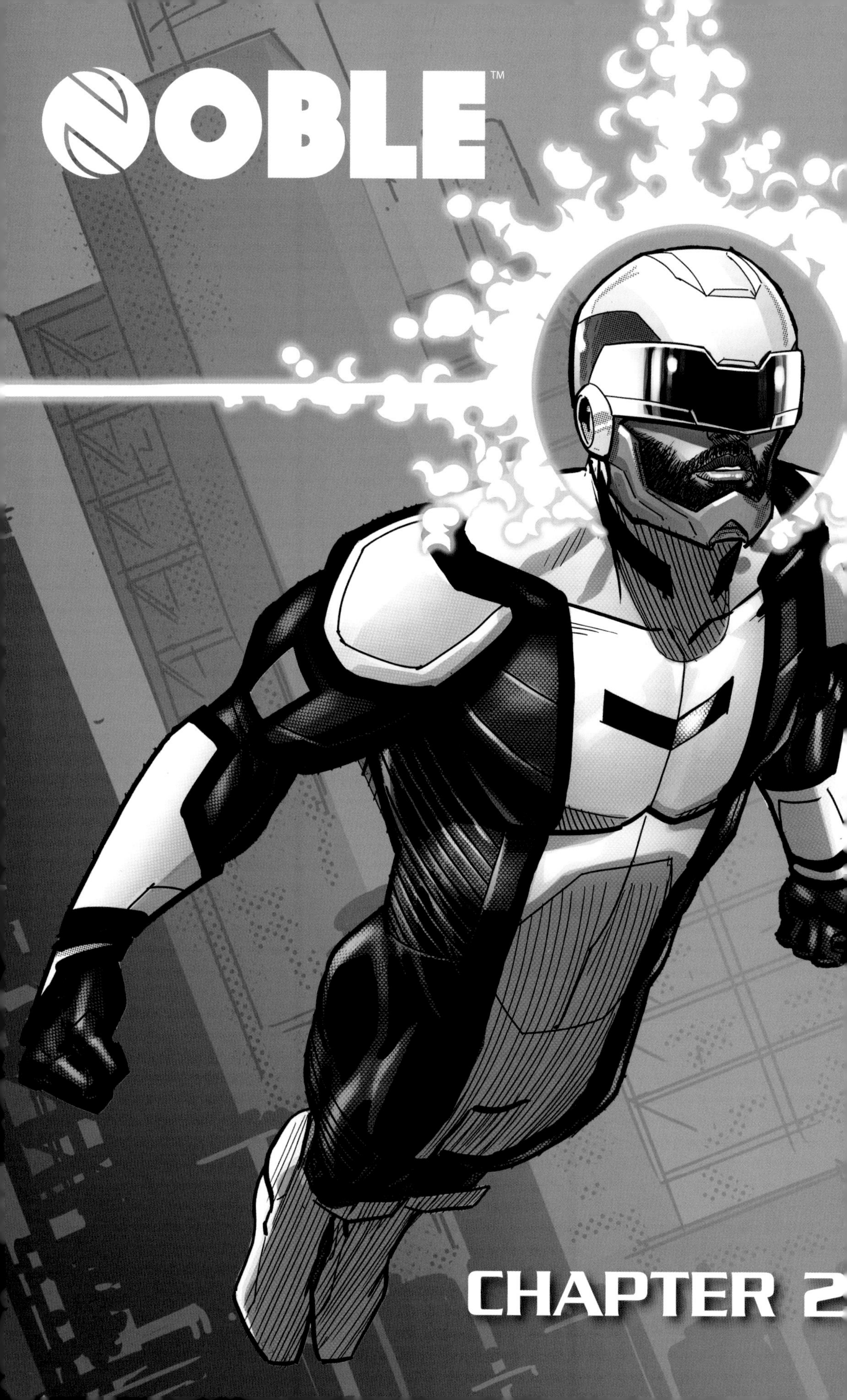
NOBLE™
CHAPTER 2

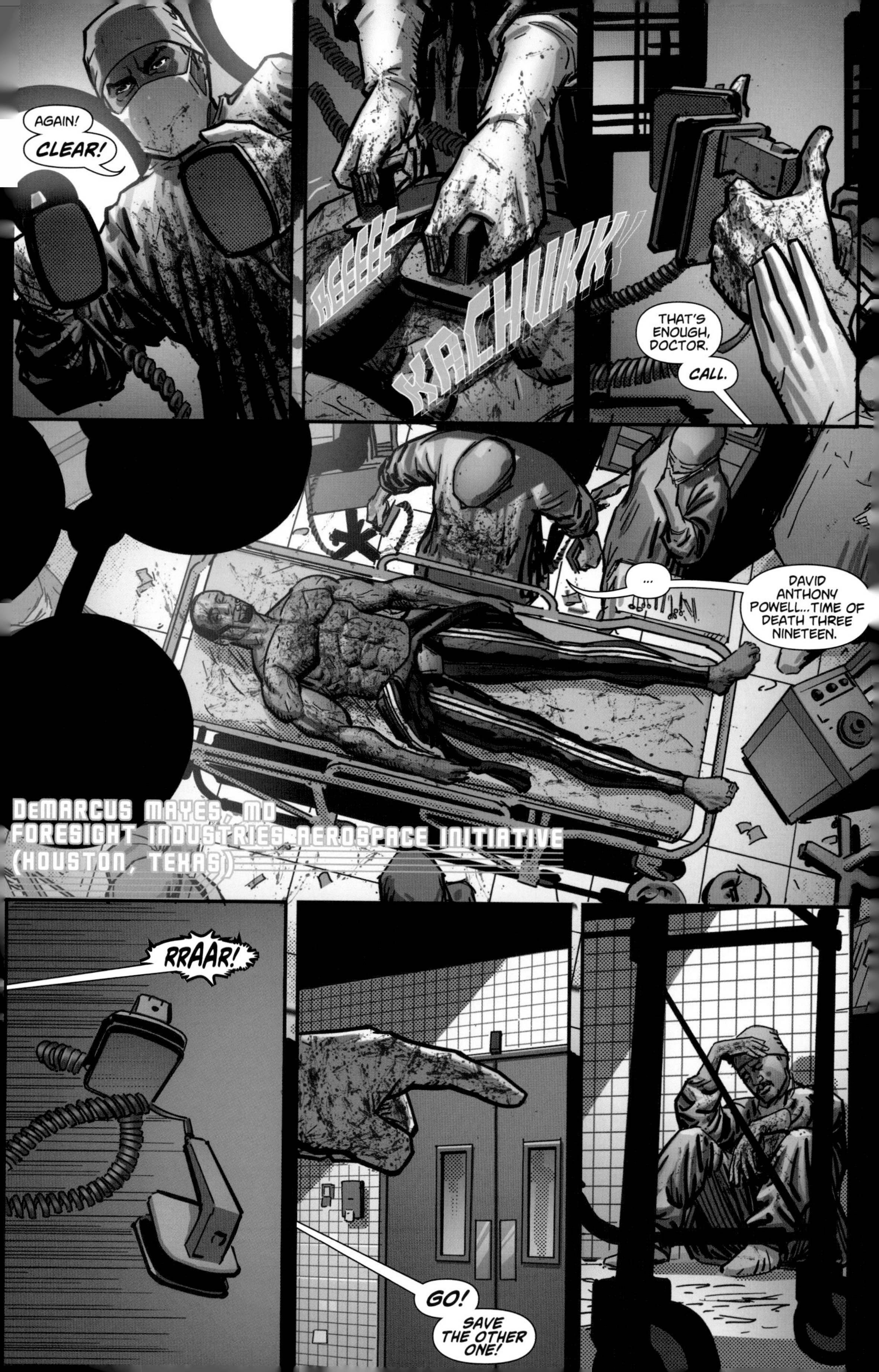

AGAIN!
CLEAR!
BEEEEE-
KACHUKK
THAT'S ENOUGH, DOCTOR.
CALL.
...
DAVID ANTHONY POWELL...TIME OF DEATH THREE NINETEEN.
DeMARCUS MAYES, MD
FORESIGHT INDUSTRIES AEROSPACE INITIATIVE
(HOUSTON, TEXAS)
RRAAR!
GO!
SAVE THE OTHER ONE!

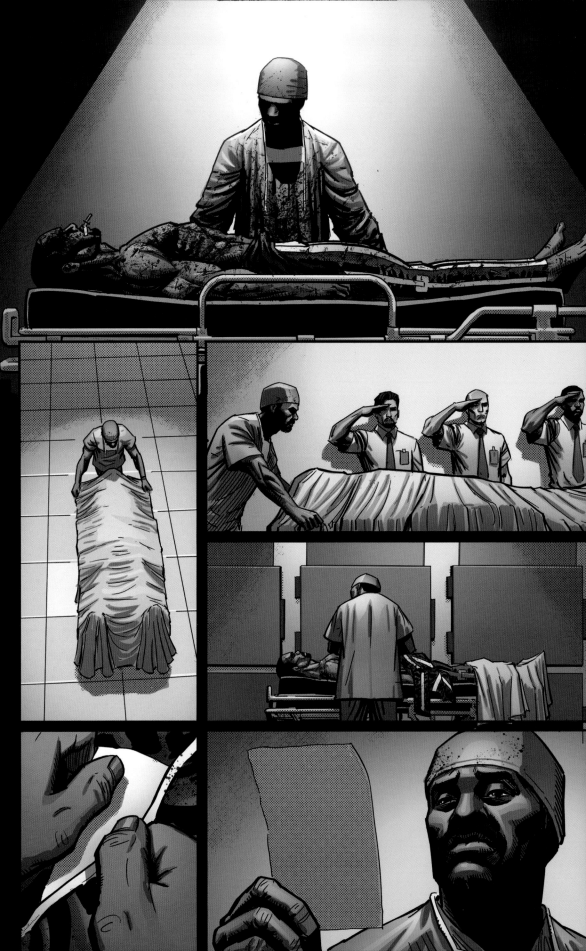

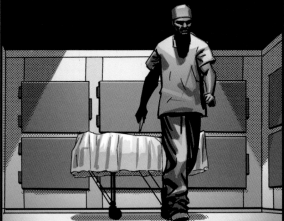

HUH...

HUGH!

≥COUGH-COUGH
...COUGH--≤

MR. POWELL--
DAVID! DAVID--
MY NAME IS MAYES,
*DEMARCUS
MAYES.*

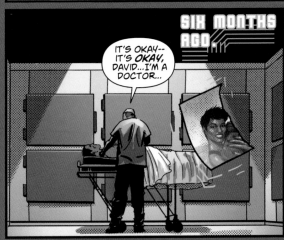

SIX MONTHS
AGO

IT'S OKAY--
IT'S *OKAY,*
DAVID...I'M A
DOCTOR...

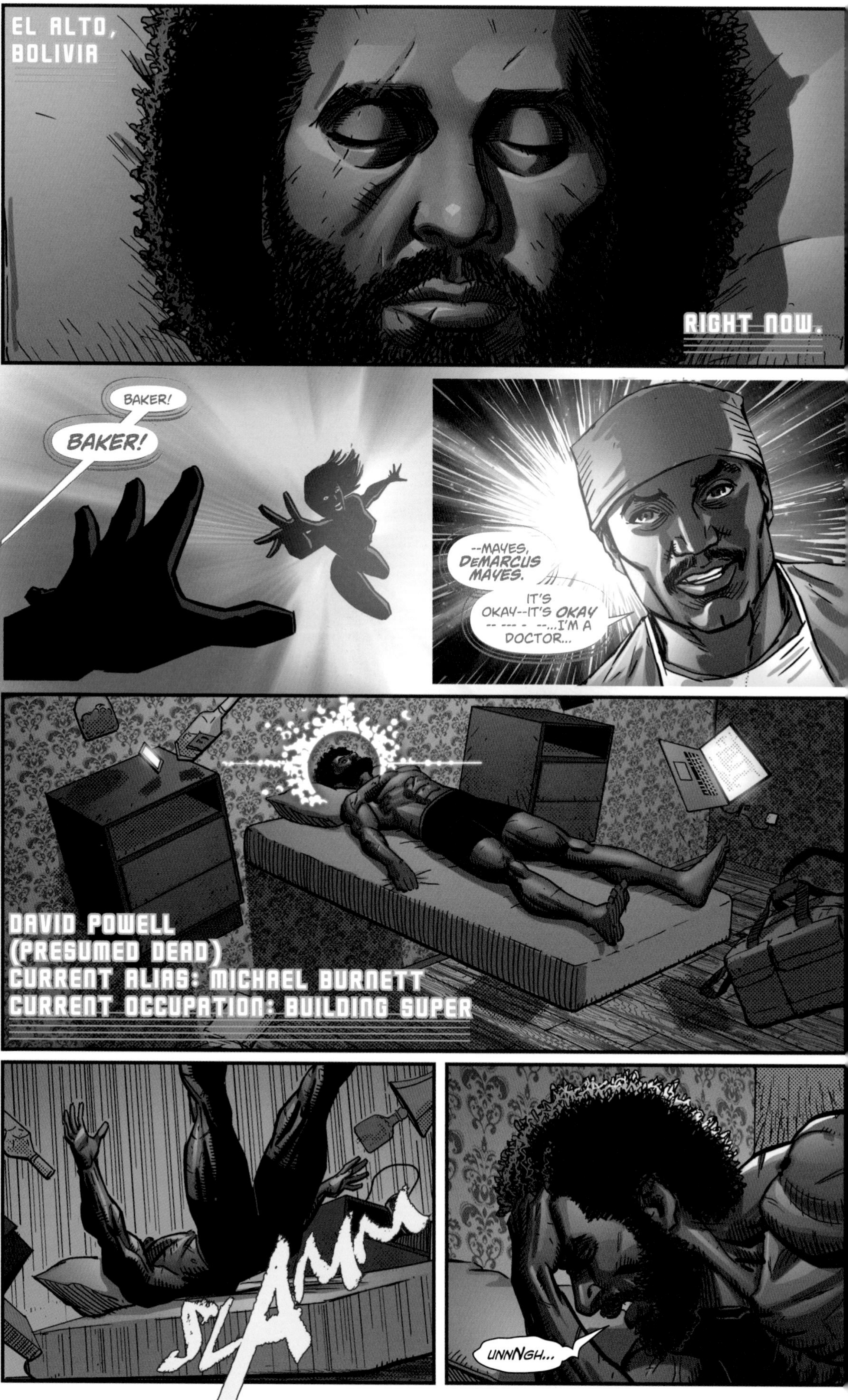

EL ALTO, BOLIVIA
RIGHT NOW.
BAKER!
BAKER!
--MAYES, DeMARCUS MAYES.
IT'S OKAY--IT'S OKAY -- --- - --...I'M A DOCTOR...
DAVID POWELL
(PRESUMED DEAD)
CURRENT ALIAS: MICHAEL BURNETT
CURRENT OCCUPATION: BUILDING SUPER
SLAMM
UNNNGH...

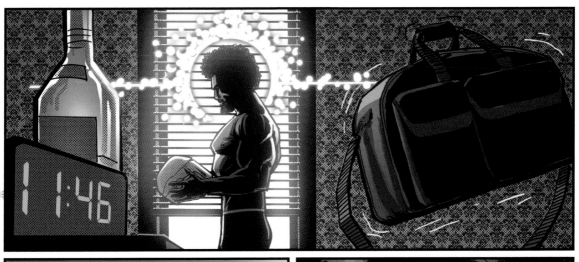

HMM.

SOON.

MICHAEL. YOU ALMOST DIDN'T MAKE IT.

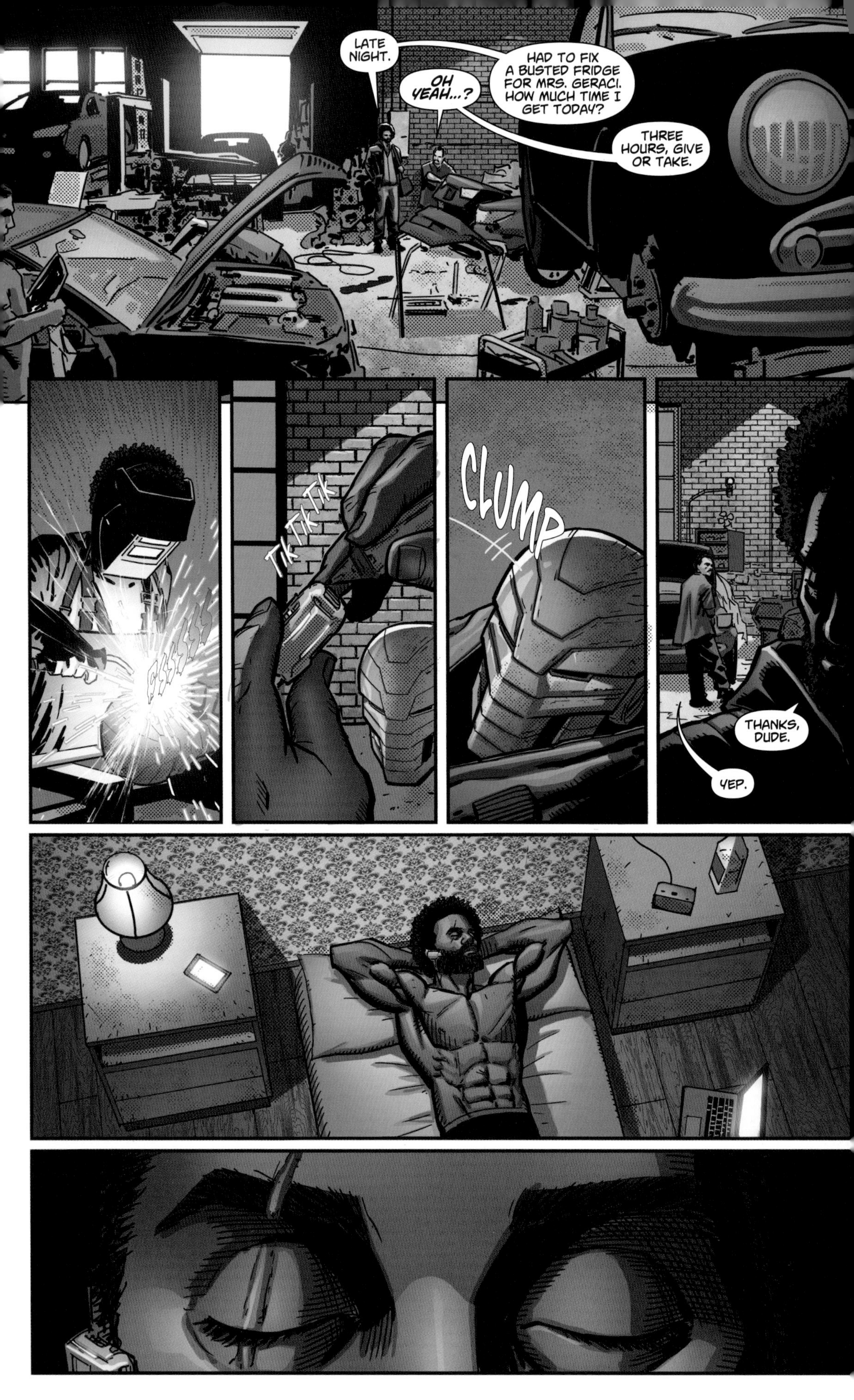
LATE NIGHT.
HAD TO FIX A BUSTED FRIDGE FOR MRS. GERACI. HOW MUCH TIME I GET TODAY?
OH YEAH...?
THREE HOURS, GIVE OR TAKE.
TIK TIK TIK
CLUMP
THANKS, DUDE.
YEP.

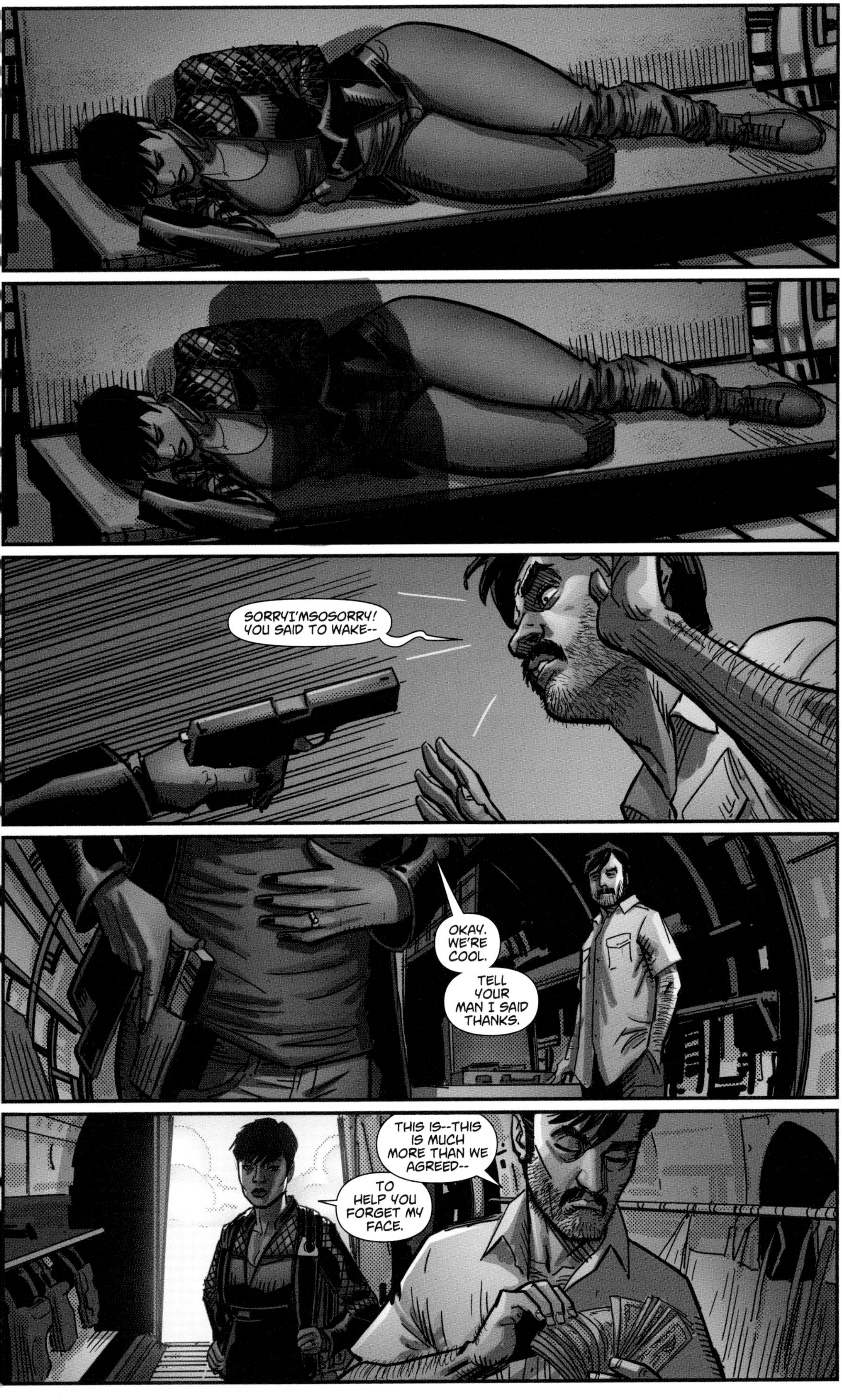
SORRYI'MSOSORRY! YOU SAID TO WAKE--
OKAY. WE'RE COOL.
TELL YOUR MAN I SAID THANKS.
THIS IS--THIS IS MUCH MORE THAN WE AGREED--
TO HELP YOU FORGET MY FACE.

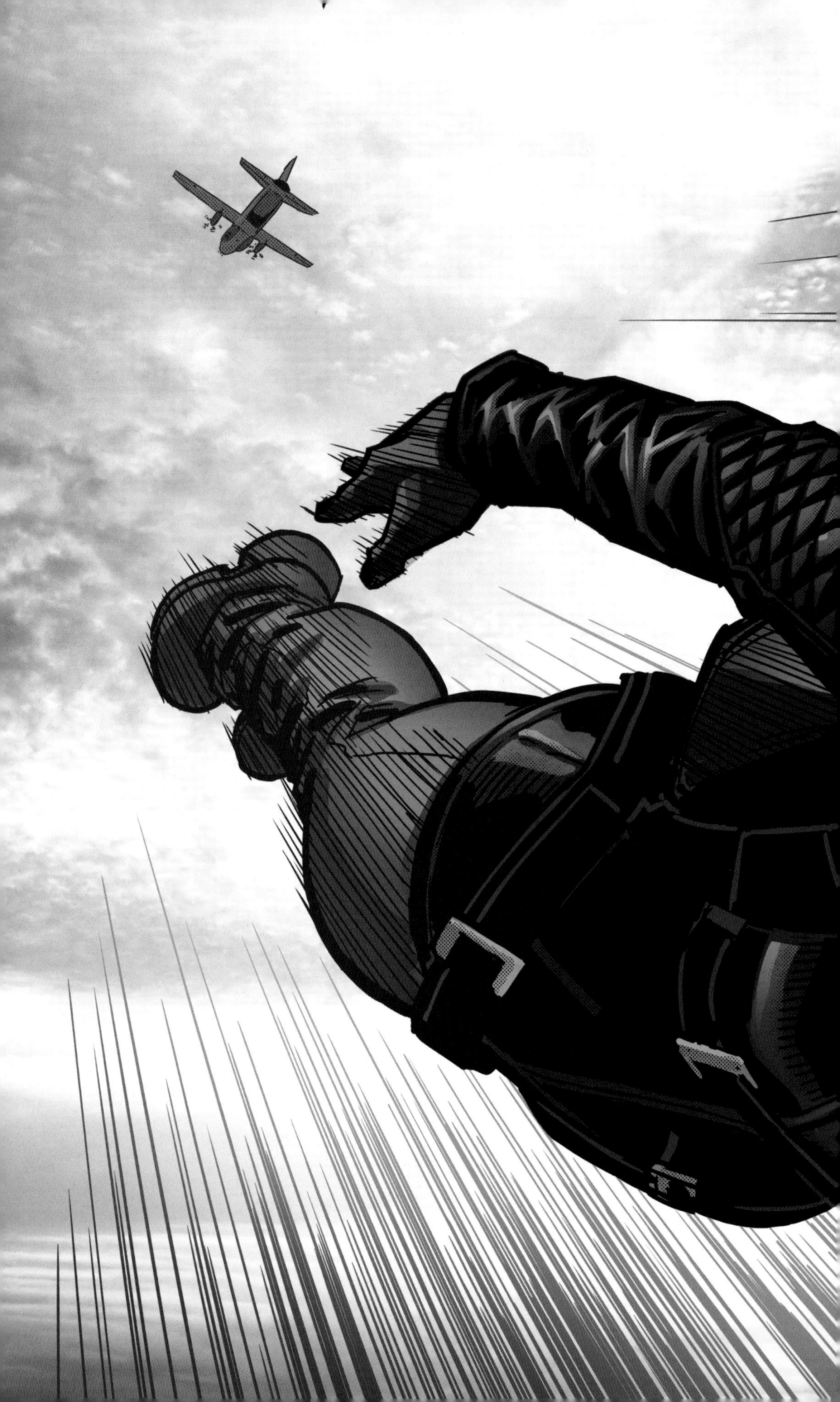

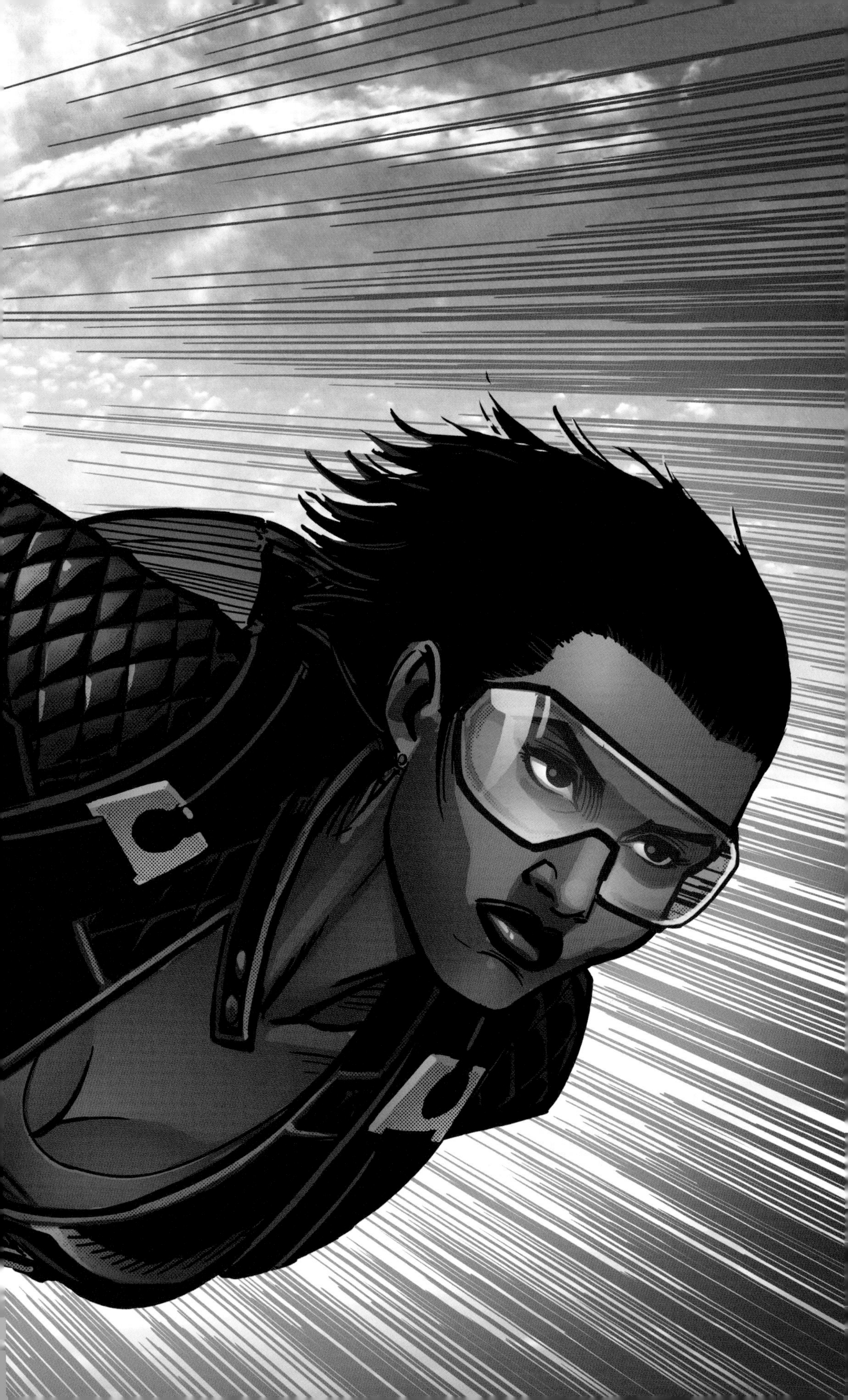

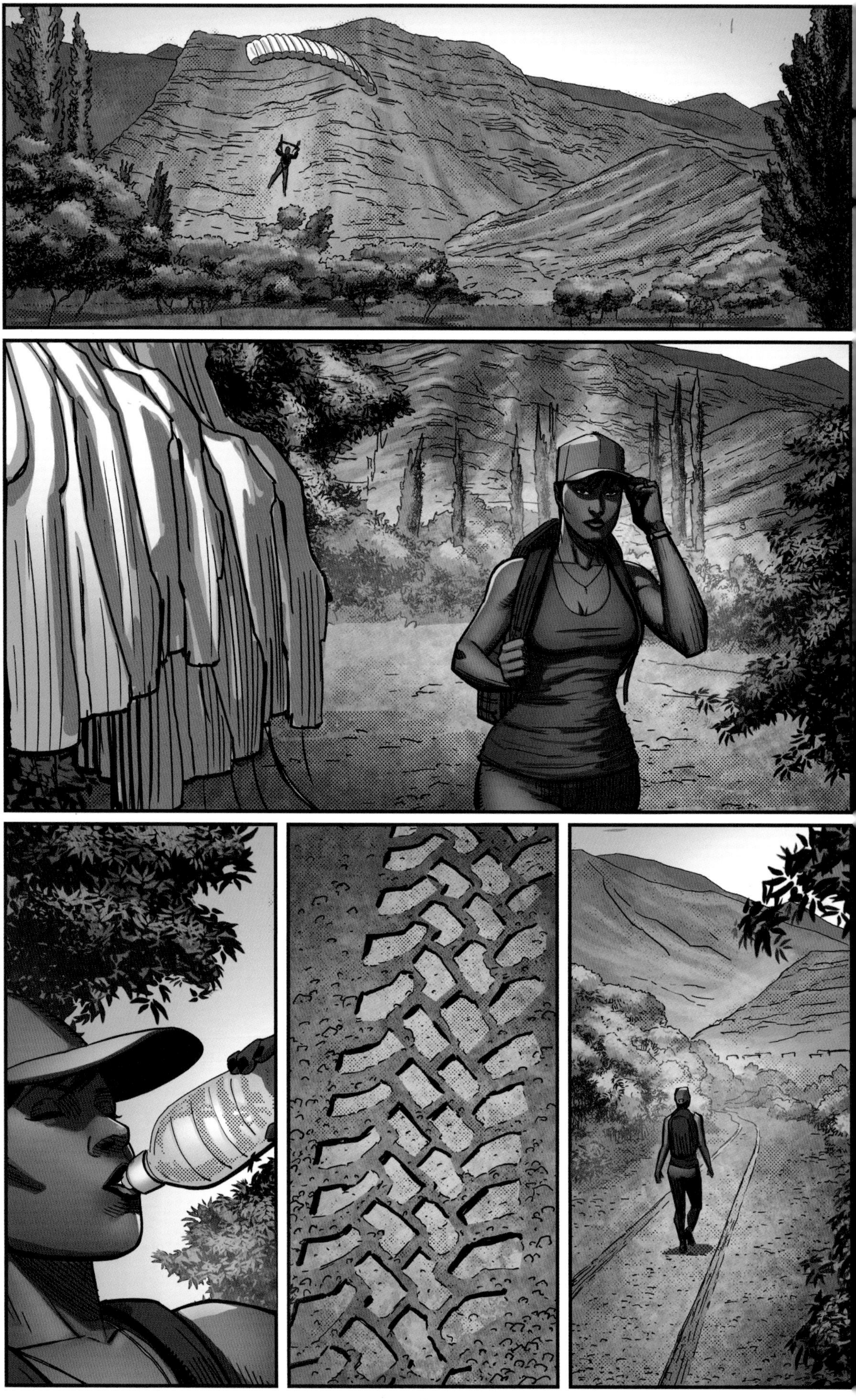

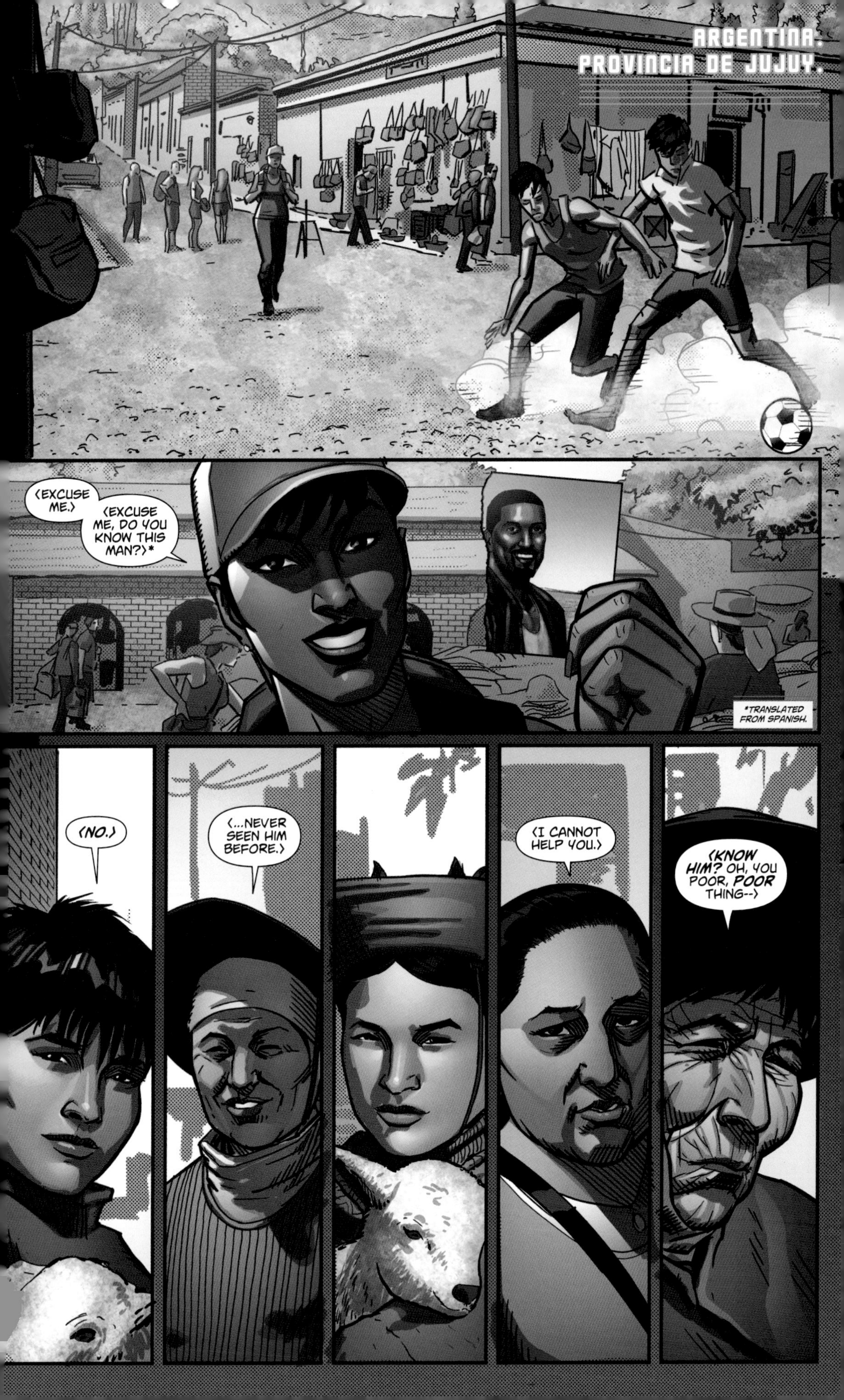
ARGENTINA.
PROVINCIA DE JUJUY.
‹EXCUSE ME.›
‹EXCUSE ME, DO YOU KNOW THIS MAN?›*
*TRANSLATED FROM SPANISH.
‹NO.›
‹...NEVER SEEN HIM BEFORE.›
‹I CANNOT HELP YOU.›
‹KNOW HIM? OH, YOU POOR, POOR THING--›

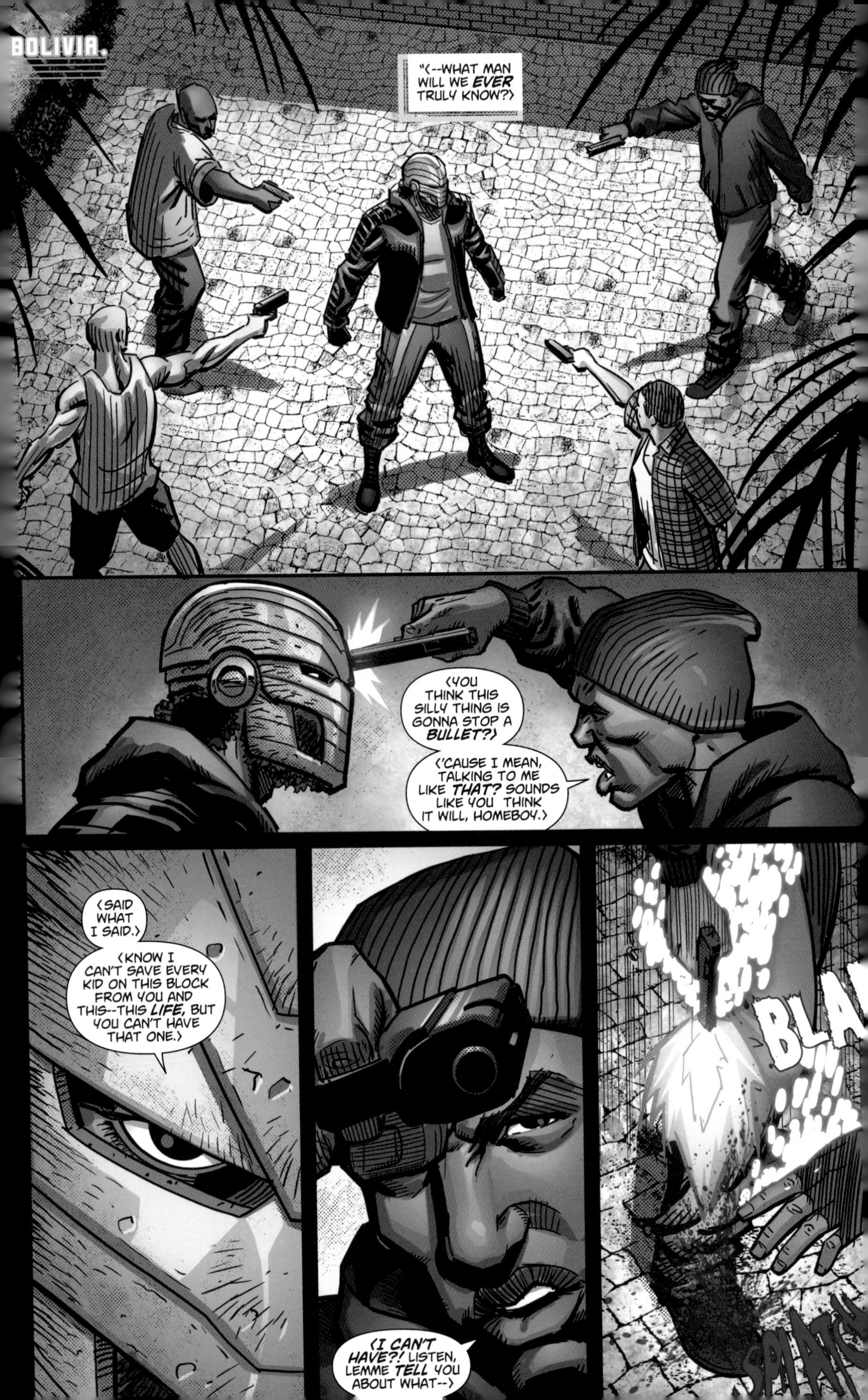
BOLIVIA.
"<--WHAT MAN WILL WE EVER TRULY KNOW?>
<YOU THINK THIS SILLY THING IS GONNA STOP A BULLET?>
<'CAUSE I MEAN, TALKING TO ME LIKE THAT? SOUNDS LIKE YOU THINK IT WILL, HOMEBOY.>
<SAID WHAT I SAID.>
<KNOW I CAN'T SAVE EVERY KID ON THIS BLOCK FROM YOU AND THIS--THIS LIFE, BUT YOU CAN'T HAVE THAT ONE.>
<I CAN'T HAVE?! LISTEN, LEMME TELL YOU ABOUT WHAT-->
BLA
SPLATCH

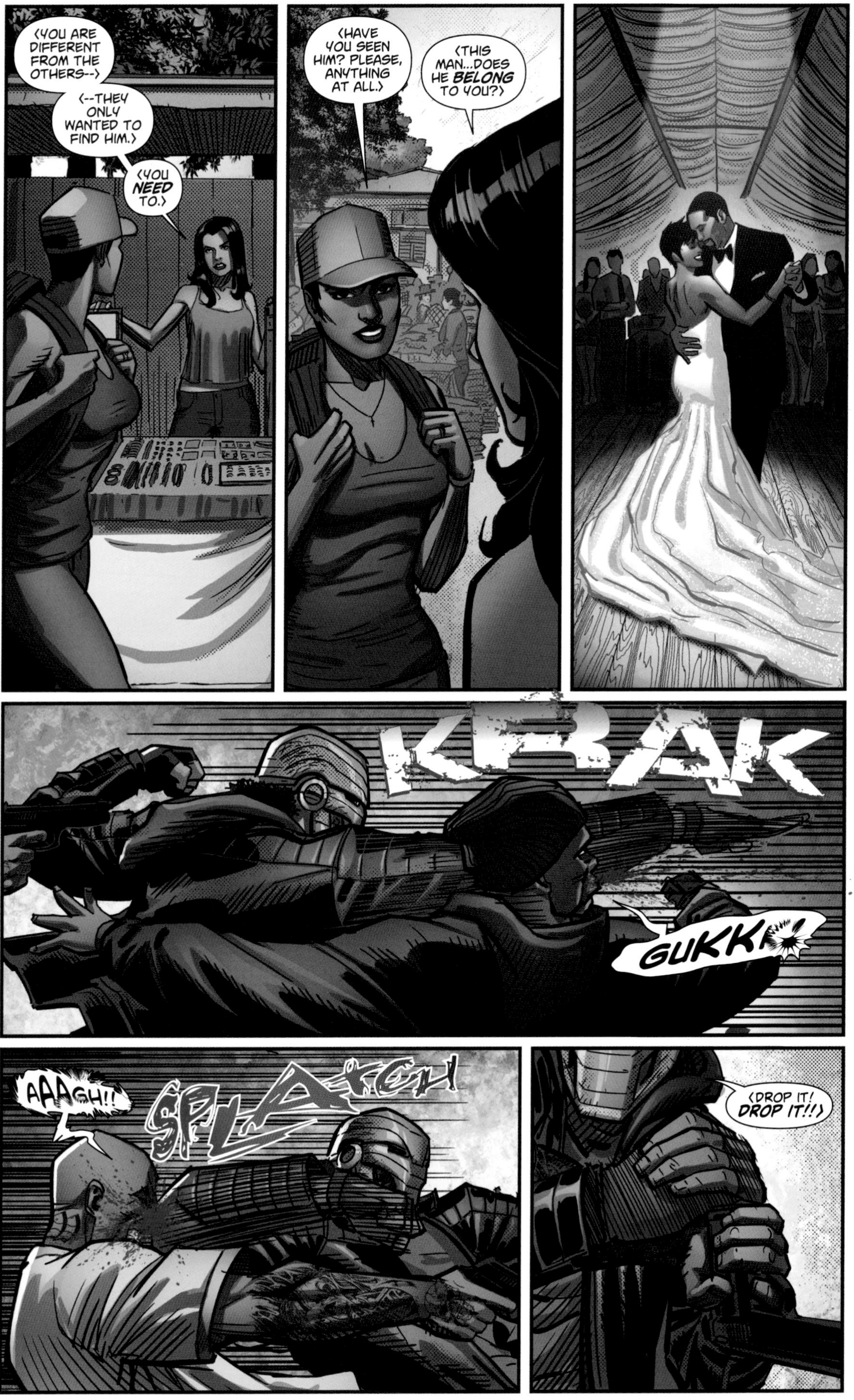

‹YOU ARE DIFFERENT FROM THE OTHERS--›
‹--THEY ONLY WANTED TO FIND HIM.›
‹YOU *NEED* TO.›
‹HAVE YOU SEEN HIM? PLEASE, ANYTHING AT ALL.›
‹THIS MAN...DOES HE *BELONG* TO YOU?›
KRAK
GUKK
AAAGH!!
SPLATCH
‹DROP IT! *DROP IT!!*›

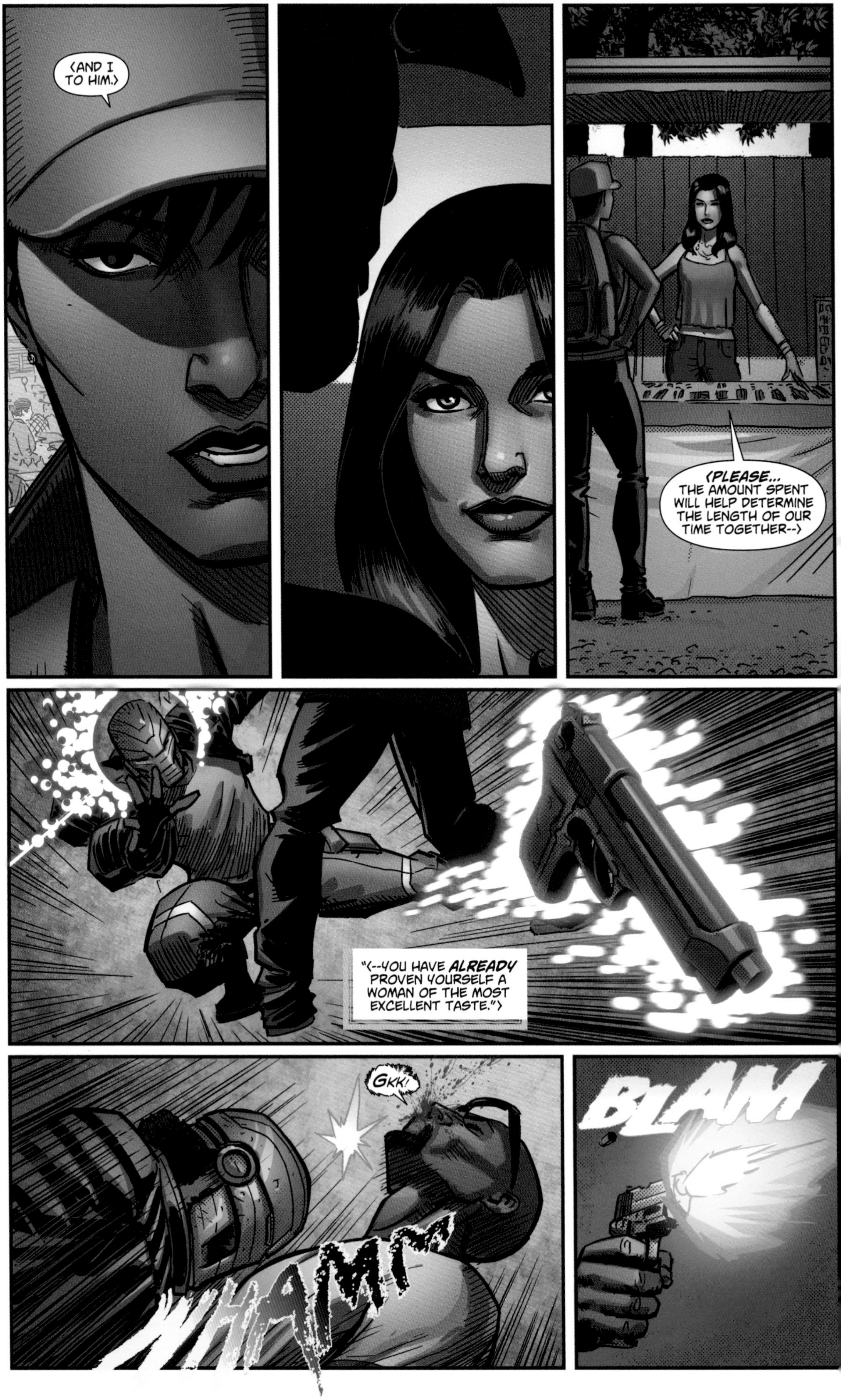
‹AND I TO HIM.›
‹PLEASE... THE AMOUNT SPENT WILL HELP DETERMINE THE LENGTH OF OUR TIME TOGETHER--›
"‹--YOU HAVE ALREADY PROVEN YOURSELF A WOMAN OF THE MOST EXCELLENT TASTE."›
GKK!
WHAMM
BLAM

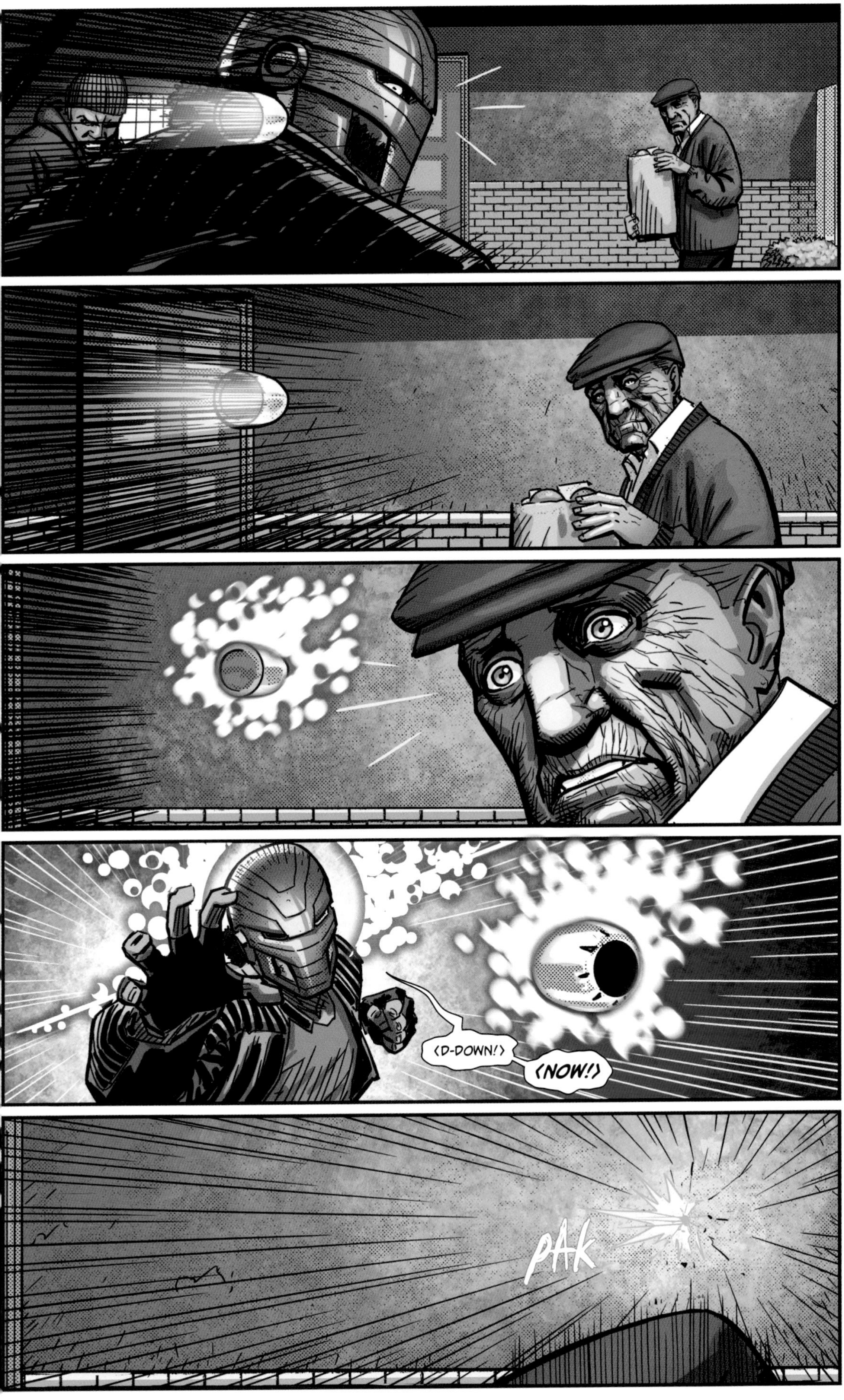

‹D-DOWN!›
‹NOW!›
PAK

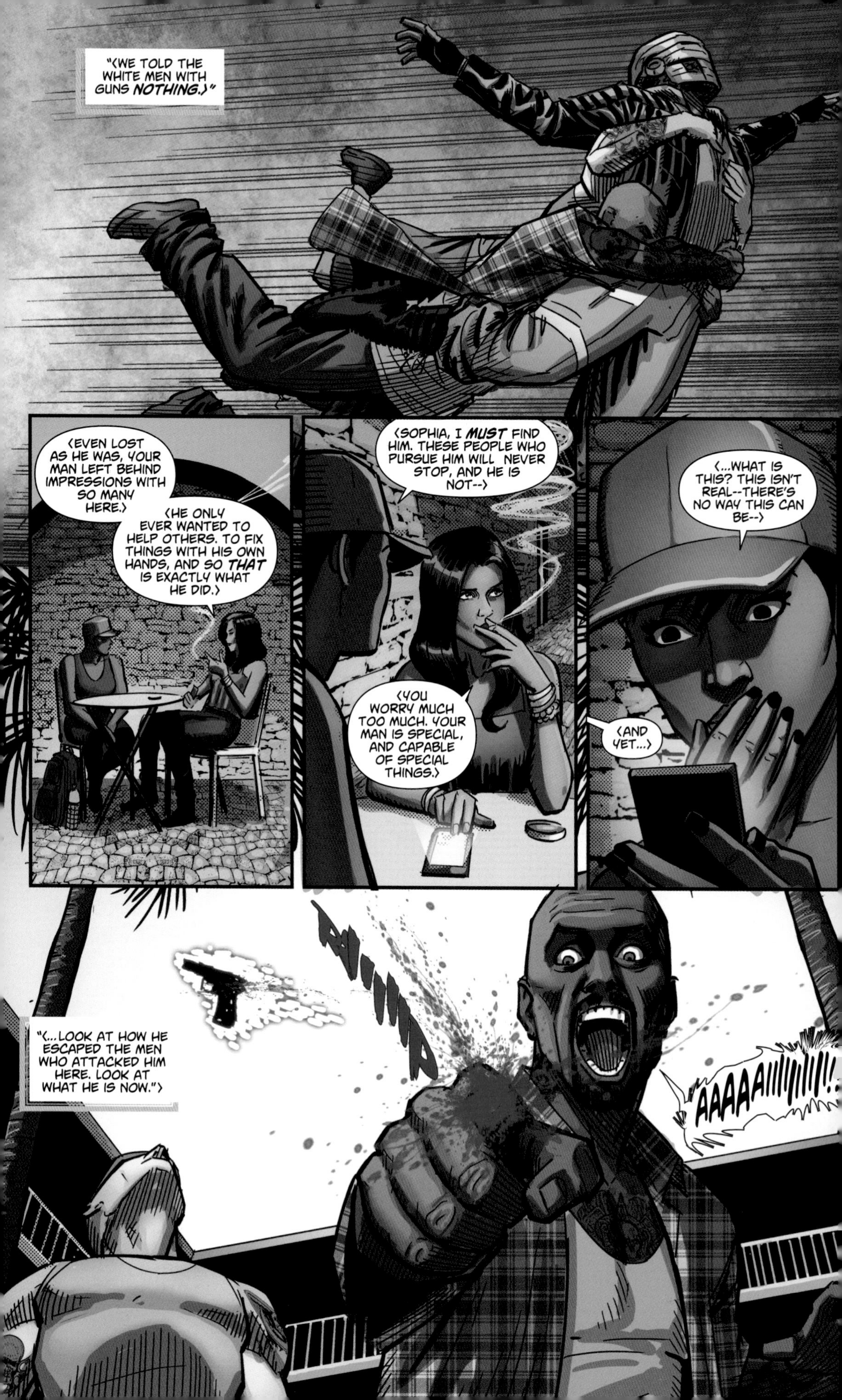
"‹WE TOLD THE WHITE MEN WITH GUNS NOTHING.›"
‹EVEN LOST AS HE WAS, YOUR MAN LEFT BEHIND IMPRESSIONS WITH SO MANY HERE.›
‹HE ONLY EVER WANTED TO HELP OTHERS. TO FIX THINGS WITH HIS OWN HANDS, AND SO THAT IS EXACTLY WHAT HE DID.›
‹SOPHIA, I MUST FIND HIM. THESE PEOPLE WHO PURSUE HIM WILL NEVER STOP, AND HE IS NOT--›
‹YOU WORRY MUCH TOO MUCH. YOUR MAN IS SPECIAL, AND CAPABLE OF SPECIAL THINGS.›
‹...WHAT IS THIS? THIS ISN'T REAL--THERE'S NO WAY THIS CAN BE--›
‹AND YET...›
"‹...LOOK AT HOW HE ESCAPED THE MEN WHO ATTACKED HIM HERE. LOOK AT WHAT HE IS NOW."›
AAAAAIIIIII!

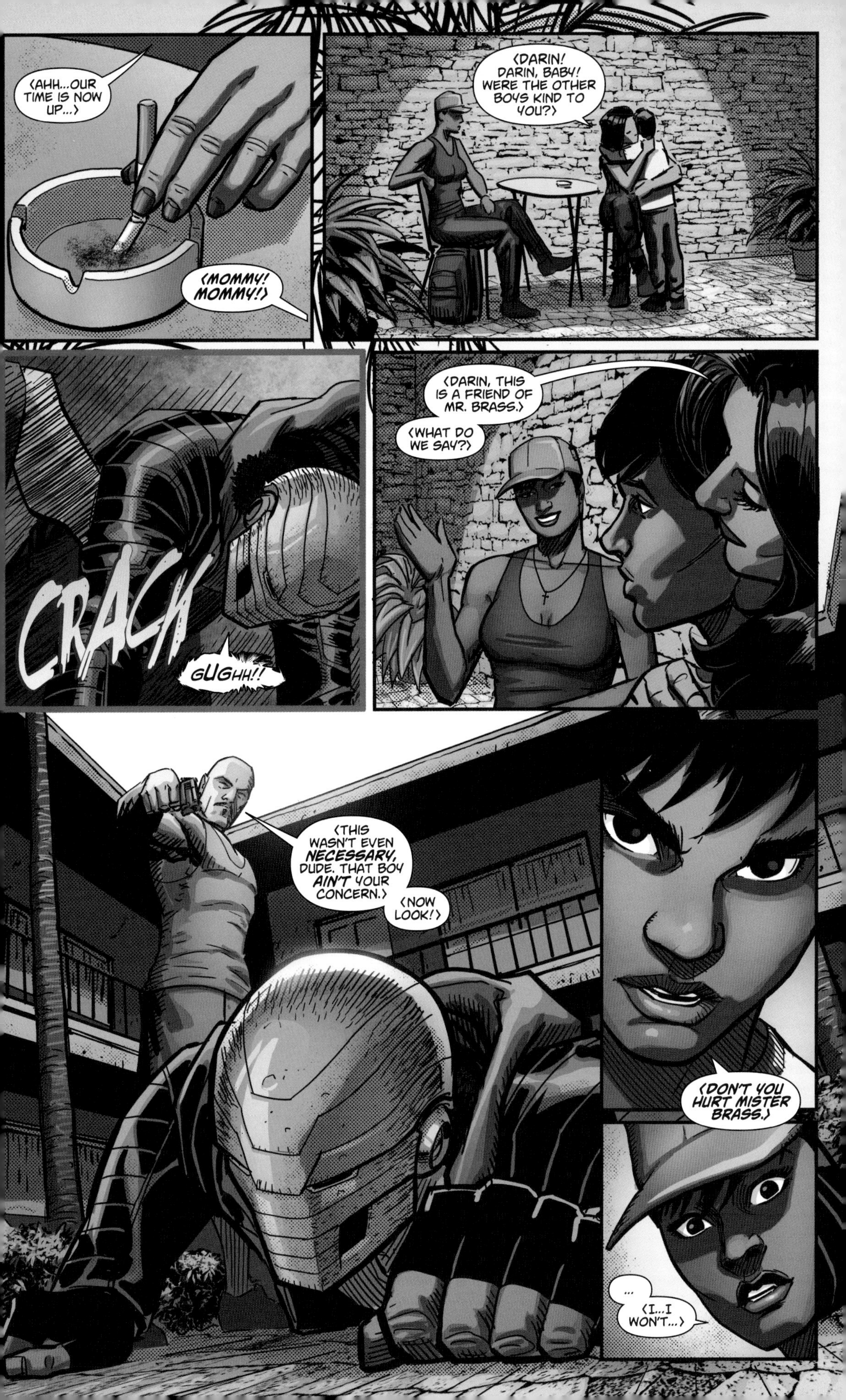

⟨AHH...OUR TIME IS NOW UP...⟩
⟨MOMMY! MOMMY!⟩
⟨DARIN! DARIN, BABY! WERE THE OTHER BOYS KIND TO YOU?⟩
CRACK
GUGHH!!
⟨DARIN, THIS IS A FRIEND OF MR. BRASS.⟩
⟨WHAT DO WE SAY?⟩
⟨THIS WASN'T EVEN NECESSARY, DUDE. THAT BOY AIN'T YOUR CONCERN.⟩
⟨NOW LOOK!⟩
⟨DON'T YOU HURT MISTER BRASS.⟩
...
⟨I...I WON'T...⟩

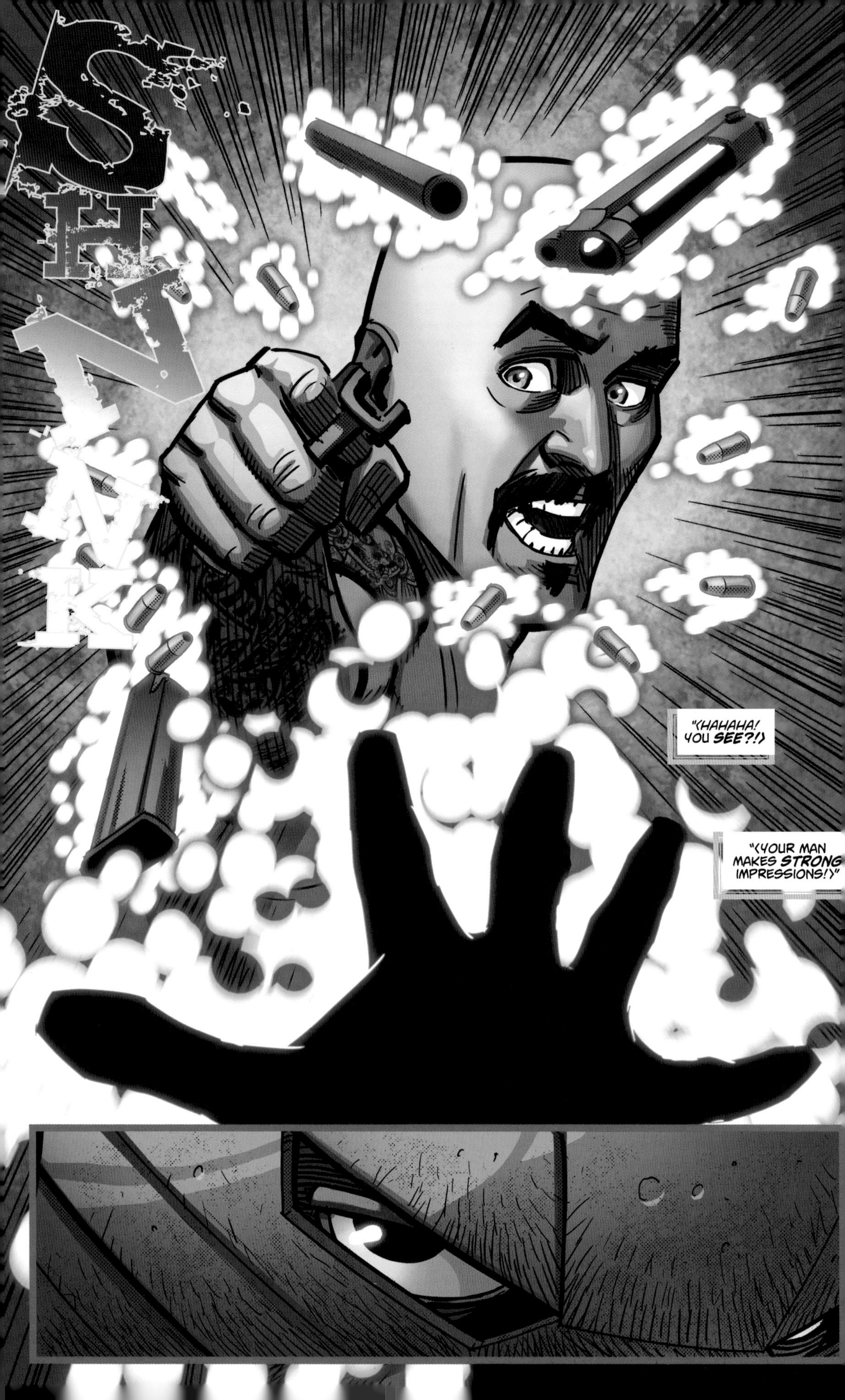
SHANK
"‹HAHAHA! YOU SEE?!›
"‹YOUR MAN MAKES STRONG IMPRESSIONS!›"

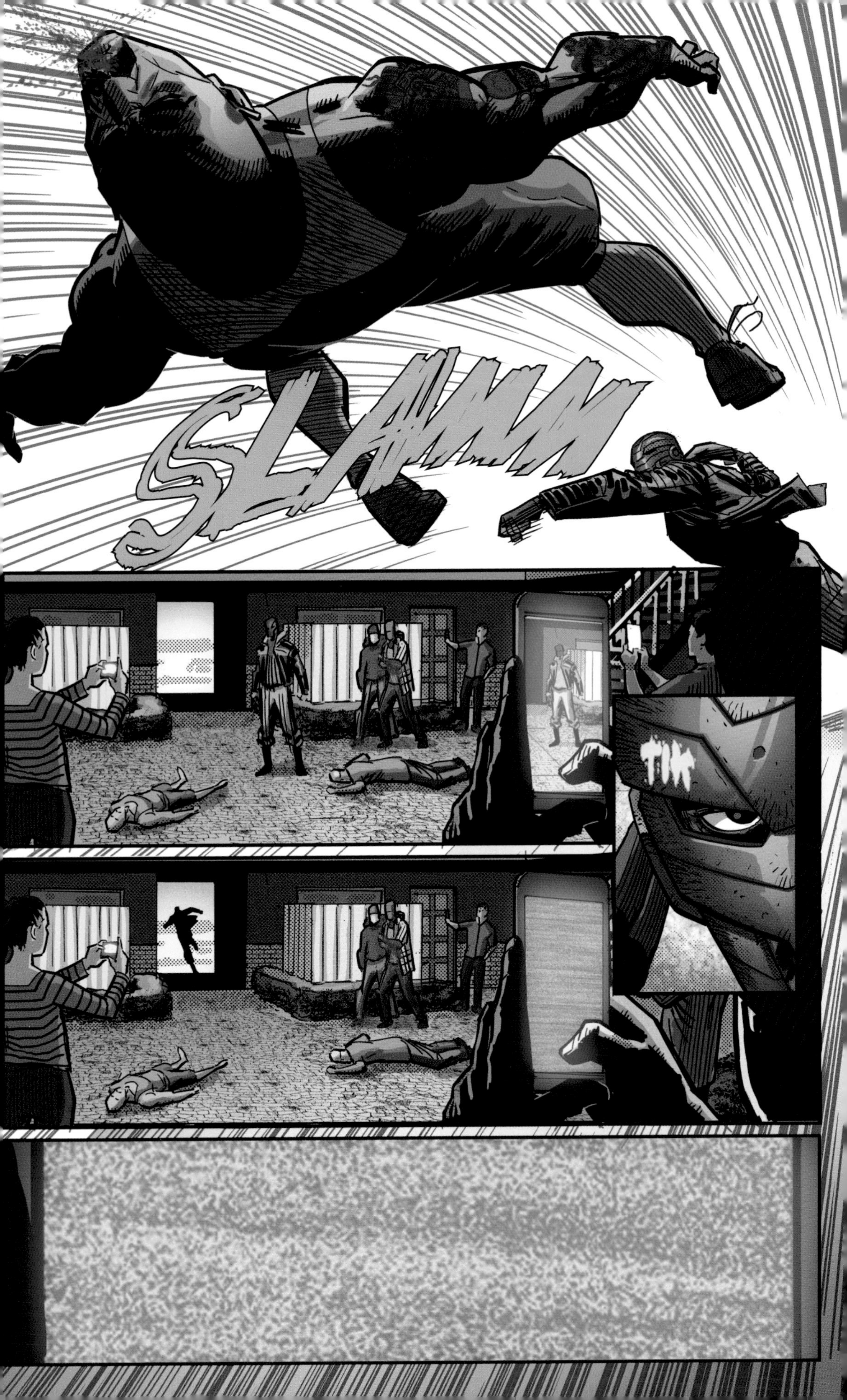
SLAMM
TIM

UNNGHH... HUUH... UNNNG--

⟨MR. RENDOZA, SIR?⟩

⟨HE'S READY FOR YOU NOW.⟩

⟨SORRY ABOUT THAT, MAN...IT HAS BEEN A DAY.⟩

⟨WE'LL DO OUR BEST TO GET YOU IN AND OUT OF HERE QUICK, OKAY?⟩

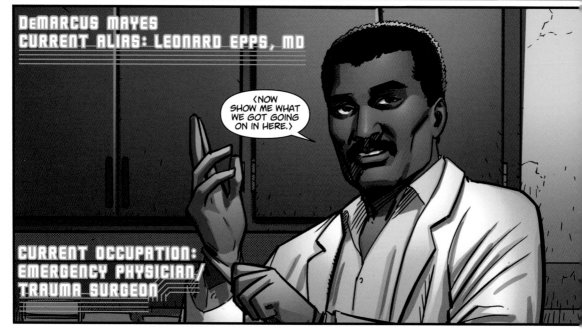

DeMARCUS MAYES
CURRENT ALIAS: LEONARD EPPS, MD

⟨NOW SHOW ME WHAT WE GOT GOING ON IN HERE.⟩

CURRENT OCCUPATION:
EMERGENCY PHYSICIAN/
TRAUMA SURGEON

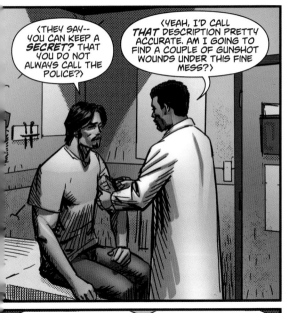

⟨THEY SAY-- YOU CAN KEEP A *SECRET*? THAT YOU DO NOT ALWAYS CALL THE POLICE?⟩

⟨YEAH, I'D CALL *THAT* DESCRIPTION PRETTY ACCURATE. AM I GOING TO FIND A COUPLE OF GUNSHOT WOUNDS UNDER THIS FINE MESS?⟩

⟨HMM... SOMETHING SHARPER, I SEE.⟩

⟨DOES ANYONE ELSE KNOW YOU CAME HERE TONIGHT? ANY FAMILY MY NURSE SHOULD CONTACT?⟩

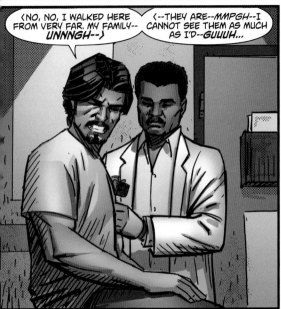

⟨NO, NO, I WALKED HERE FROM VERY FAR. MY FAMILY-- *UNNNGH*--⟩

⟨--THEY ARE--*MMPGH*--I CANNOT SEE THEM AS MUCH AS I'D--*GUUUH*...⟩

⟨*SORRY*, MR. RENDOZA... THIS'LL DEFINITELY HELP YOU WITH THAT.⟩

⟨*UUU*HH... SOMETHING IS... I FEELLL....⟩

⟨ANGIE, PLEASE BRING MY KIT DOWN AND PREP THE ROOM PLEASE--⟩

⟨I AGREE THAT HE'LL BE ABSOLUTELY *PERFECT*.⟩

⟨THANK YOU, DOCTOR. GOOD LUCK TO YOU.⟩

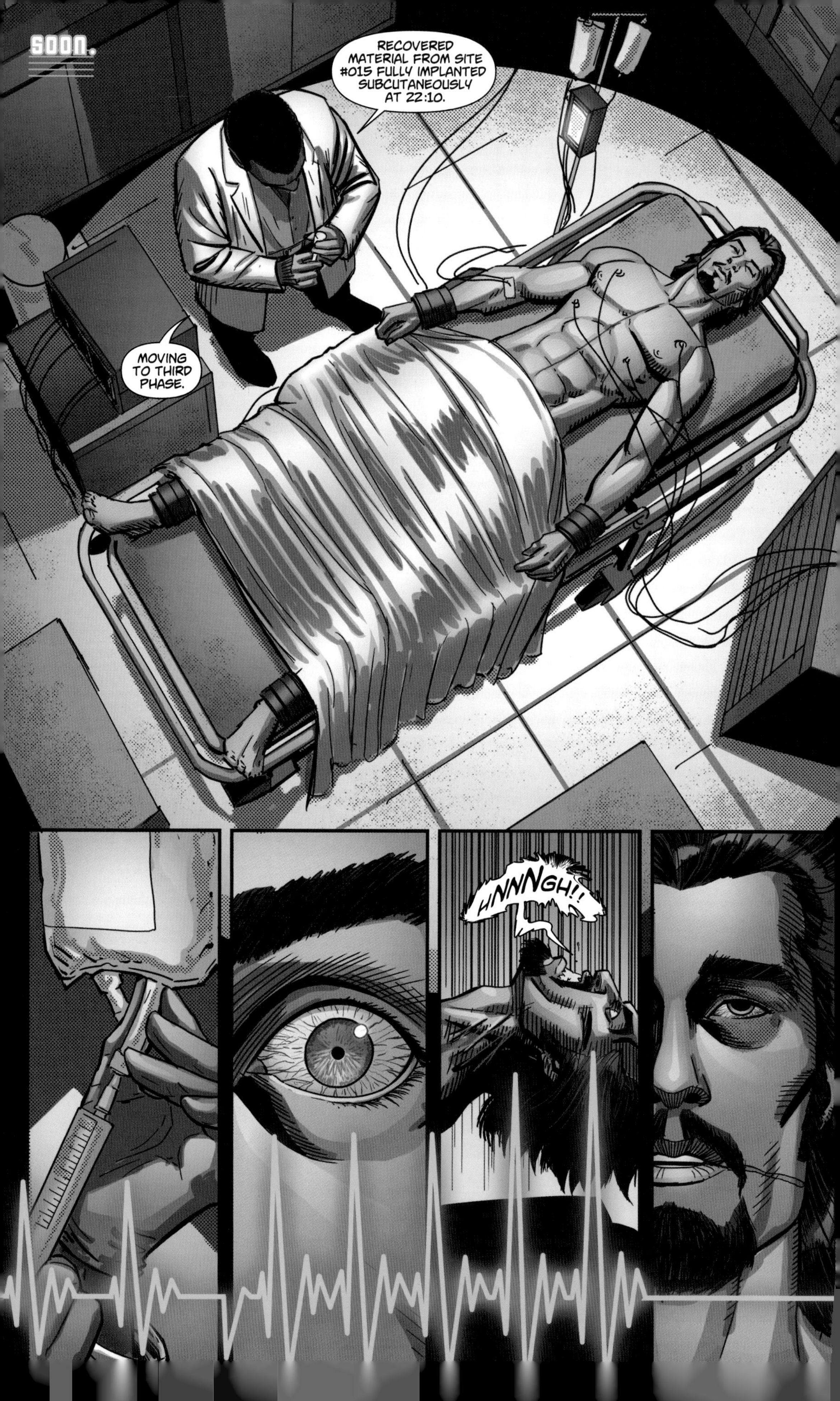
SOON.
RECOVERED MATERIAL FROM SITE #015 FULLY IMPLANTED SUBCUTANEOUSLY AT 22:10.
MOVING TO THIRD PHASE.
HNNNGH!!

PHASE FOUR. BEGINNING COUNTDOWN.

5 MINS 27 SECONDS

9 MINS 13 SECONDS

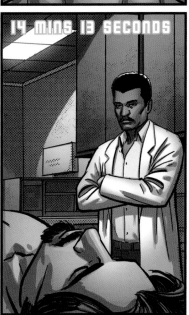

14 MINS 13 SECONDS

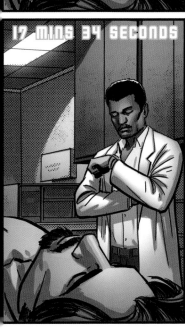

17 MINS 34 SECONDS

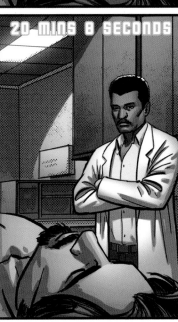

20 MINS 8 SECONDS

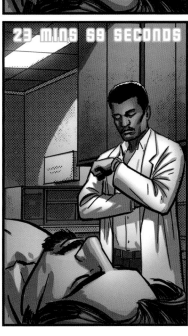

23 MINS 59 SECONDS

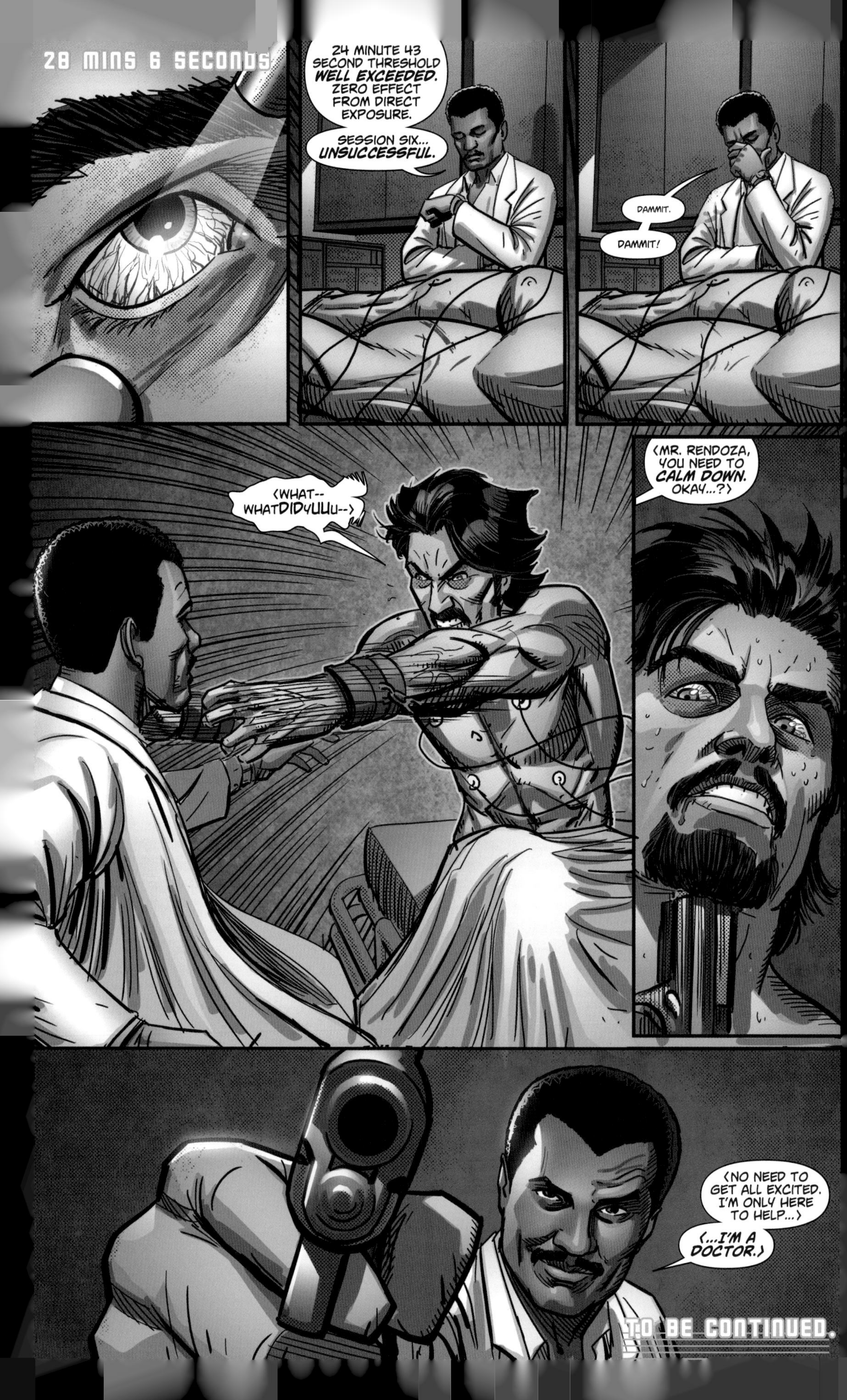
28 MINS 6 SECONDS
24 MINUTE 43 SECOND THRESHOLD WELL EXCEEDED. ZERO EFFECT FROM DIRECT EXPOSURE.
SESSION SIX... UNSUCCESSFUL.
DAMMIT.
DAMMIT!
‹WHAT-- WHATDIDYUUu--›
‹MR. RENDOZA, YOU NEED TO CALM DOWN. OKAY...?›
‹NO NEED TO GET ALL EXCITED. I'M ONLY HERE TO HELP...›
‹...I'M A DOCTOR.›
TO BE CONTINUED.

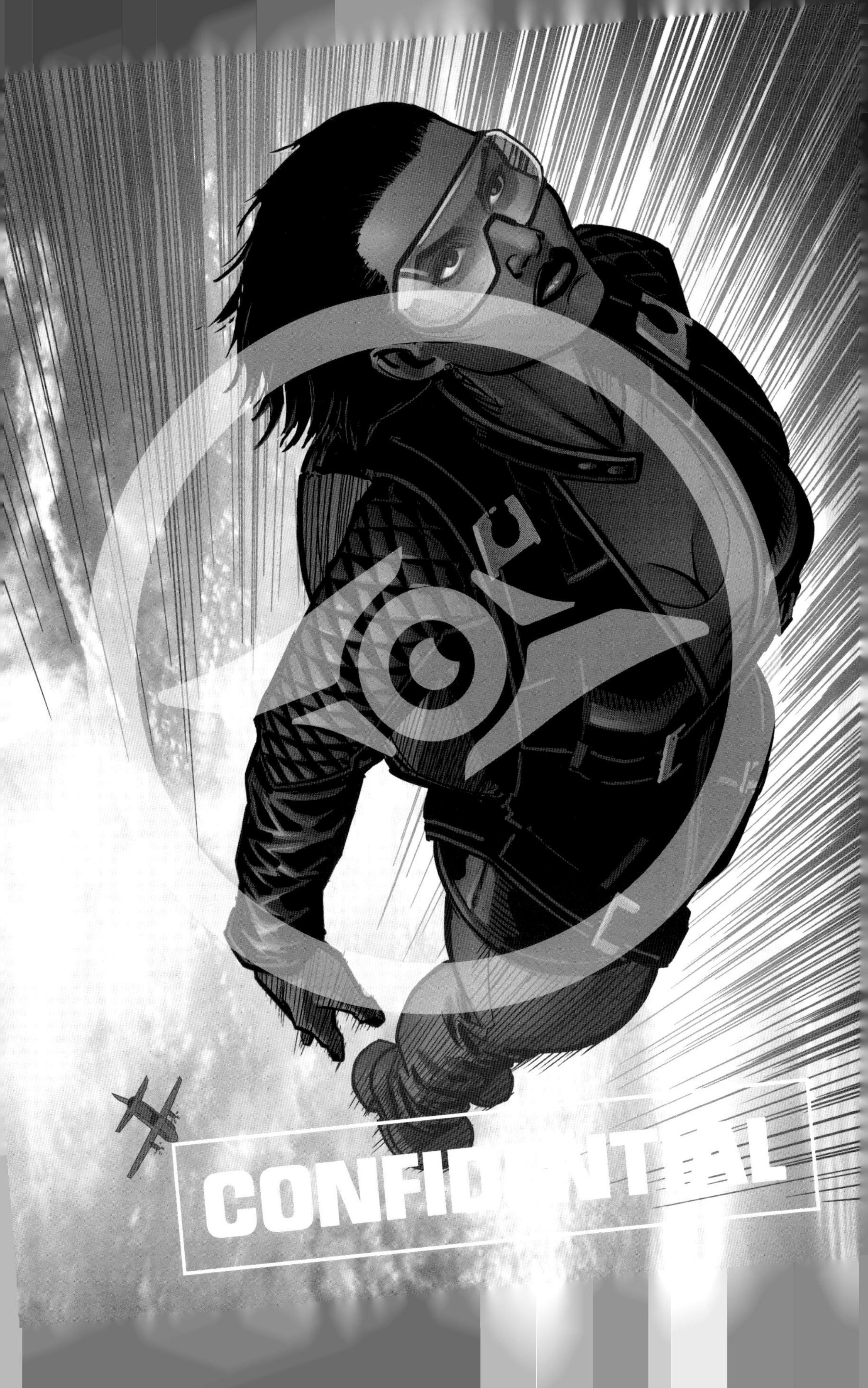
CONFIDENTIAL

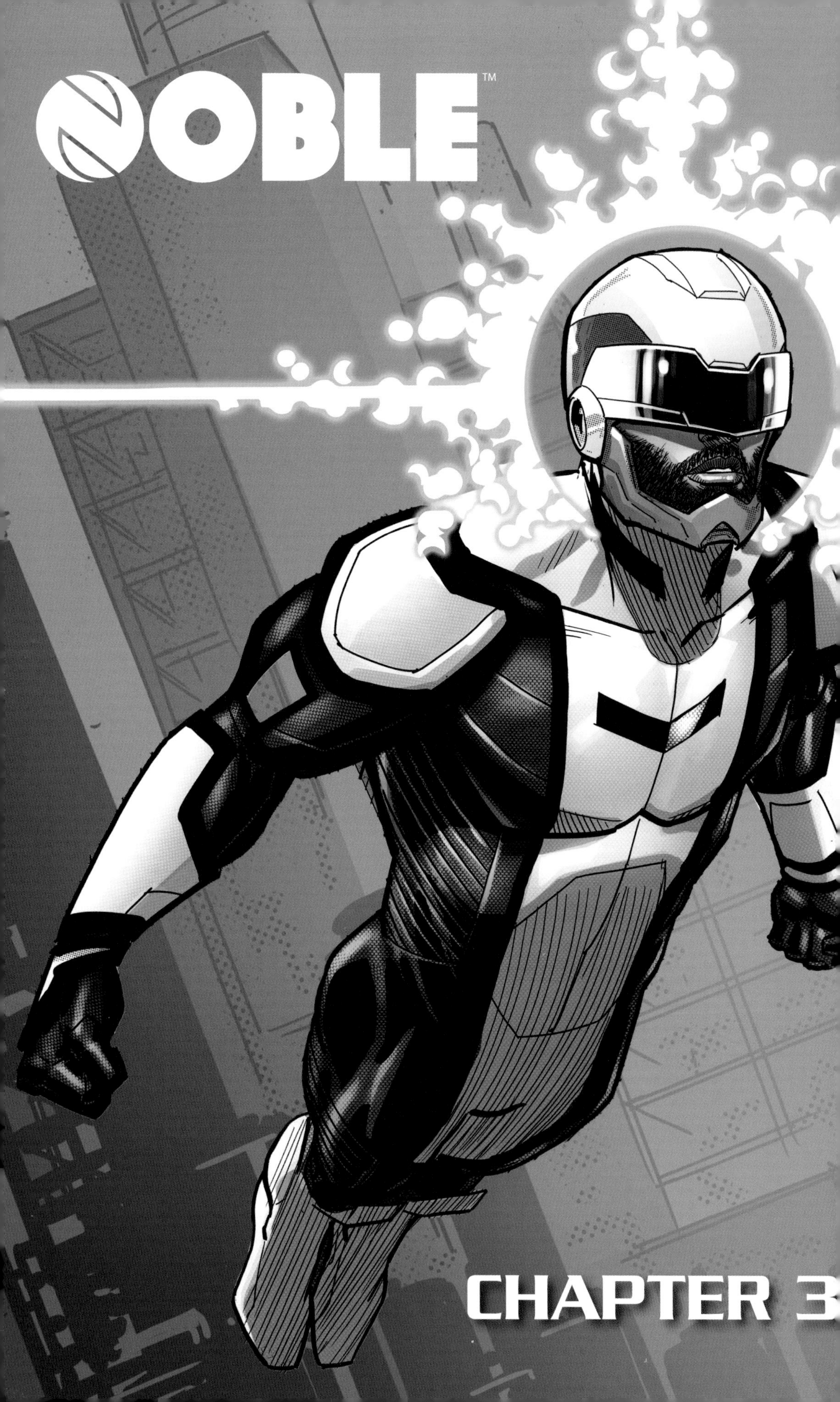
NOBLE™
CHAPTER 3

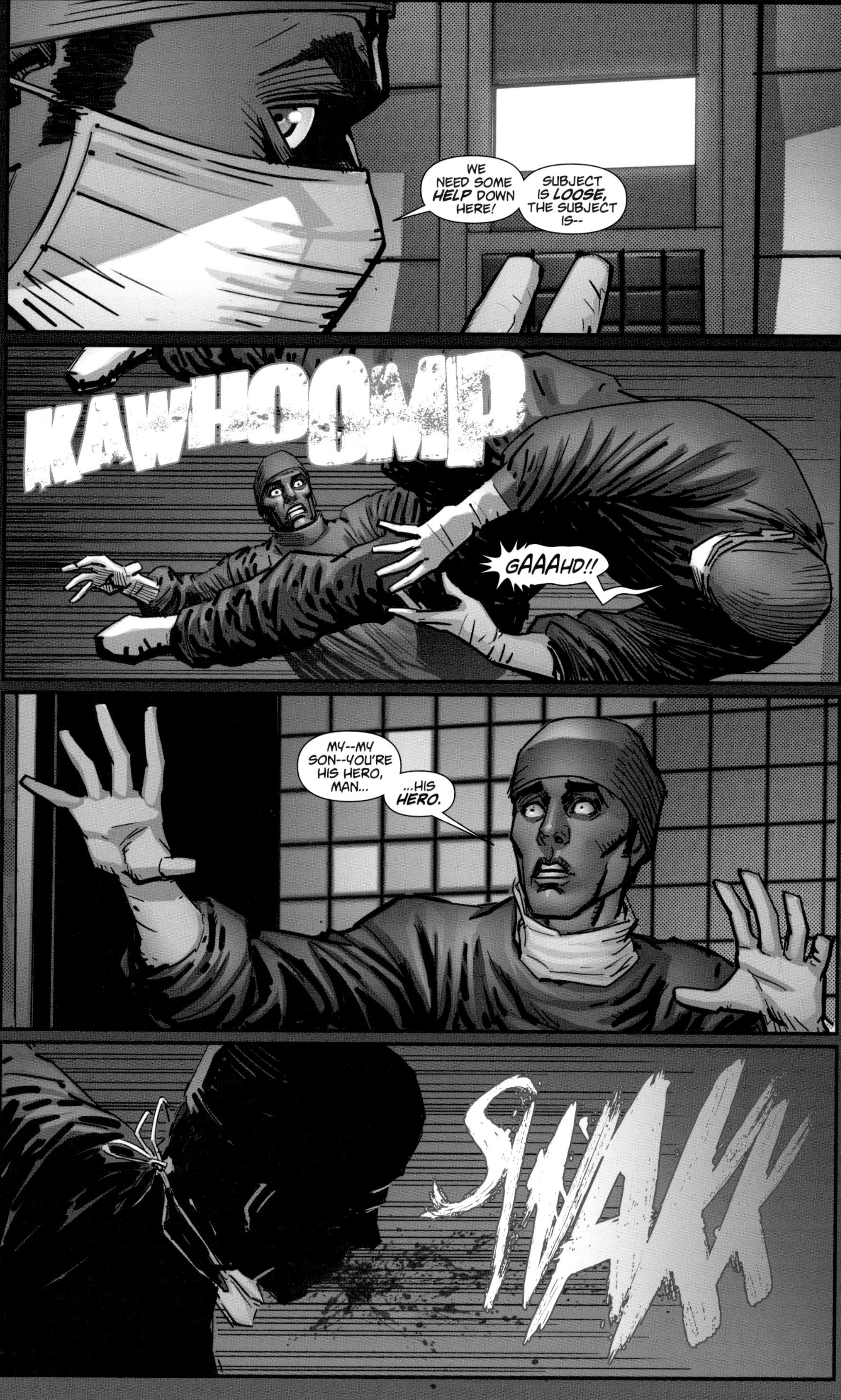
WE NEED SOME HELP DOWN HERE!
SUBJECT IS LOOSE, THE SUBJECT IS--
KAWHOOMP
GAAAHD!!
MY--MY SON--YOU'RE HIS HERO, MAN...
...HIS HERO.
SHAKK

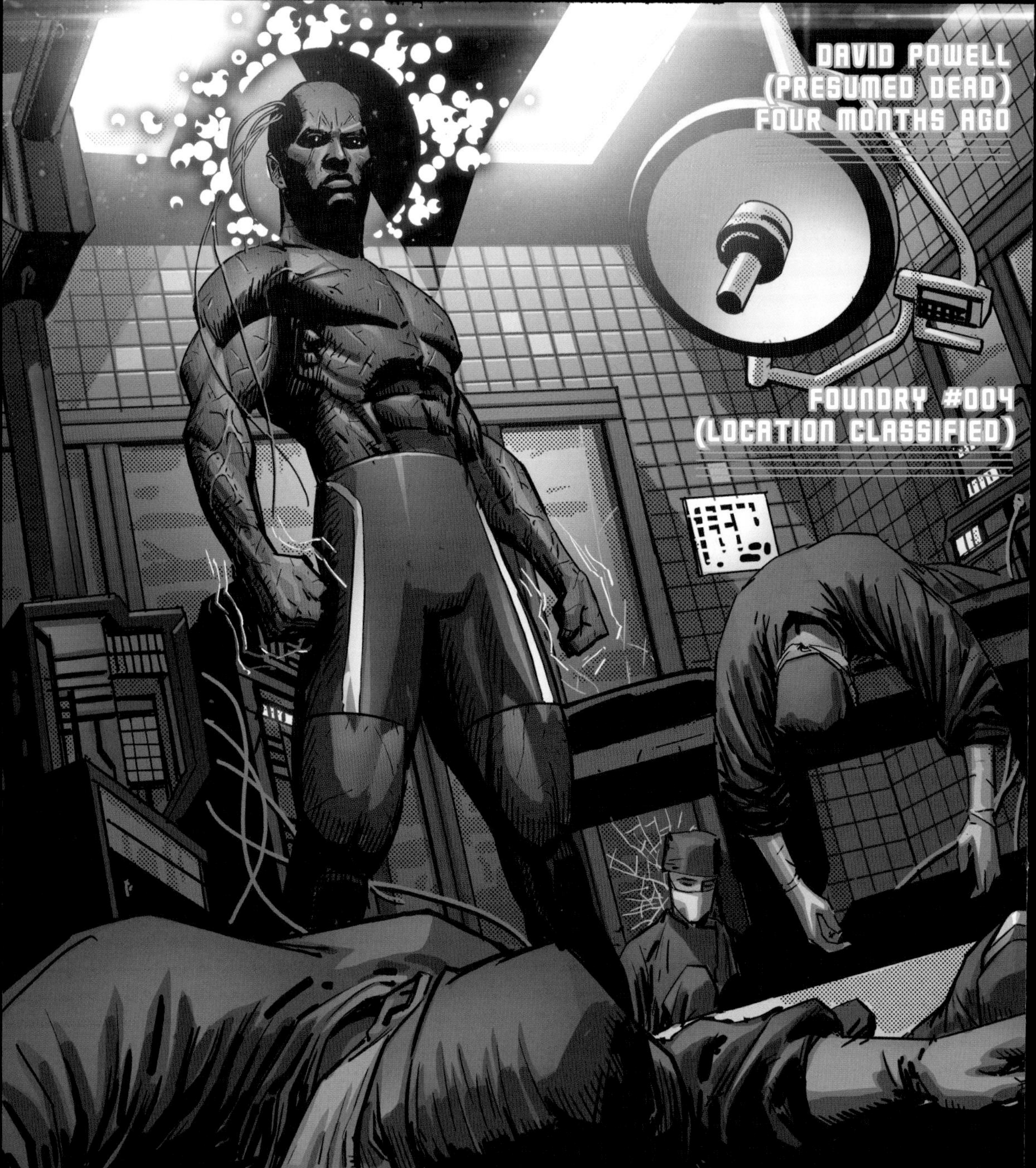
DAVID POWELL
(PRESUMED DEAD)
FOUR MONTHS AGO
FOUNDRY #004
(LOCATION CLASSIFIED)

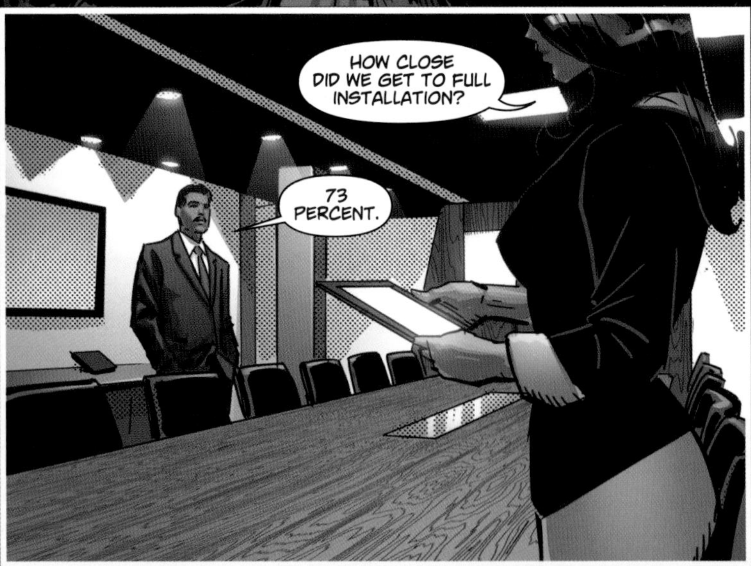
HOW CLOSE DID WE GET TO FULL INSTALLATION?
73 PERCENT.

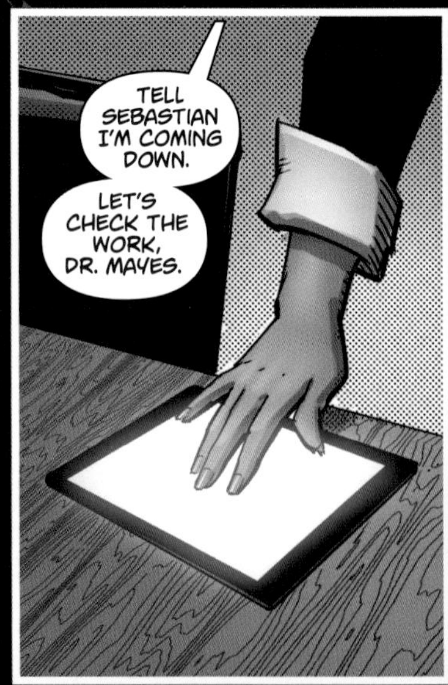
TELL SEBASTIAN I'M COMING DOWN.
LET'S CHECK THE WORK, DR. MAYES.

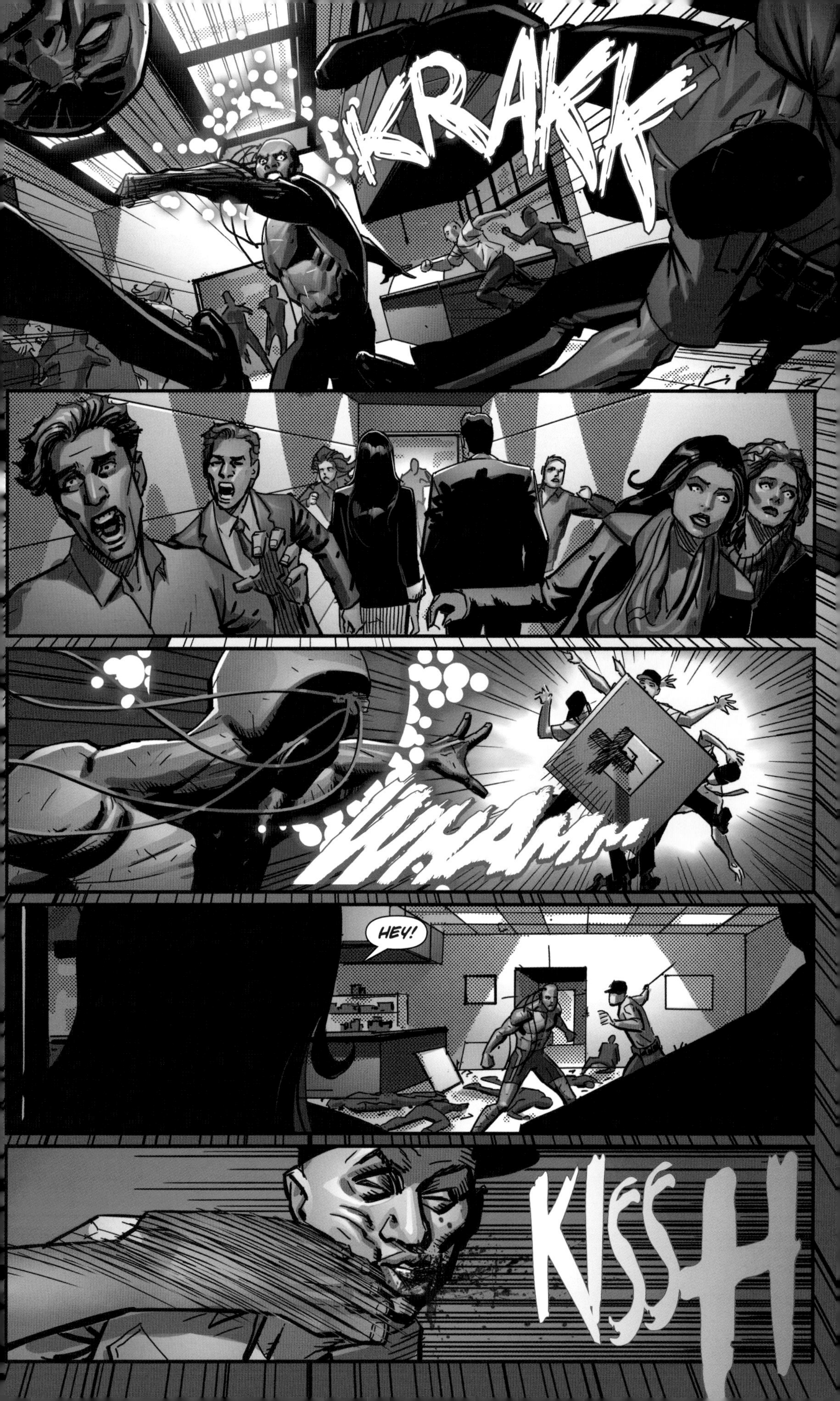
KRAKK
WHAMM
HEY!
KISSH

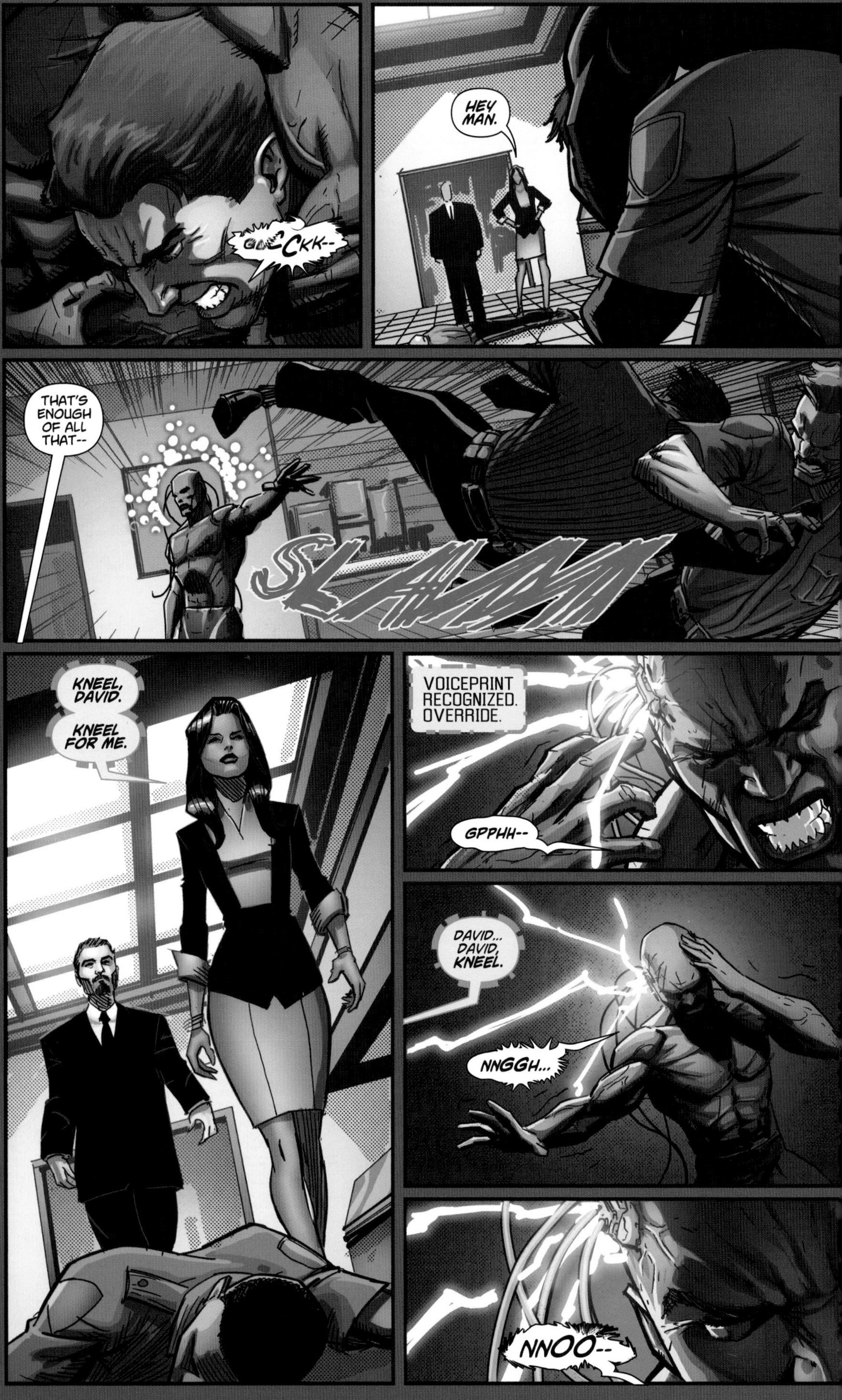
GGCCKK--
HEY MAN.
THAT'S ENOUGH OF ALL THAT--
SLAMM
KNEEL, DAVID.
KNEEL FOR ME.
VOICEPRINT RECOGNIZED. OVERRIDE.
GPPHH--
DAVID... DAVID, KNEEL.
NNGGH...
NNOO--

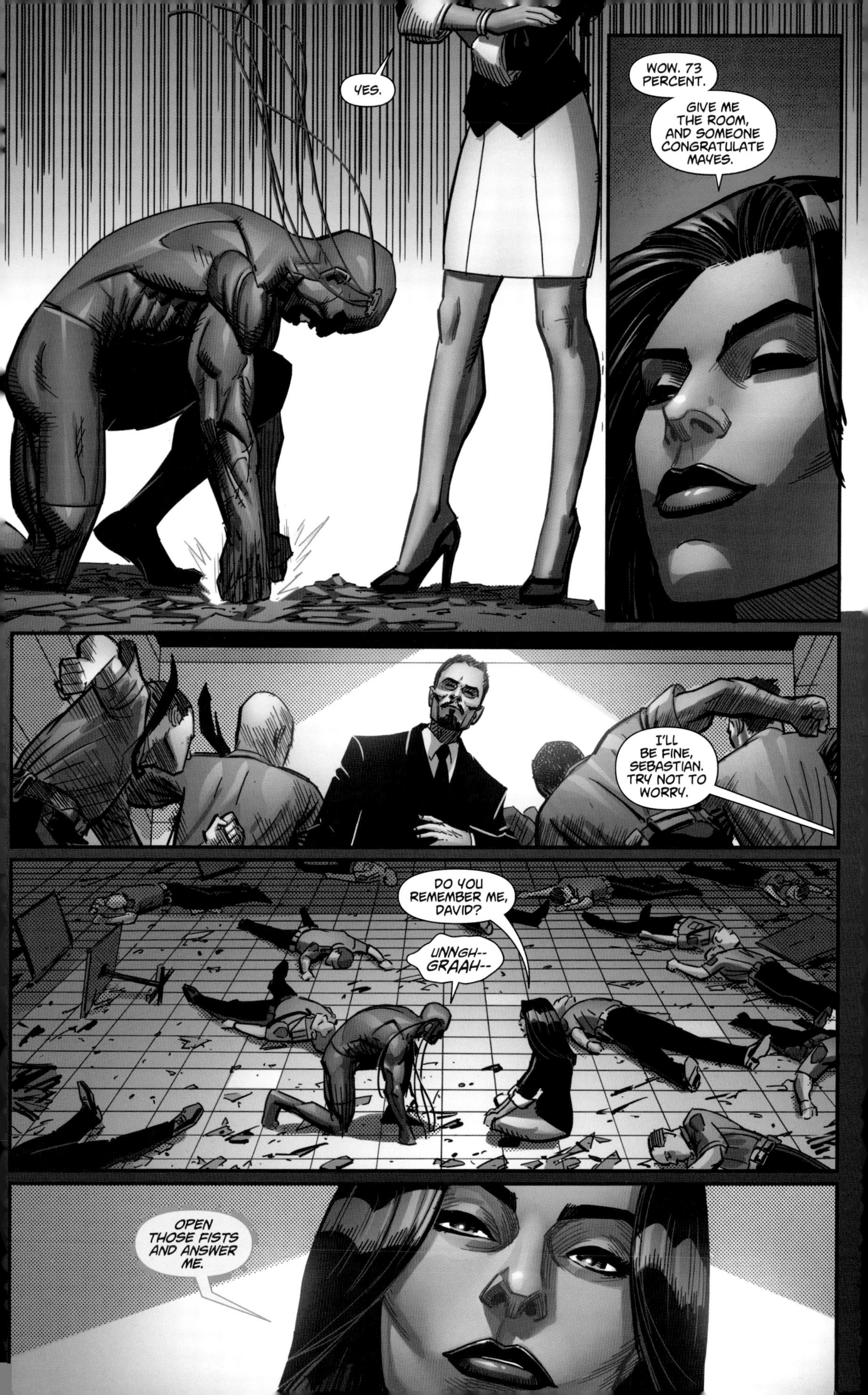
YES.
WOW. 73 PERCENT.
GIVE ME THE ROOM, AND SOMEONE CONGRATULATE MAYES.
I'LL BE FINE, SEBASTIAN. TRY NOT TO WORRY.
DO YOU REMEMBER ME, DAVID?
UNNGH-- GRAAH--
OPEN THOSE FISTS AND ANSWER ME.

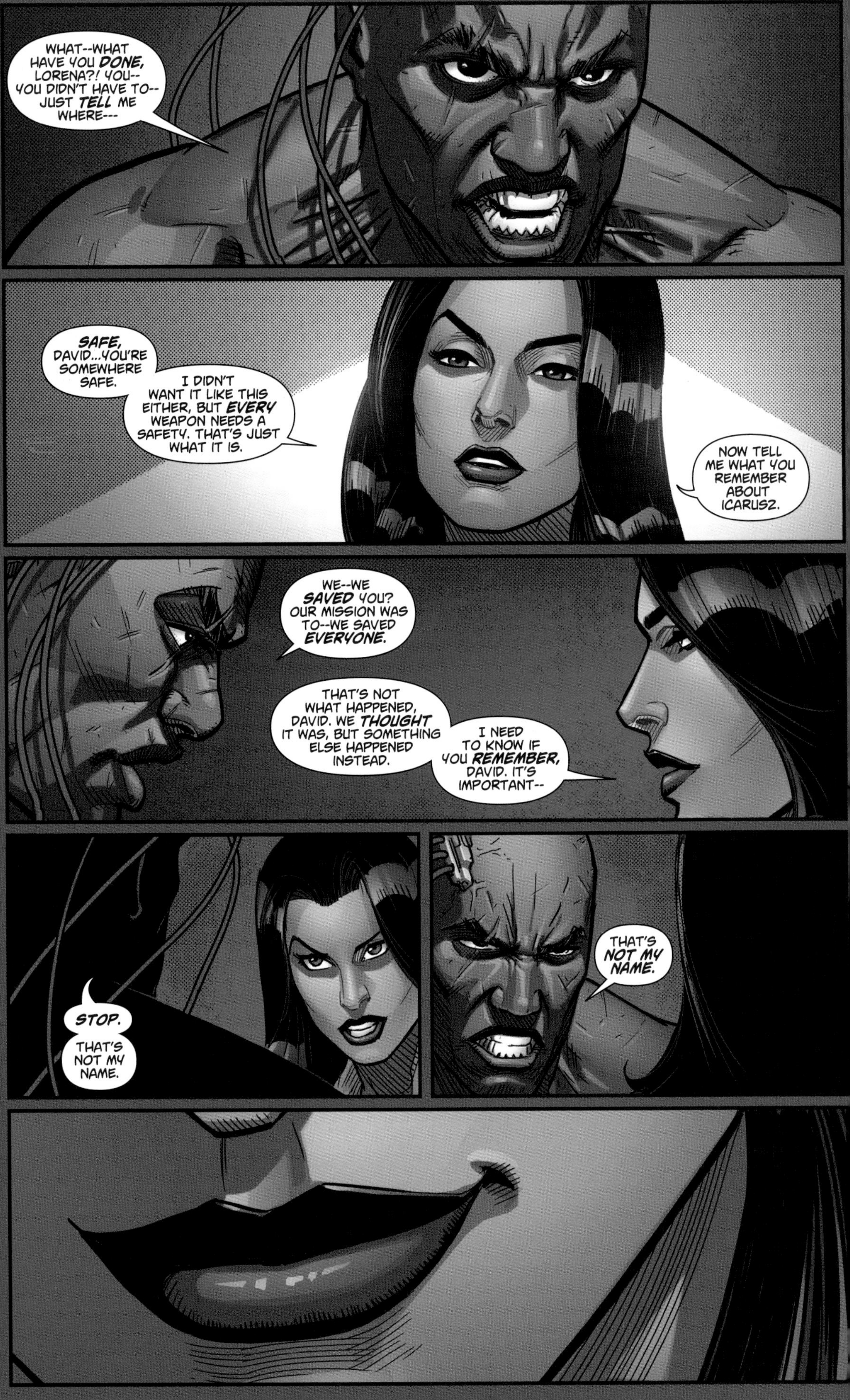
WHAT--WHAT HAVE YOU DONE, LORENA?! YOU--YOU DIDN'T HAVE TO--JUST TELL ME WHERE---
SAFE, DAVID...YOU'RE SOMEWHERE SAFE.
I DIDN'T WANT IT LIKE THIS EITHER, BUT EVERY WEAPON NEEDS A SAFETY. THAT'S JUST WHAT IT IS.
NOW TELL ME WHAT YOU REMEMBER ABOUT ICARUS2.
WE--WE SAVED YOU? OUR MISSION WAS TO--WE SAVED EVERYONE.
THAT'S NOT WHAT HAPPENED, DAVID. WE THOUGHT IT WAS, BUT SOMETHING ELSE HAPPENED INSTEAD.
I NEED TO KNOW IF YOU REMEMBER, DAVID. IT'S IMPORTANT--
STOP.
THAT'S NOT MY NAME.
THAT'S NOT MY NAME.

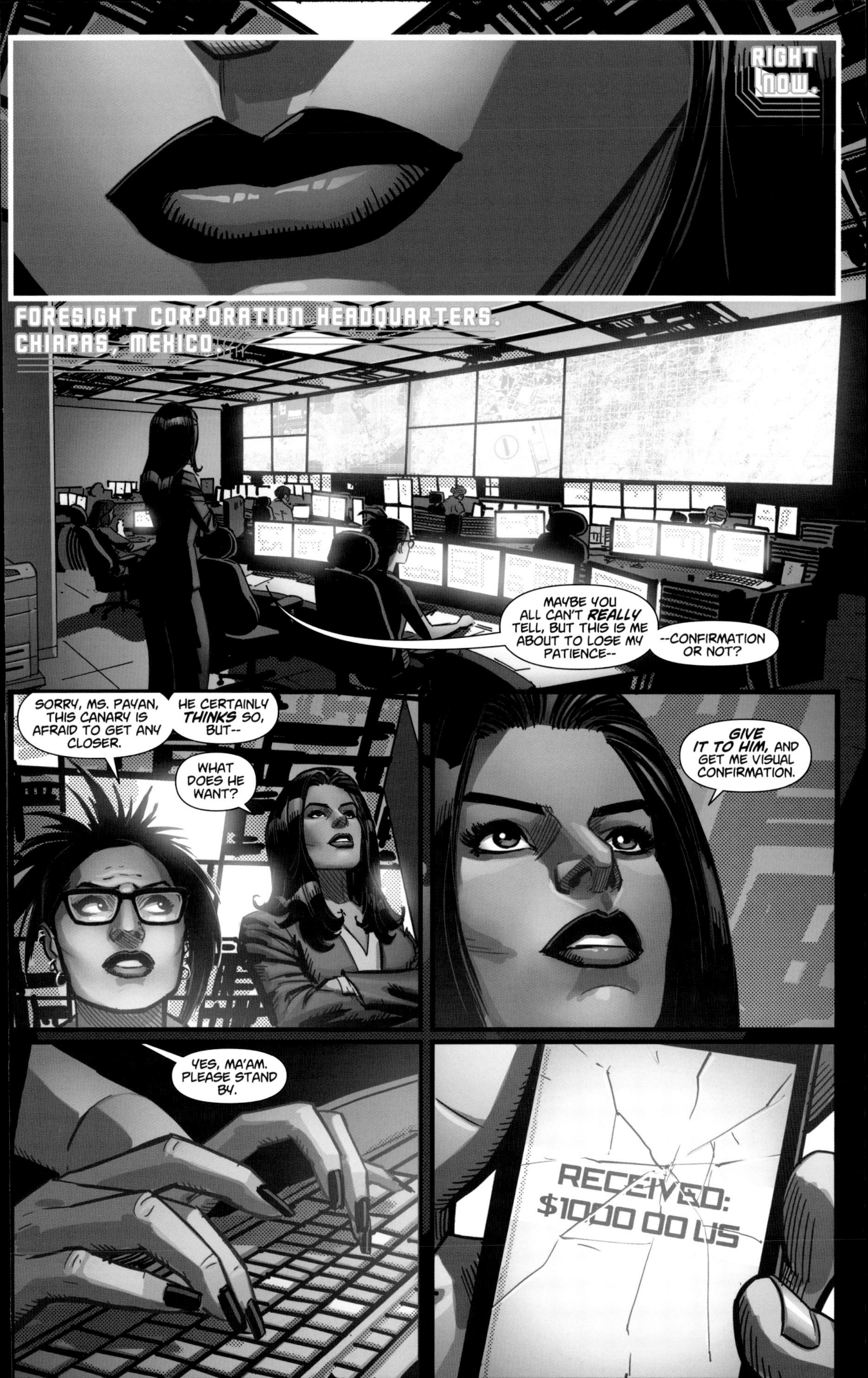
RIGHT NOW.
FORESIGHT CORPORATION HEADQUARTERS. CHIAPAS, MEXICO.
MAYBE YOU ALL CAN'T REALLY TELL, BUT THIS IS ME ABOUT TO LOSE MY PATIENCE--
--CONFIRMATION OR NOT?
SORRY, MS. PAYAN, THIS CANARY IS AFRAID TO GET ANY CLOSER.
HE CERTAINLY THINKS SO, BUT--
WHAT DOES HE WANT?
GIVE IT TO HIM, AND GET ME VISUAL CONFIRMATION.
YES, MA'AM. PLEASE STAND BY.
RECEIVED: $1000 00 US

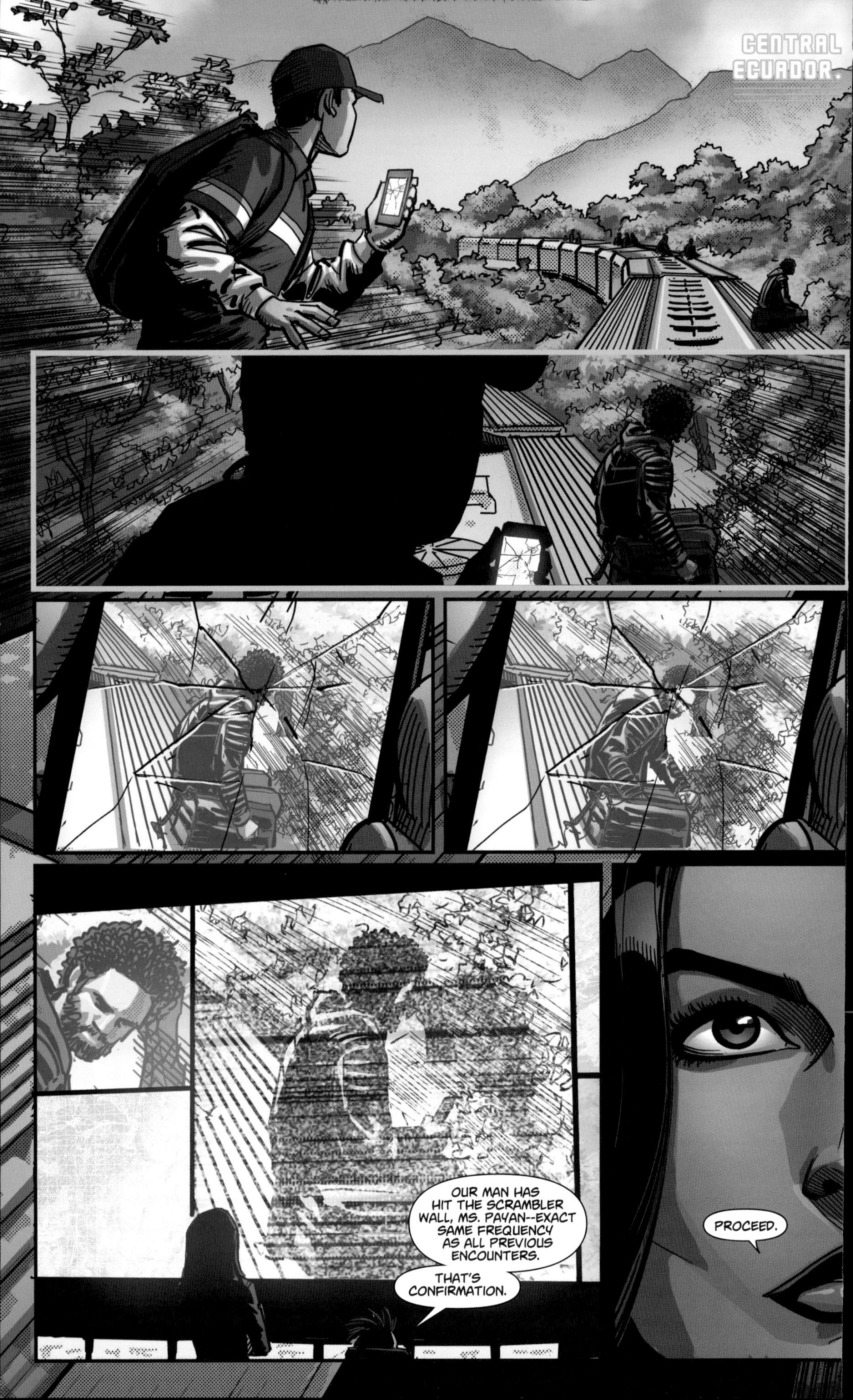
CENTRAL ECUADOR.
OUR MAN HAS HIT THE SCRAMBLER WALL, MS. PAYAN--EXACT SAME FREQUENCY AS ALL PREVIOUS ENCOUNTERS.
THAT'S CONFIRMATION.
PROCEED.

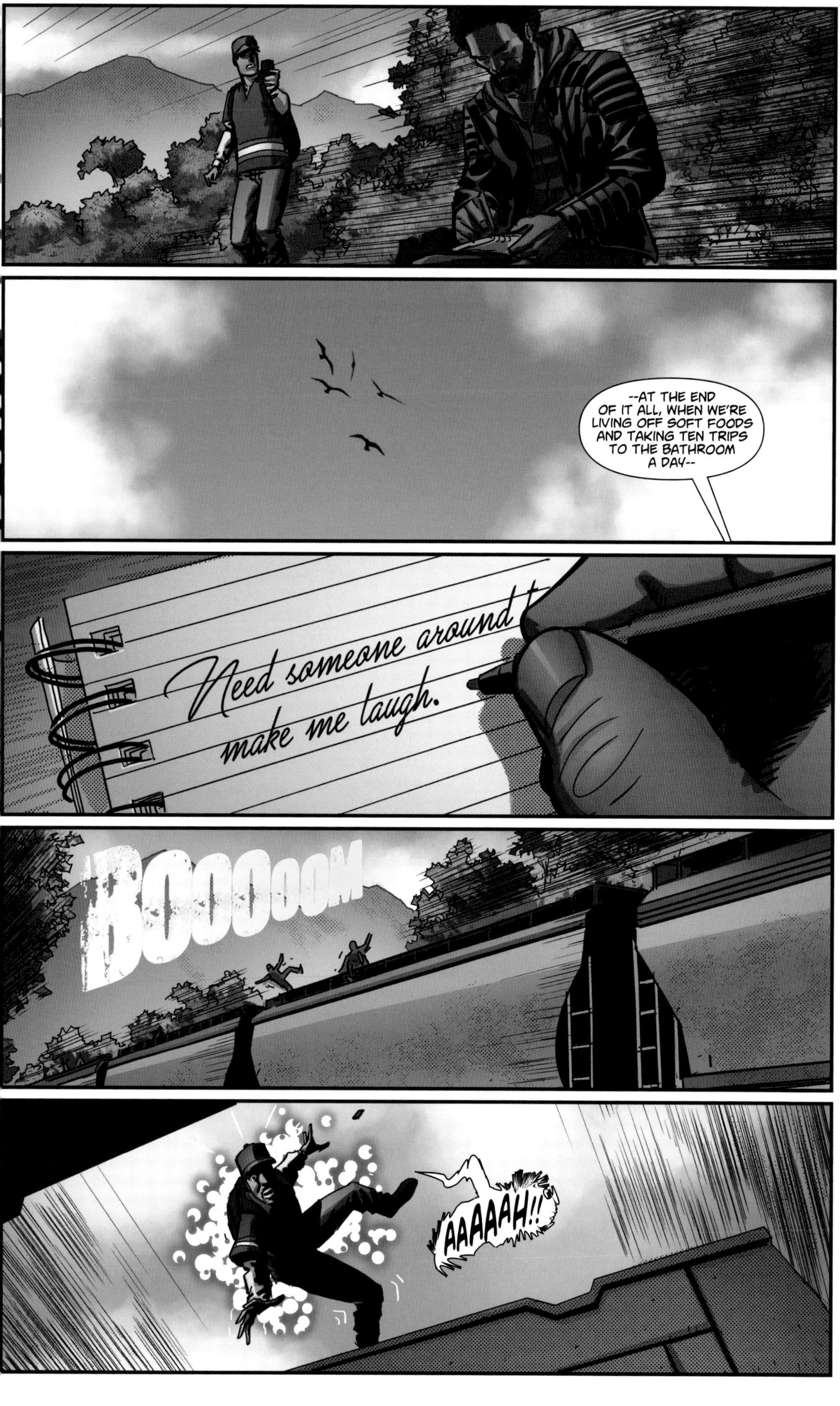
--AT THE END OF IT ALL, WHEN WE'RE LIVING OFF SOFT FOODS AND TAKING TEN TRIPS TO THE BATHROOM A DAY--
Need someone around
make me laugh.
BOOOooM
AAAAAH!!

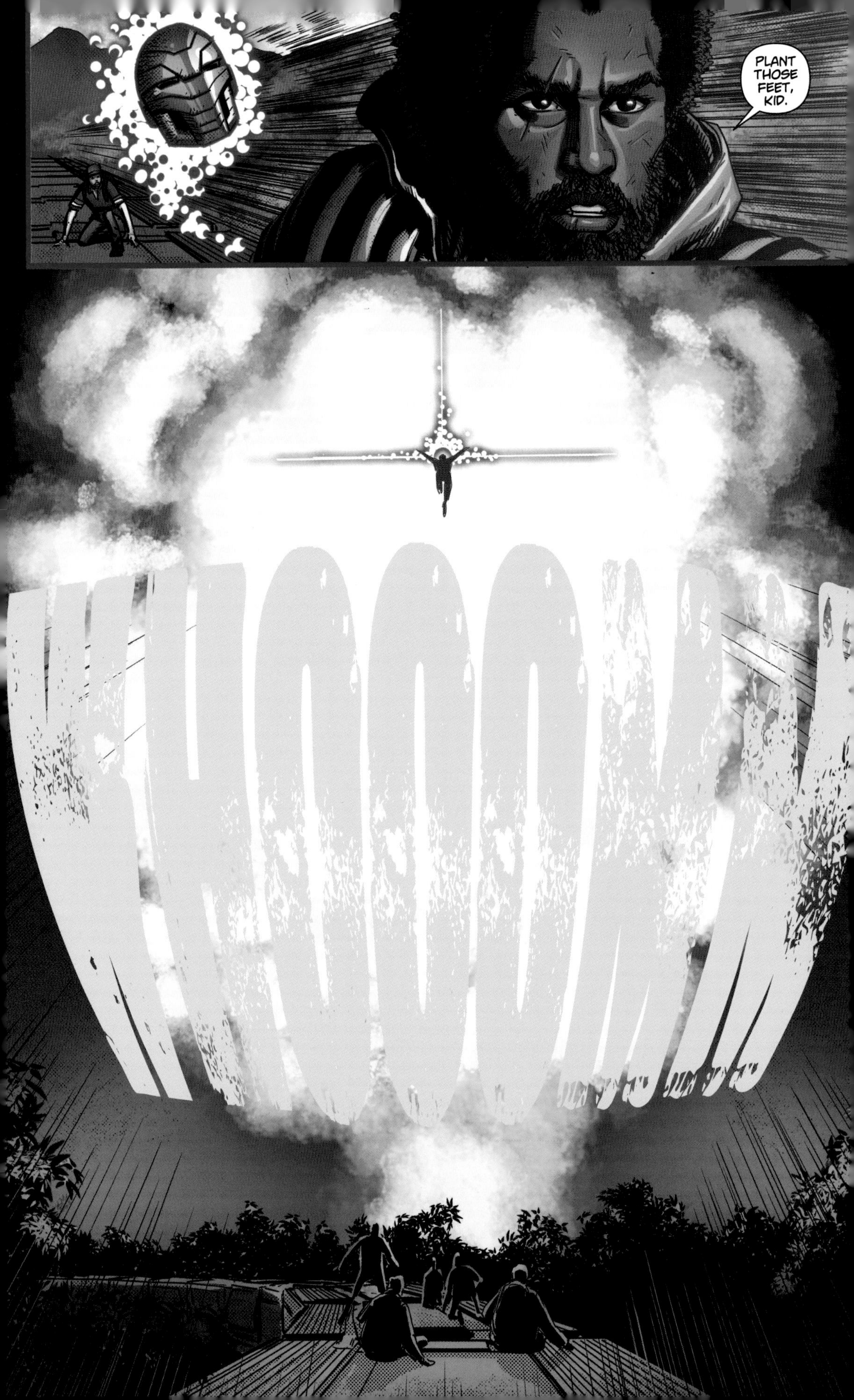
PLANT THOSE FEET, KID.

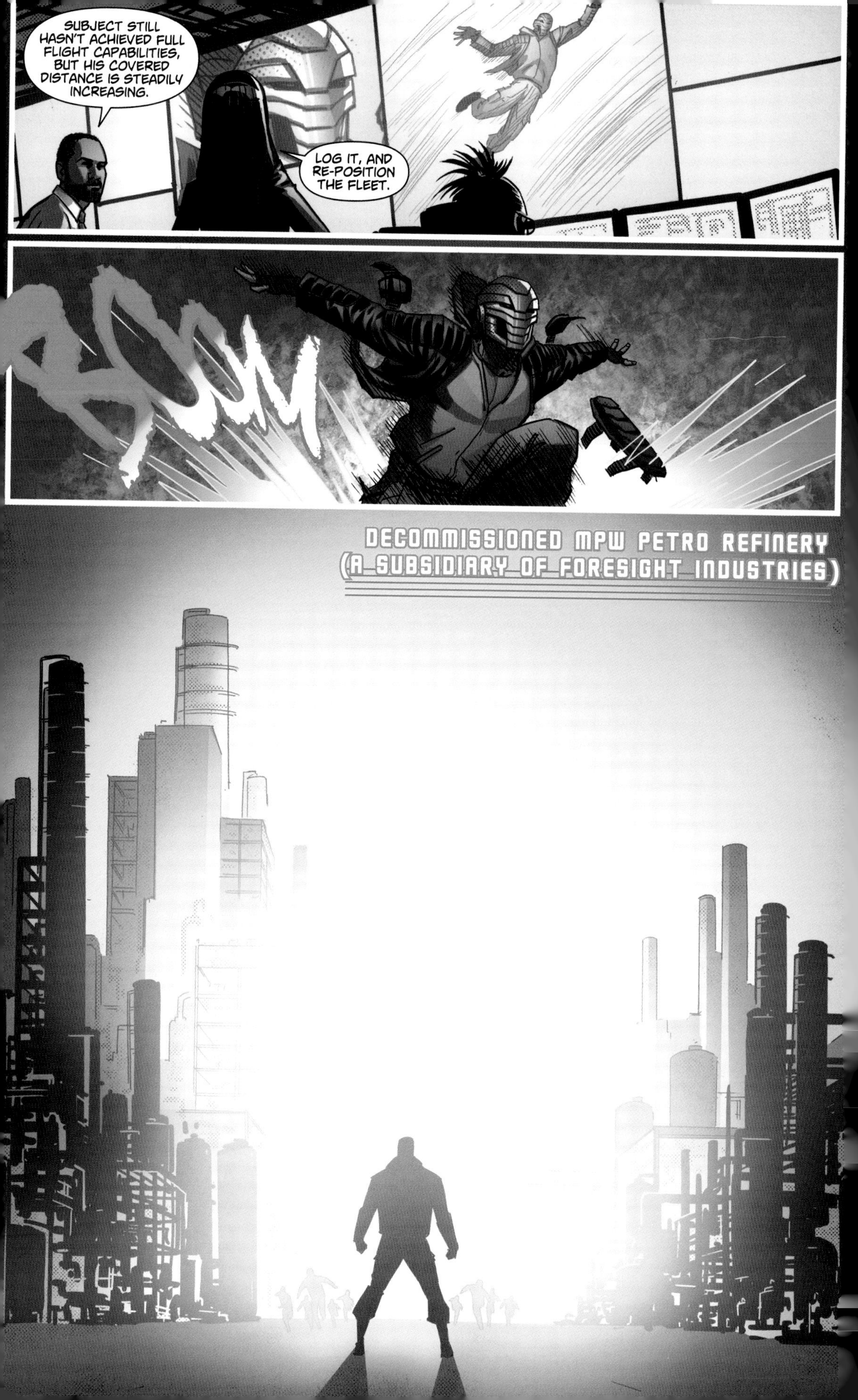
SUBJECT STILL HASN'T ACHIEVED FULL FLIGHT CAPABILITIES, BUT HIS COVERED DISTANCE IS STEADILY INCREASING.
LOG IT, AND RE-POSITION THE FLEET.
DECOMMISSIONED MPW PETRO REFINERY (A SUBSIDIARY OF FORESIGHT INDUSTRIES)

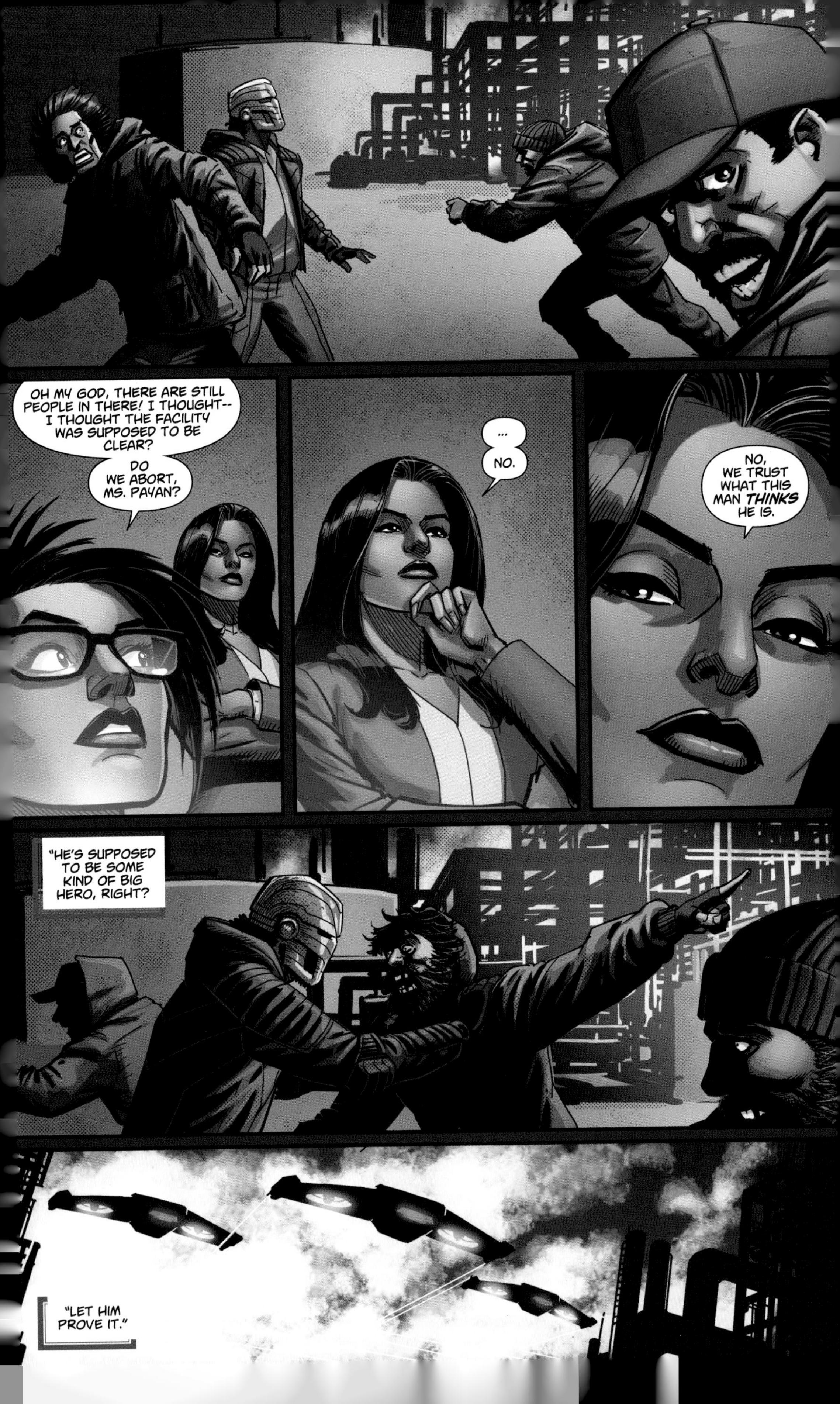
OH MY GOD, THERE ARE STILL PEOPLE IN THERE! I THOUGHT-- I THOUGHT THE FACILITY WAS SUPPOSED TO BE CLEAR?
DO WE ABORT, MS. PAYAN?
...
NO.
NO, WE TRUST WHAT THIS MAN *THINKS* HE IS.
"HE'S SUPPOSED TO BE SOME KIND OF BIG HERO, RIGHT?
"LET HIM PROVE IT."

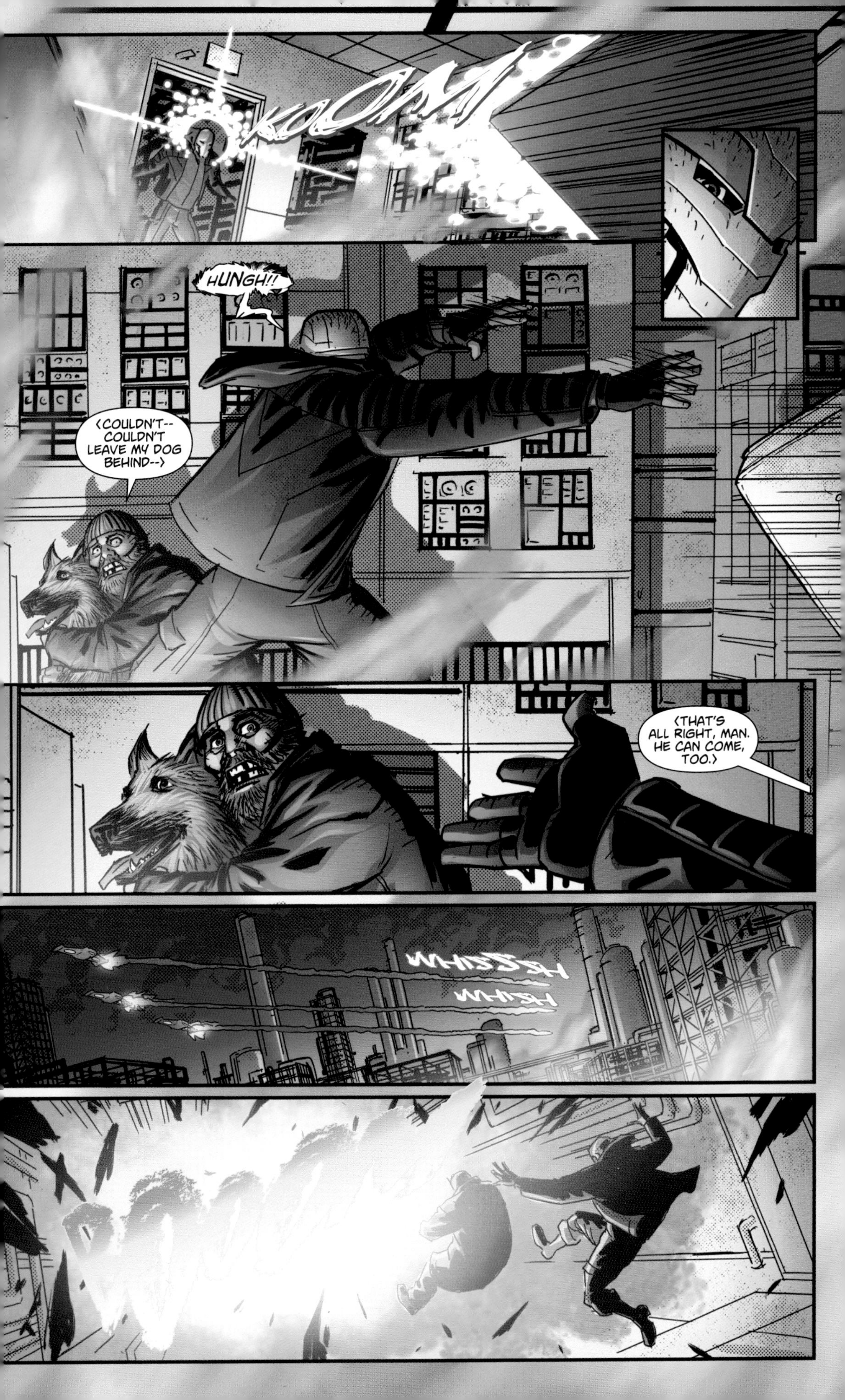
KOOM!
HUNGH!!
‹COULDN'T-- COULDN'T LEAVE MY DOG BEHIND--›
‹THAT'S ALL RIGHT, MAN. HE CAN COME, TOO.›
WHISSSH
WHISH

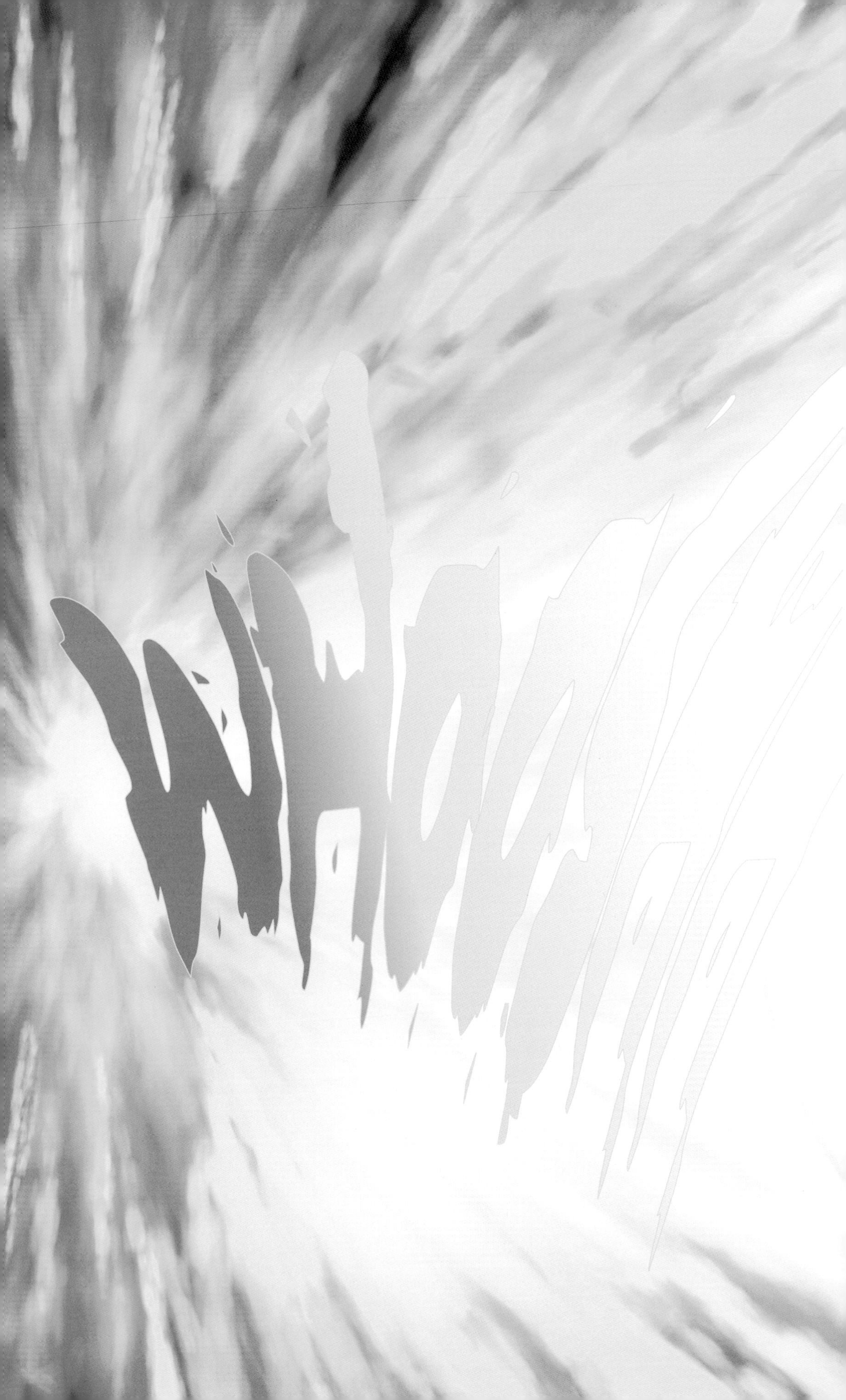

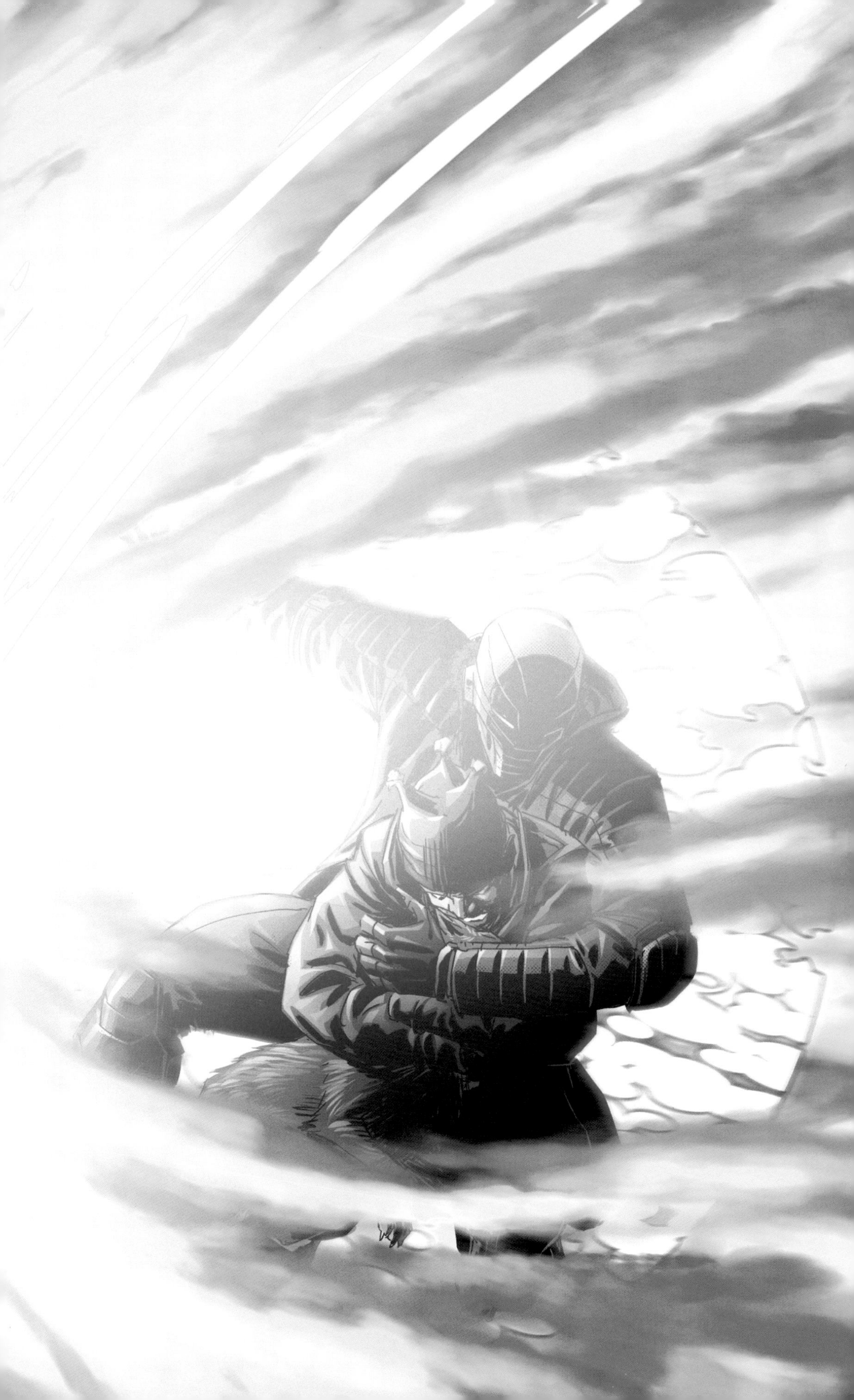

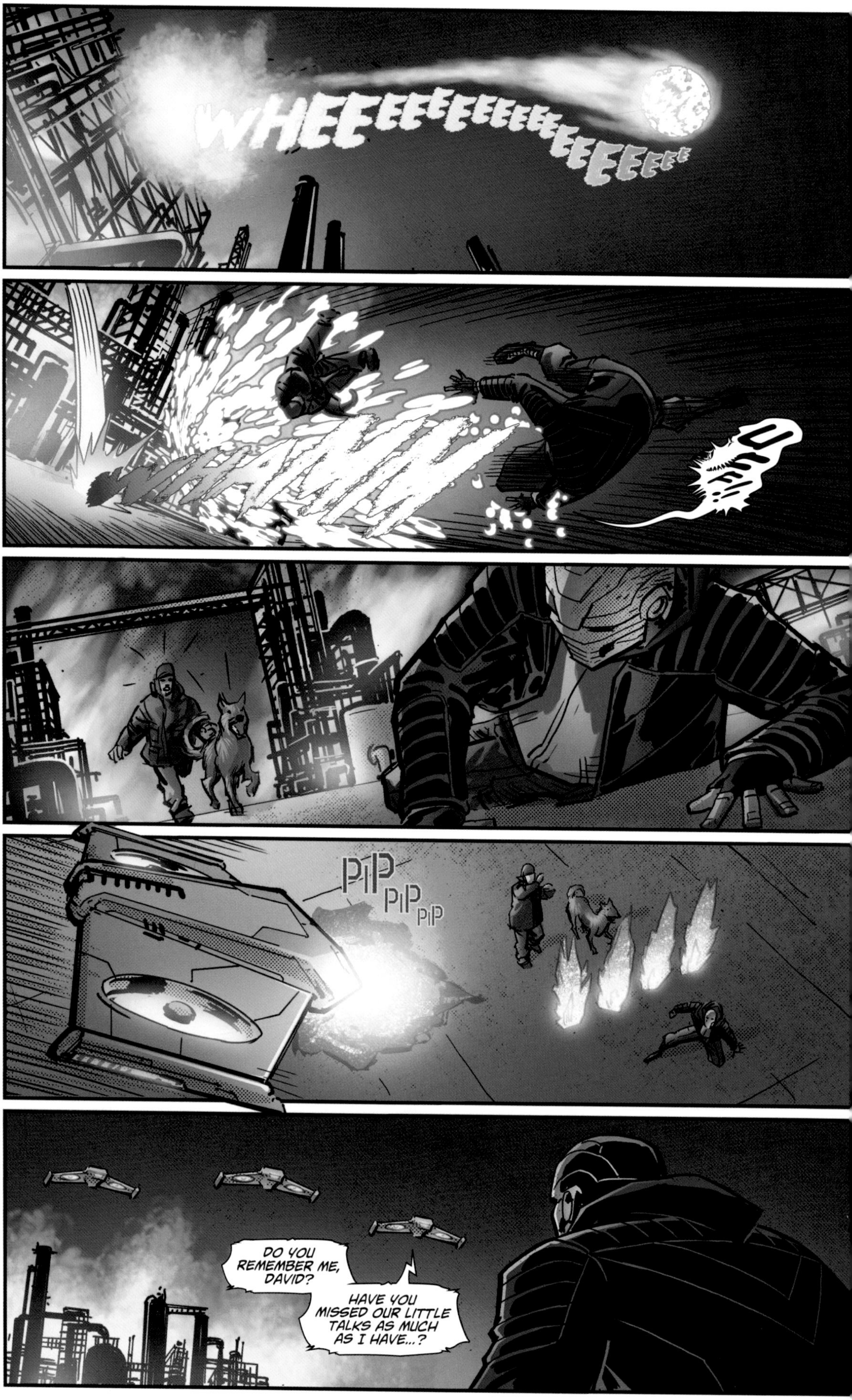
PIP PIP PIP
DO YOU REMEMBER ME, DAVID?
HAVE YOU MISSED OUR LITTLE TALKS AS MUCH AS I HAVE...?

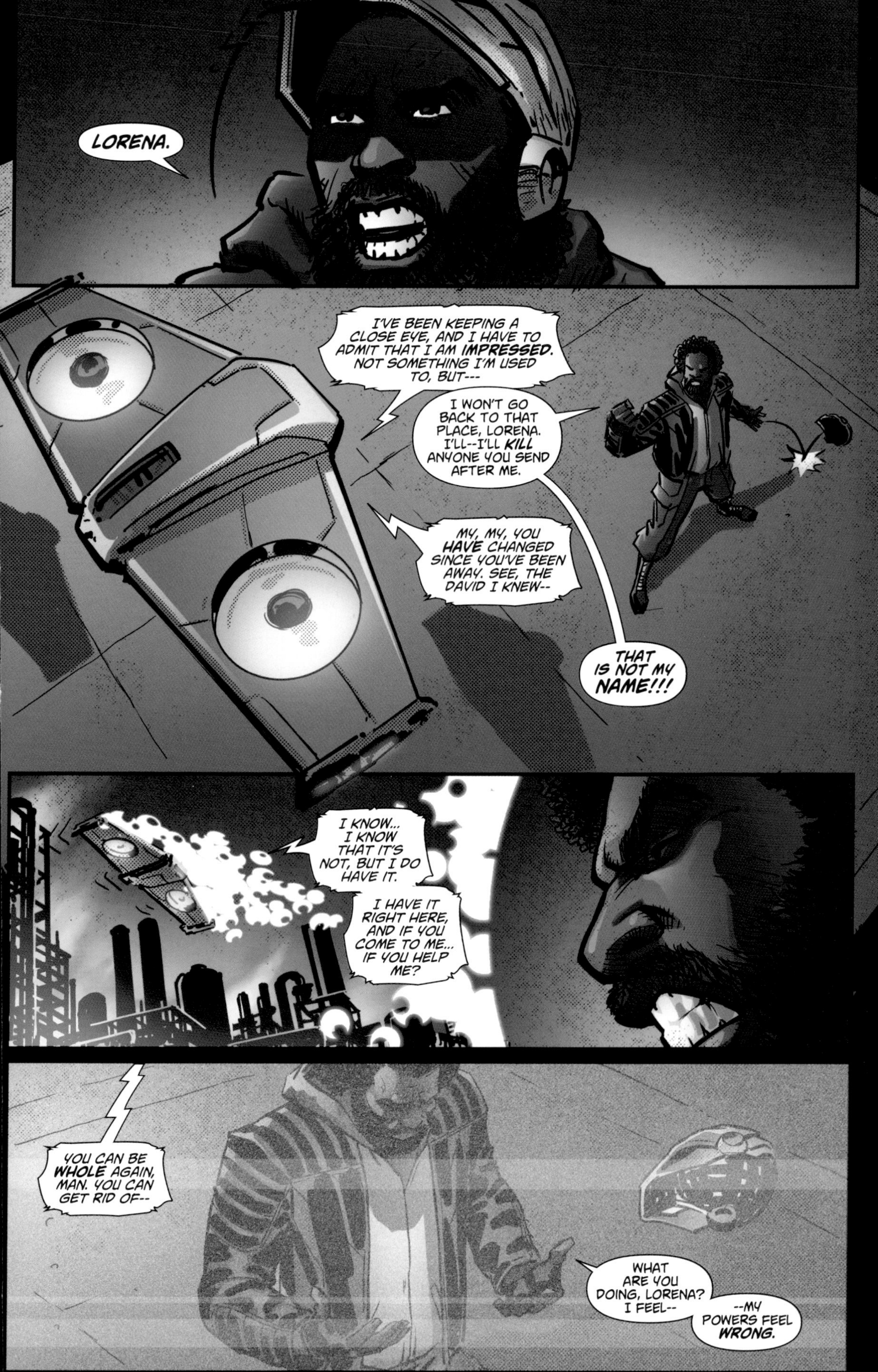
LORENA.
I'VE BEEN KEEPING A CLOSE EYE, AND I HAVE TO ADMIT THAT I AM IMPRESSED. NOT SOMETHING I'M USED TO, BUT---
I WON'T GO BACK TO THAT PLACE, LORENA. I'LL--I'LL KILL ANYONE YOU SEND AFTER ME.
MY, MY, YOU HAVE CHANGED SINCE YOU'VE BEEN AWAY. SEE, THE DAVID I KNEW--
THAT IS NOT MY NAME!!!
I KNOW... I KNOW THAT IT'S NOT, BUT I DO HAVE IT.
I HAVE IT RIGHT HERE, AND IF YOU COME TO ME... IF YOU HELP ME?
YOU CAN BE WHOLE AGAIN, MAN. YOU CAN GET RID OF--
WHAT ARE YOU DOING, LORENA? I FEEL--
--MY POWERS FEEL WRONG.

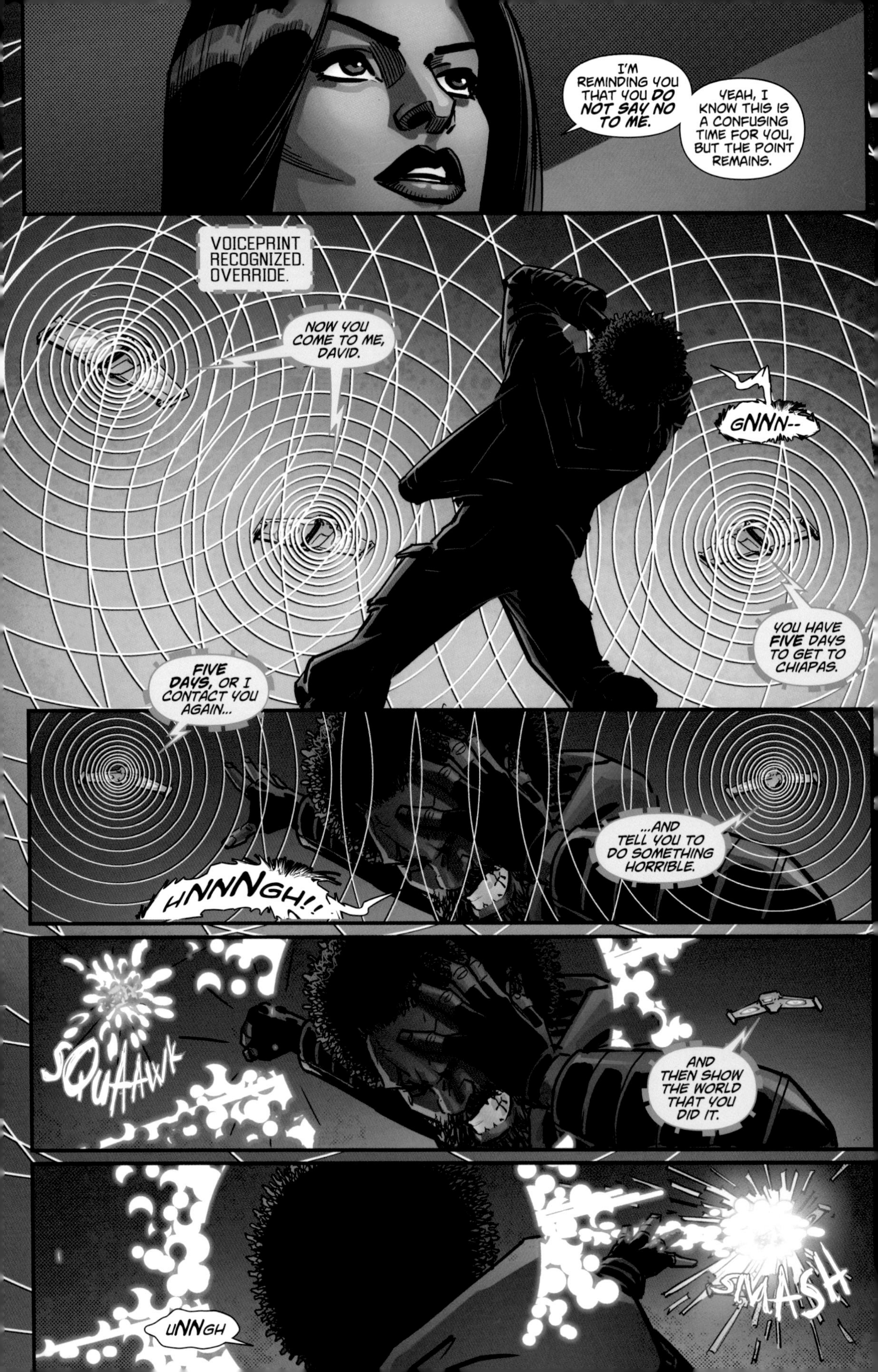
I'M REMINDING YOU THAT YOU DO NOT SAY NO TO ME.
YEAH, I KNOW THIS IS A CONFUSING TIME FOR YOU, BUT THE POINT REMAINS.
VOICEPRINT RECOGNIZED. OVERRIDE.
NOW YOU COME TO ME, DAVID.
GNNN--
YOU HAVE FIVE DAYS TO GET TO CHIAPAS.
FIVE DAYS, OR I CONTACT YOU AGAIN...
...AND TELL YOU TO DO SOMETHING HORRIBLE.
HNNNGH!!
SQUAAWK
AND THEN SHOW THE WORLD THAT YOU DID IT.
SMASH
UNNGH

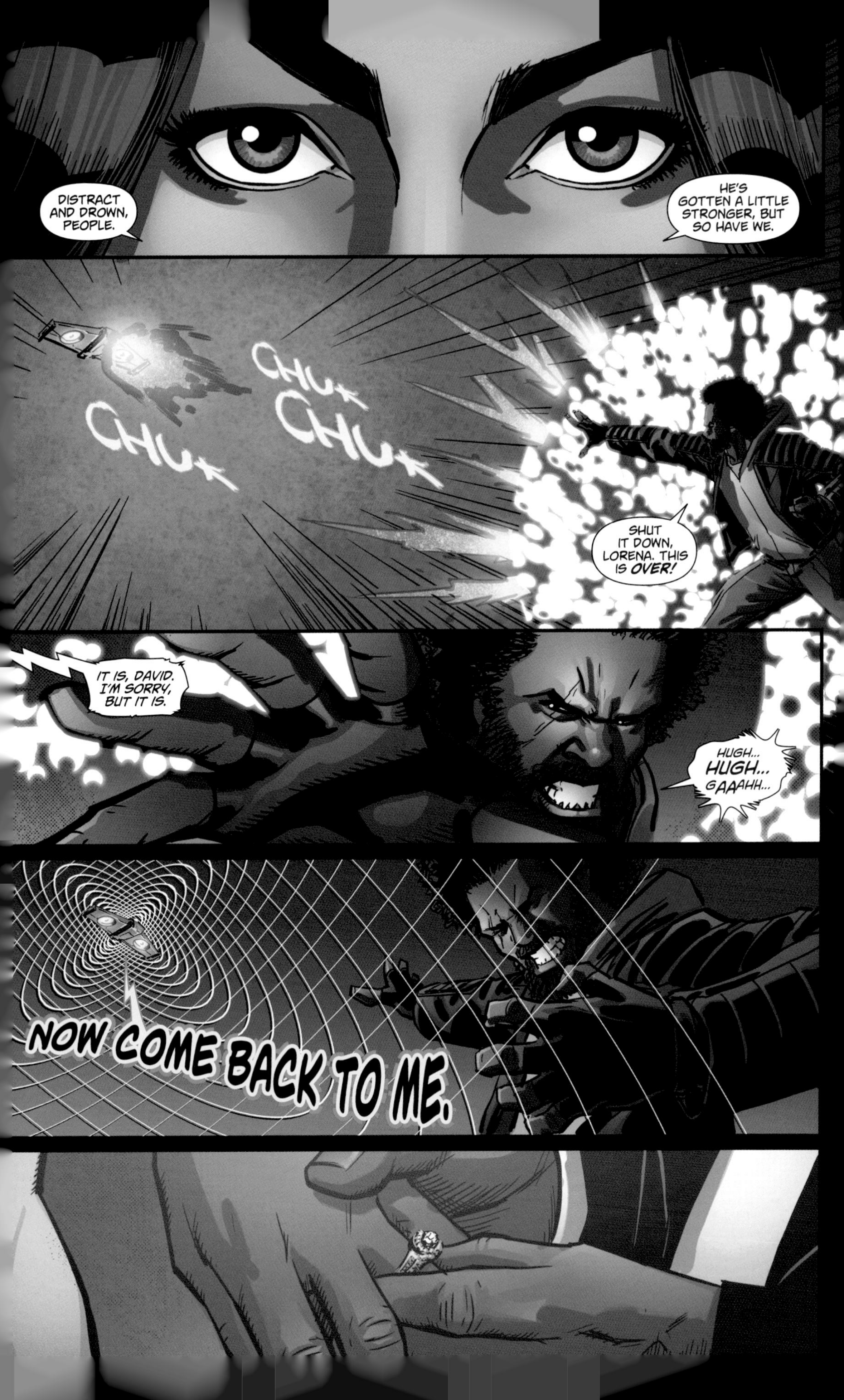
DISTRACT AND DROWN, PEOPLE.
HE'S GOTTEN A LITTLE STRONGER, BUT SO HAVE WE.
CHUK
CHUK
CHUK
SHUT IT DOWN, LORENA. THIS IS OVER!
IT IS, DAVID. I'M SORRY, BUT IT IS.
HUGH... HUGH... GAAAHH...
NOW COME BACK TO ME.

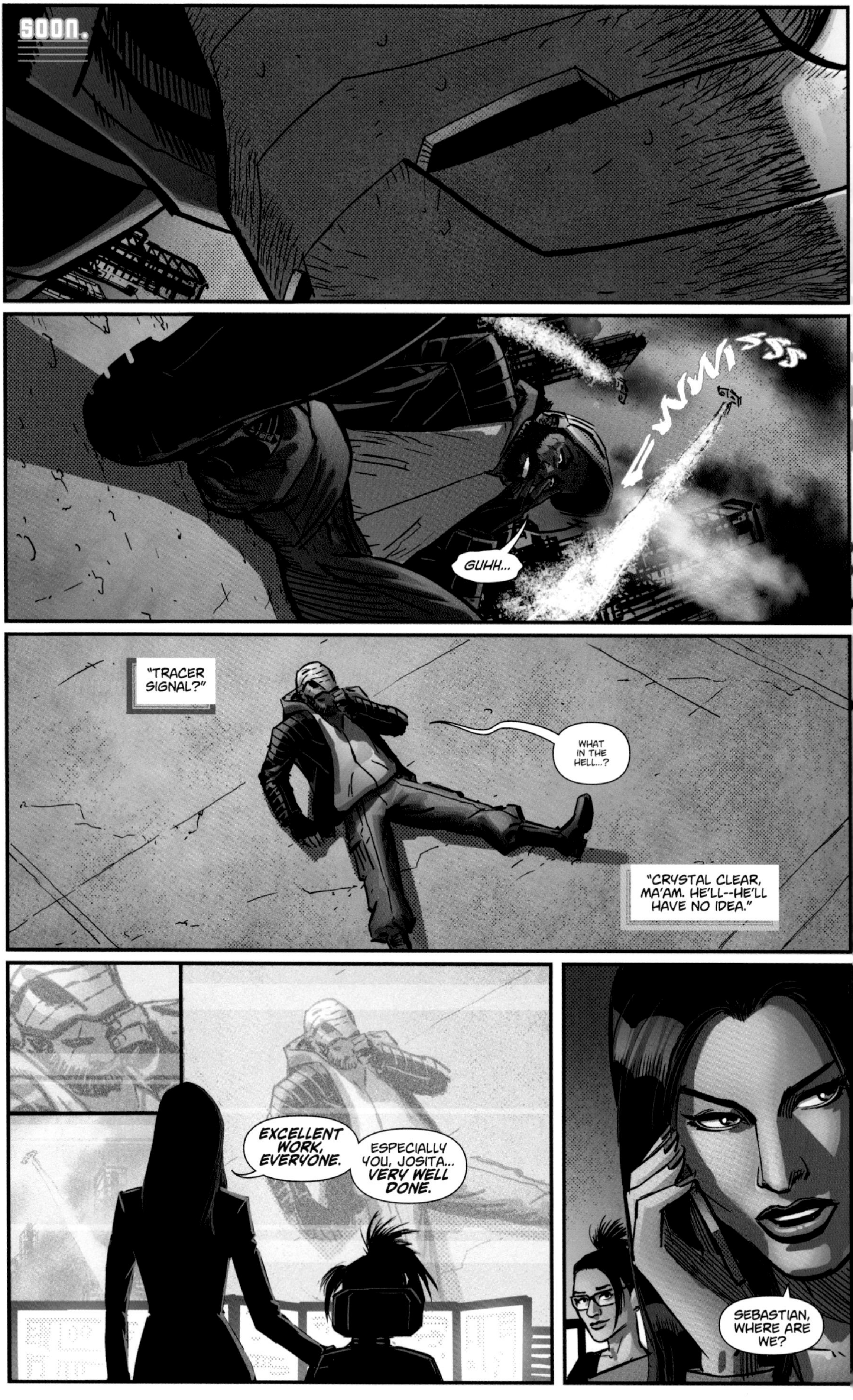
SOON.
SWISSS
GUHH...
"TRACER SIGNAL?"
WHAT IN THE HELL...?
"CRYSTAL CLEAR, MA'AM. HE'LL--HE'LL HAVE NO IDEA."
EXCELLENT WORK, EVERYONE.
ESPECIALLY YOU, JOSITA... VERY WELL DONE.
SEBASTIAN, WHERE ARE WE?

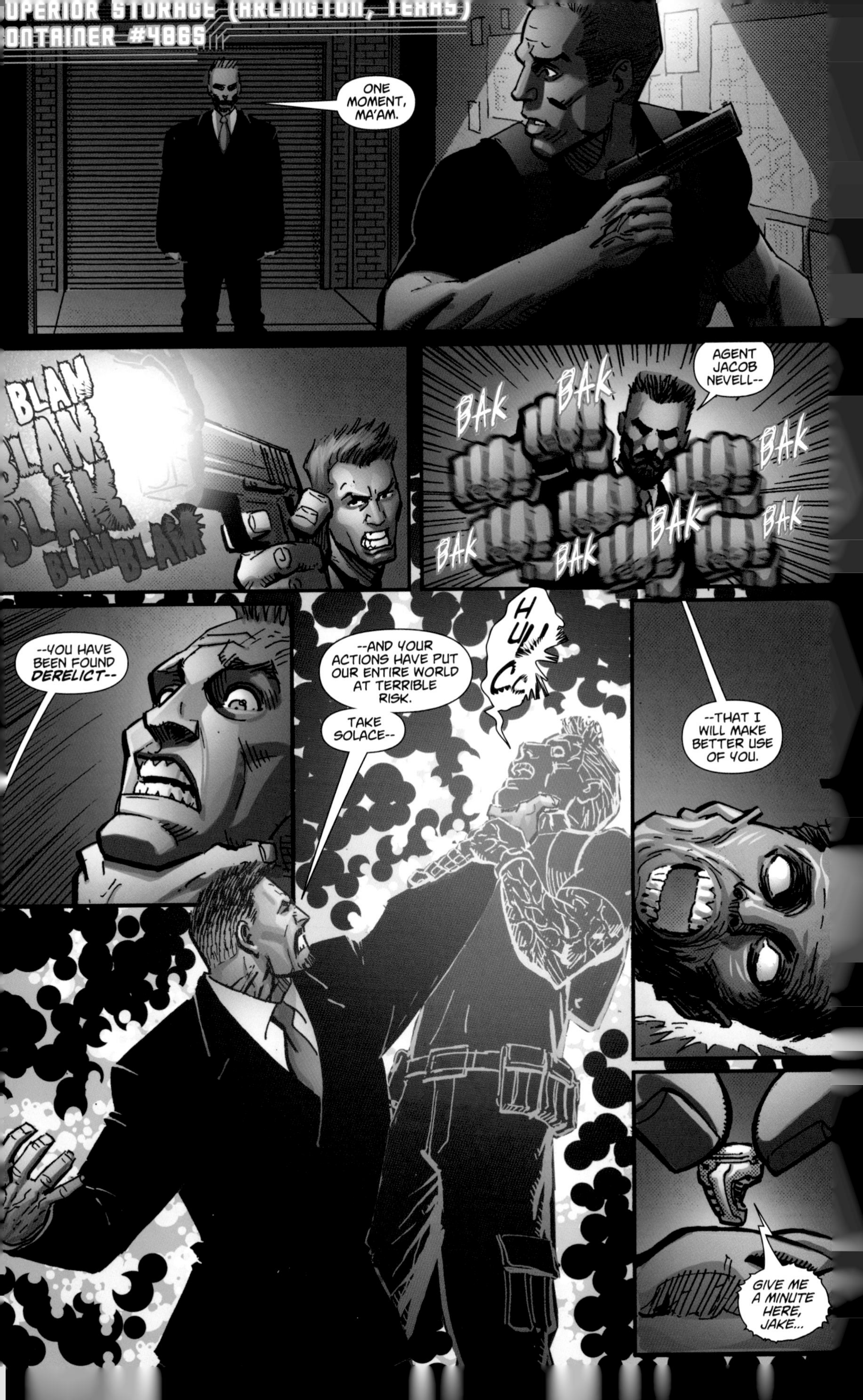

UPERIOR STORAGE (ARLINGTON, TEXAS)
ONTAINER #4865
ONE MOMENT, MA'AM.
BLAM BLAM BLAM BLAM BLAM BLAM
BAK BAK
AGENT JACOB NEVELL--
BAK BAK BAK BAK BAK
--YOU HAVE BEEN FOUND DERELICT--
--AND YOUR ACTIONS HAVE PUT OUR ENTIRE WORLD AT TERRIBLE RISK.
TAKE SOLACE--
HU... CC
--THAT I WILL MAKE BETTER USE OF YOU.
GIVE ME A MINUTE HERE, JAKE...

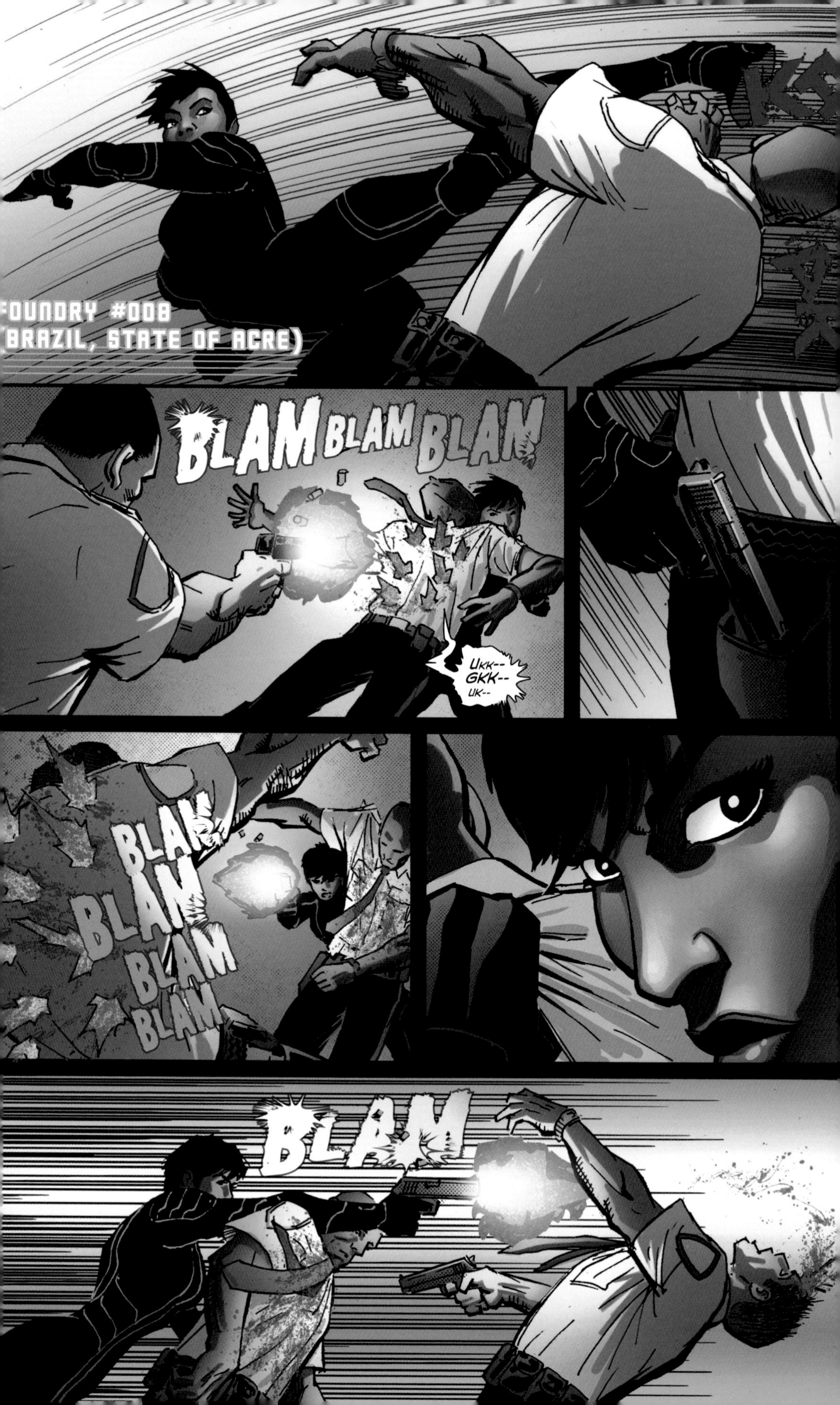
FOUNDRY #008
(BRAZIL, STATE OF ACRE)
BLAM BLAM BLAM
UKK-- GKK-- UK--
BLAM BLAM BLAM BLAM
BLAM

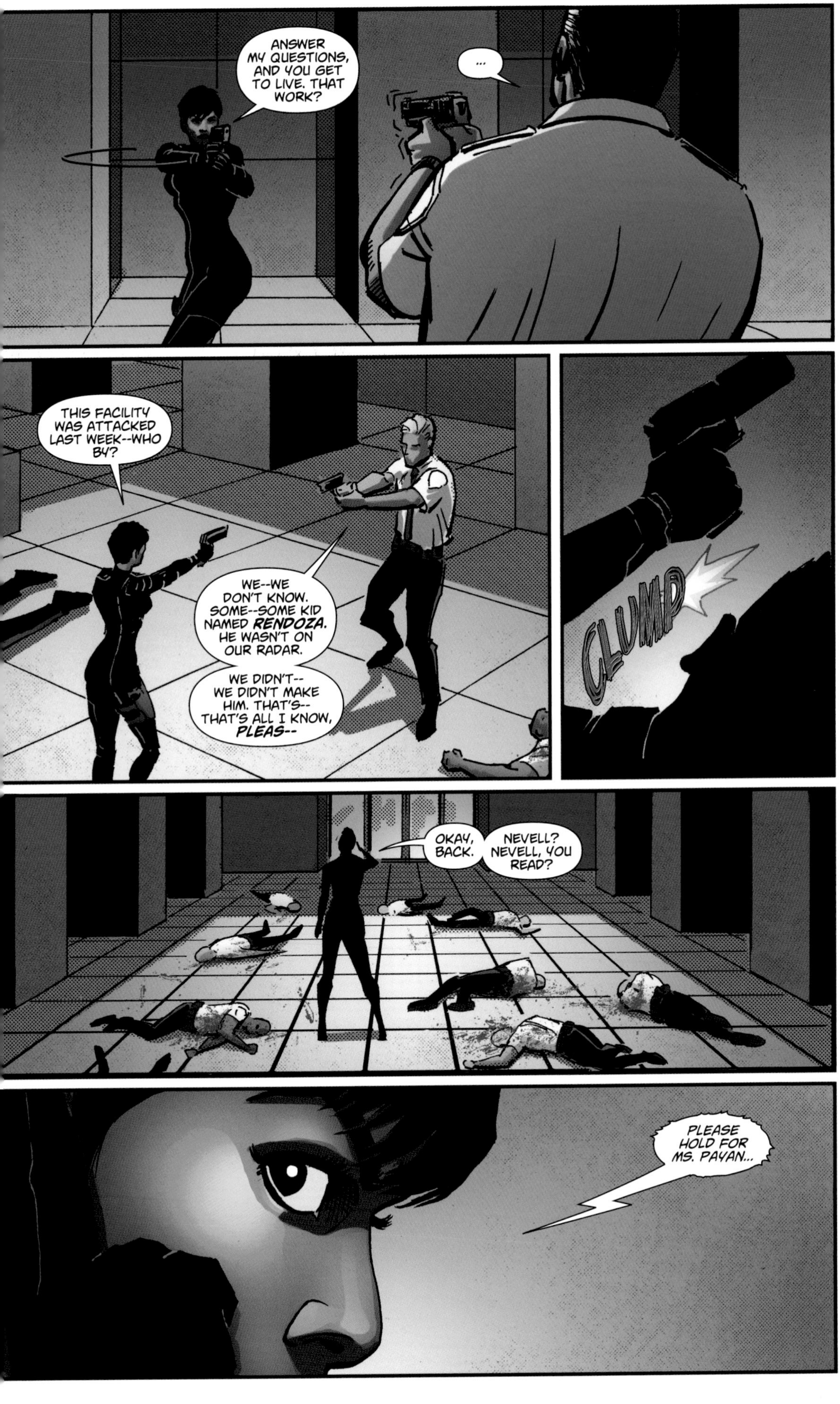
ANSWER MY QUESTIONS, AND YOU GET TO LIVE. THAT WORK?
...
THIS FACILITY WAS ATTACKED LAST WEEK--WHO BY?
WE--WE DON'T KNOW. SOME--SOME KID NAMED **RENDOZA**. HE WASN'T ON OUR RADAR.
WE DIDN'T-- WE DIDN'T MAKE HIM. THAT'S-- THAT'S ALL I KNOW, **PLEAS--**
CLUMP
OKAY, BACK.
NEVELL? NEVELL, YOU READ?
PLEASE HOLD FOR MS. PAYAN...

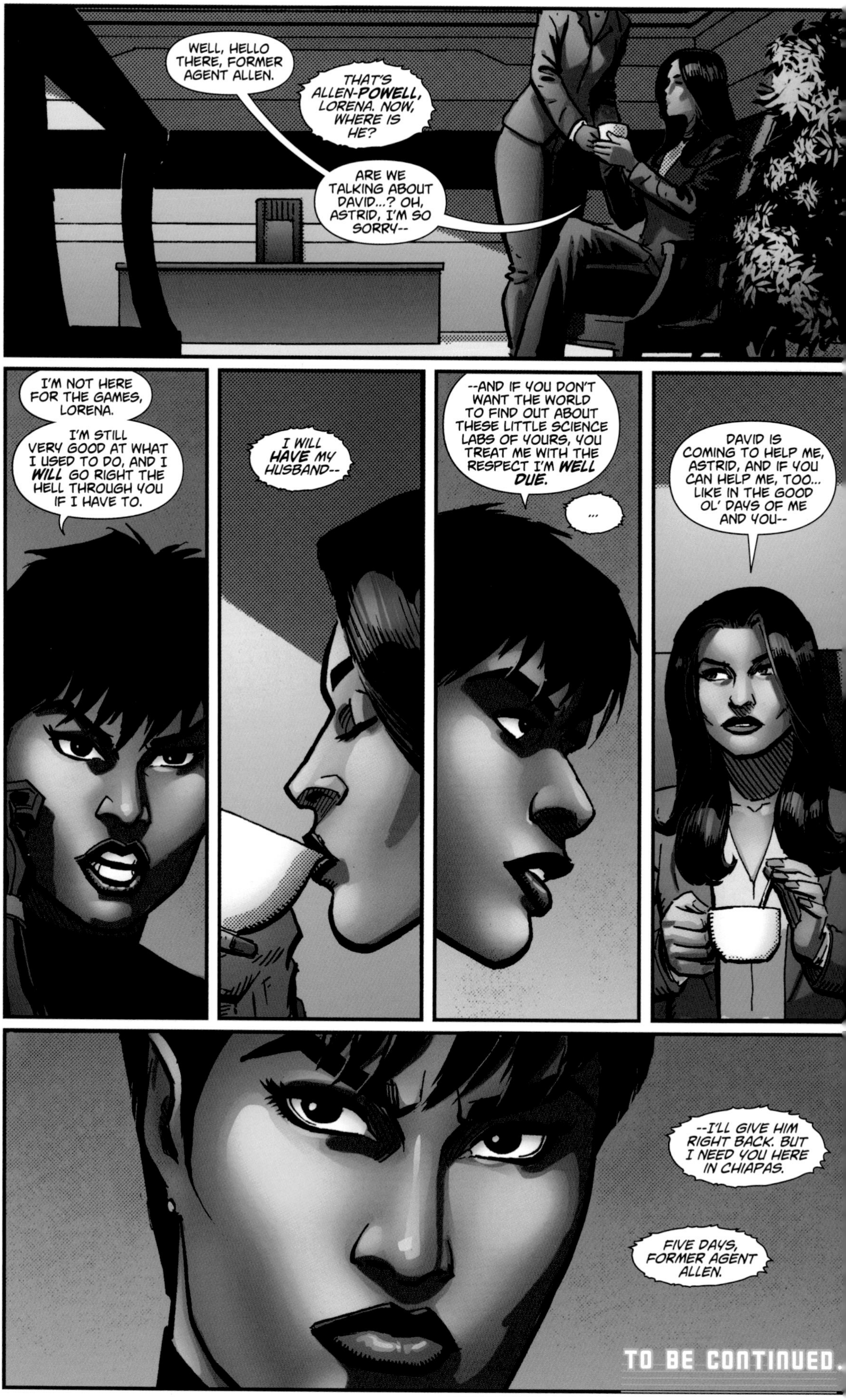
WELL, HELLO THERE, FORMER AGENT ALLEN.
THAT'S ALLEN-POWELL, LORENA. NOW, WHERE IS HE?
ARE WE TALKING ABOUT DAVID...? OH, ASTRID, I'M SO SORRY--
I'M NOT HERE FOR THE GAMES, LORENA.
I'M STILL VERY GOOD AT WHAT I USED TO DO, AND I WILL GO RIGHT THE HELL THROUGH YOU IF I HAVE TO.
I WILL HAVE MY HUSBAND--
--AND IF YOU DON'T WANT THE WORLD TO FIND OUT ABOUT THESE LITTLE SCIENCE LABS OF YOURS, YOU TREAT ME WITH THE RESPECT I'M WELL DUE.
...
DAVID IS COMING TO HELP ME, ASTRID, AND IF YOU CAN HELP ME, TOO... LIKE IN THE GOOD OL' DAYS OF ME AND YOU--
--I'LL GIVE HIM RIGHT BACK. BUT I NEED YOU HERE IN CHIAPAS.
FIVE DAYS, FORMER AGENT ALLEN.
TO BE CONTINUED...

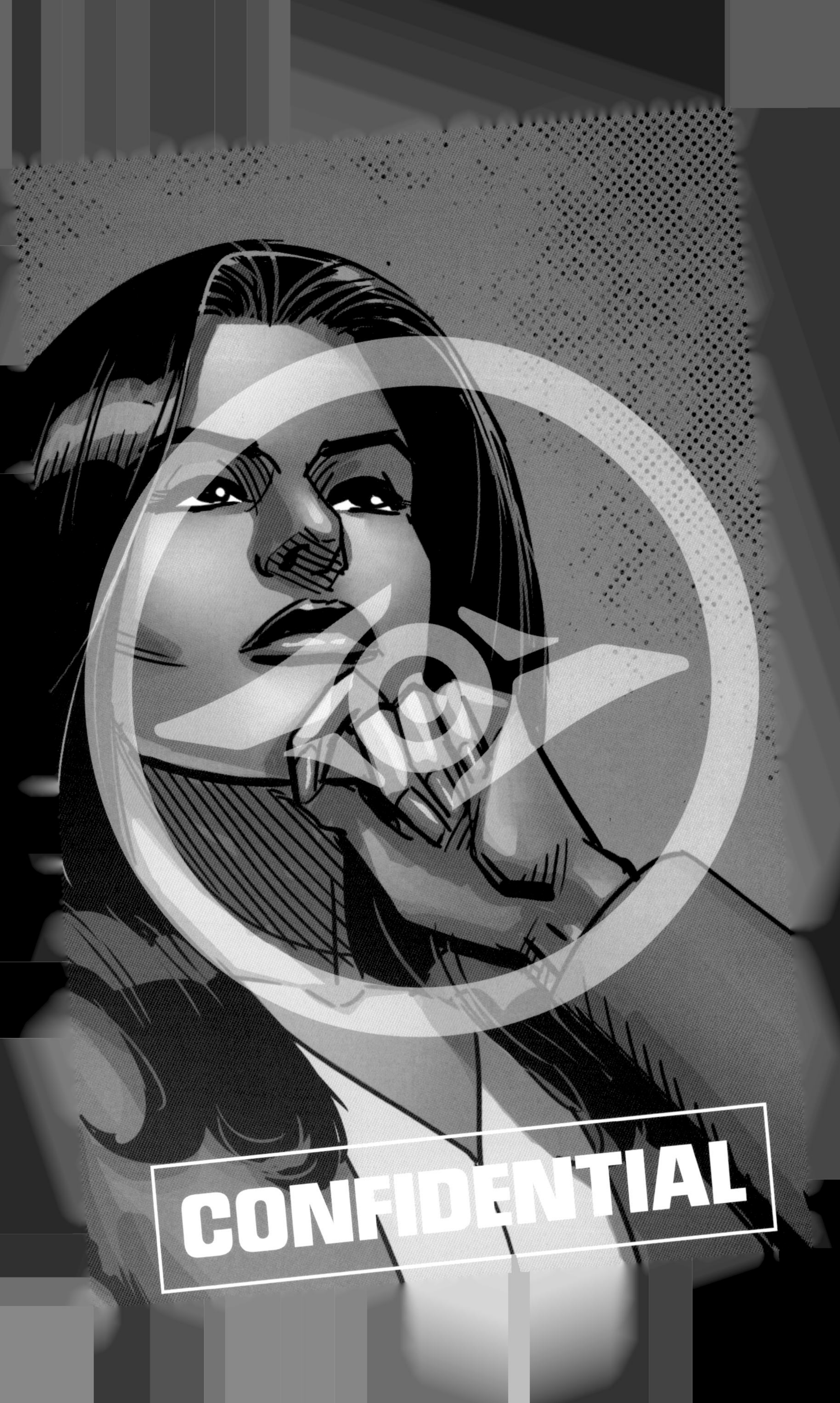
CONFIDENTIAL

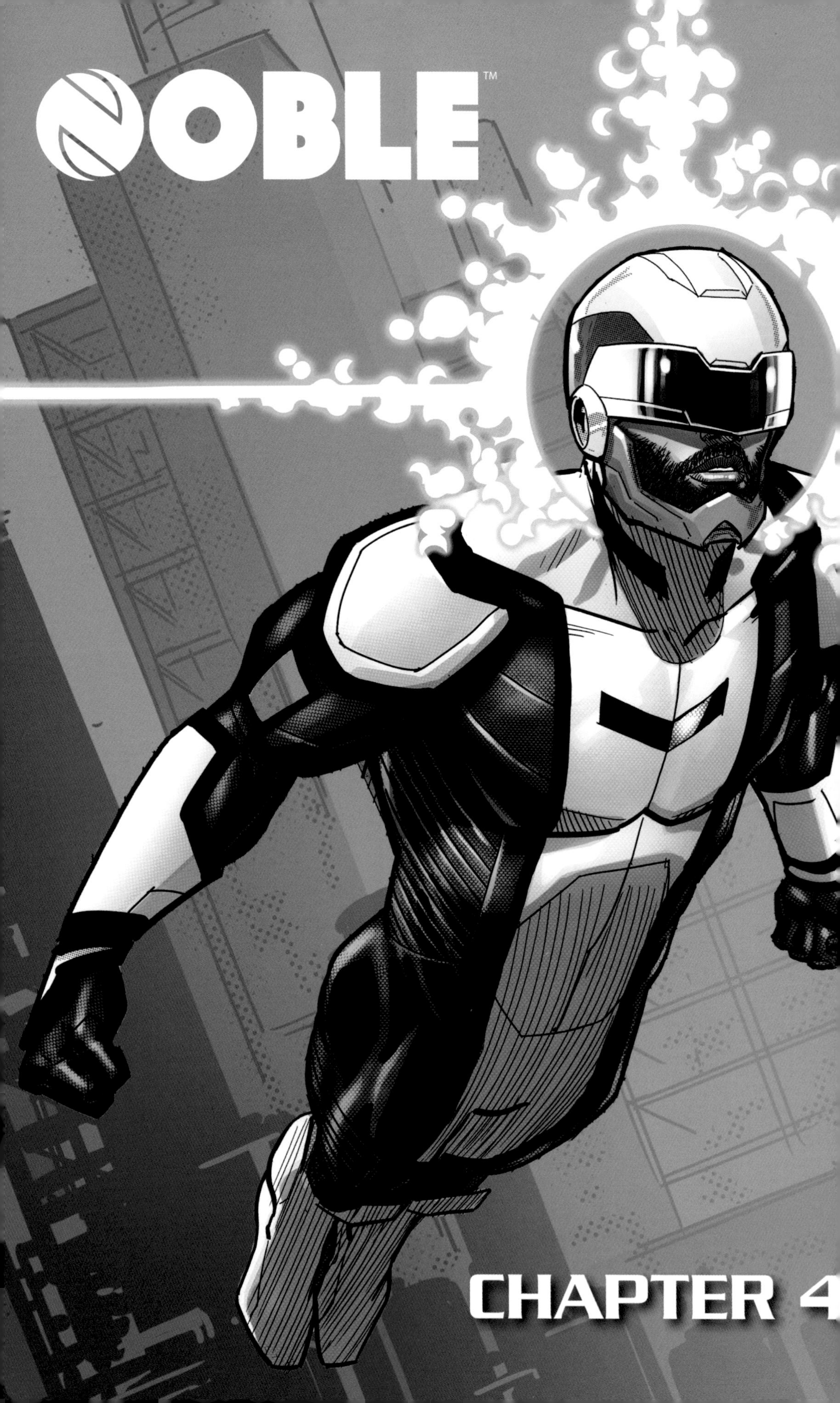
NOBLE™
CHAPTER 4

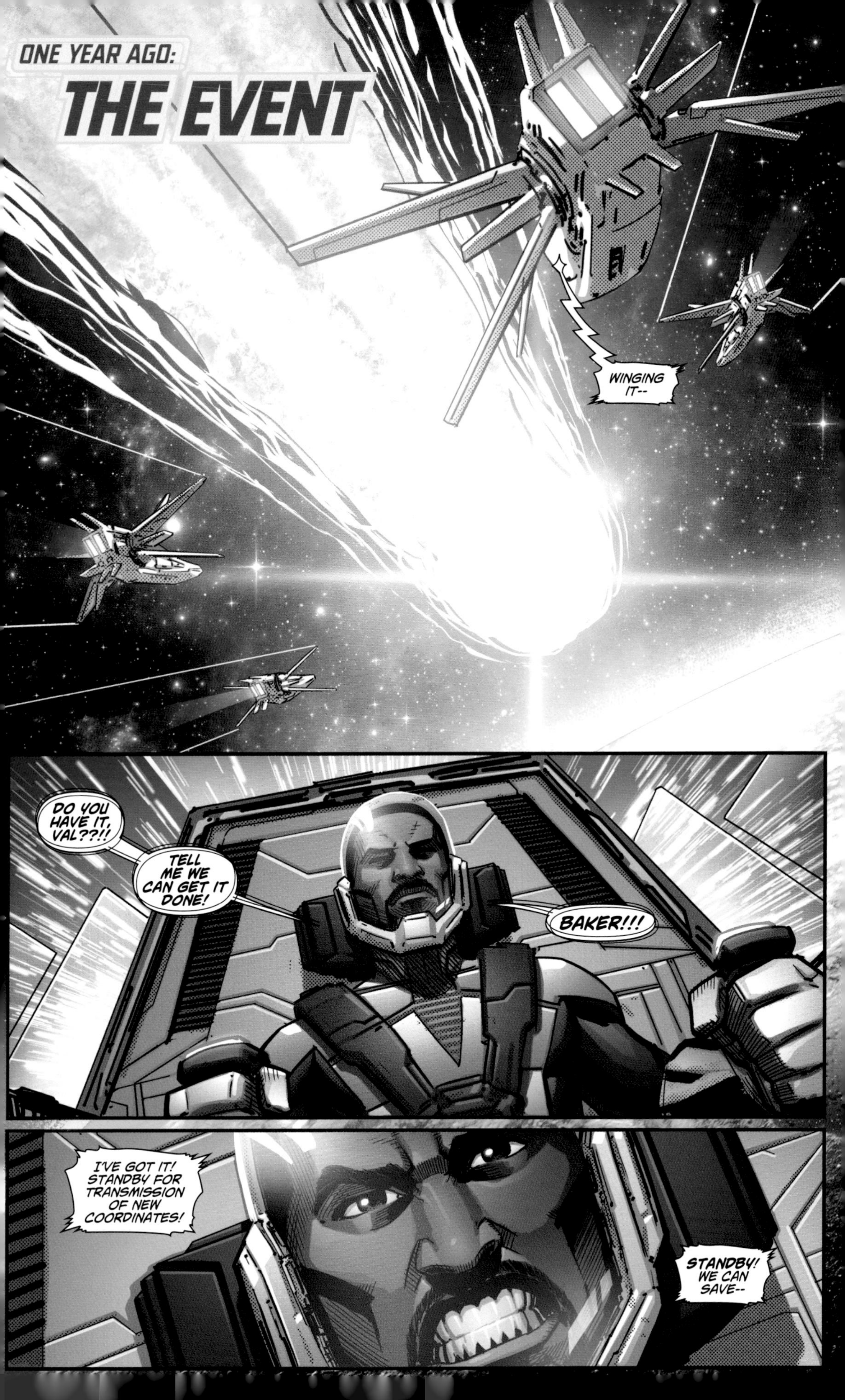
ONE YEAR AGO:
THE EVENT
WINGING IT--
DO YOU HAVE IT, VAL??!!
TELL ME WE CAN GET IT DONE!
BAKER!!!
I'VE GOT IT! STANDBY FOR TRANSMISSION OF NEW COORDINATES!
STANDBY! WE CAN SAVE--

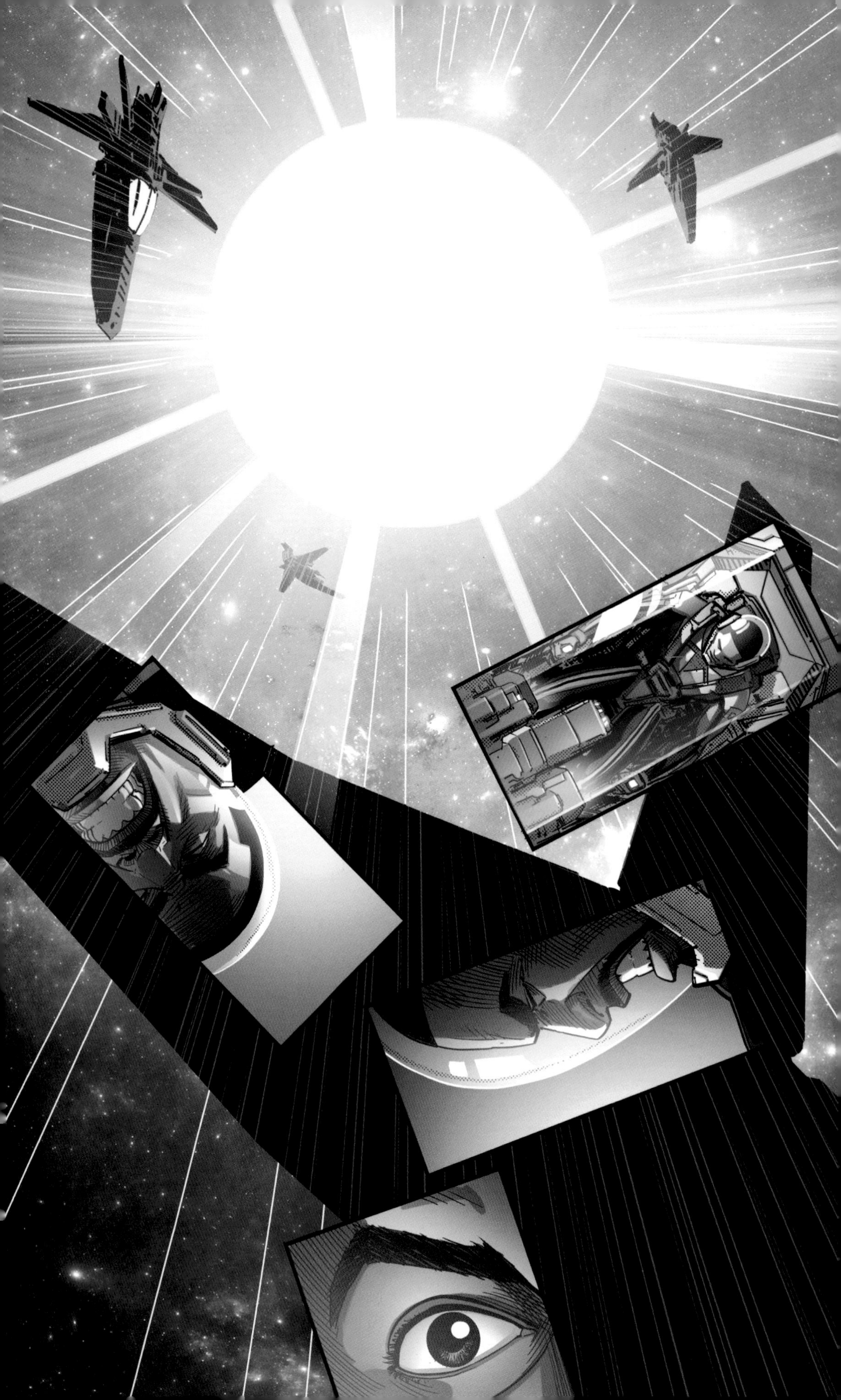

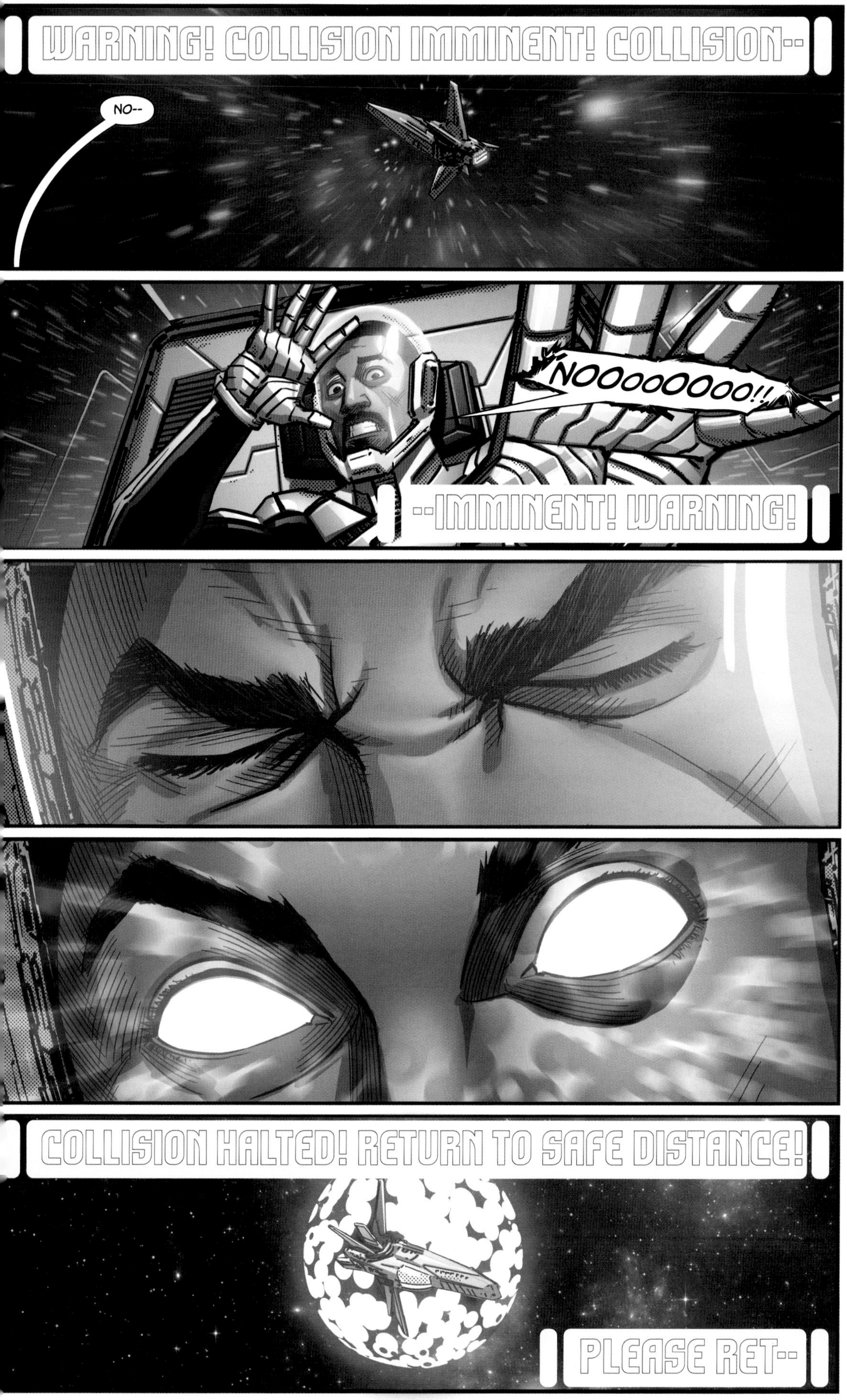
WARNING! COLLISION IMMINENT! COLLISION--
NO--
NOOOOOOOO!!
--IMMINENT! WARNING!
COLLISION HALTED! RETURN TO SAFE DISTANCE!
PLEASE RET--

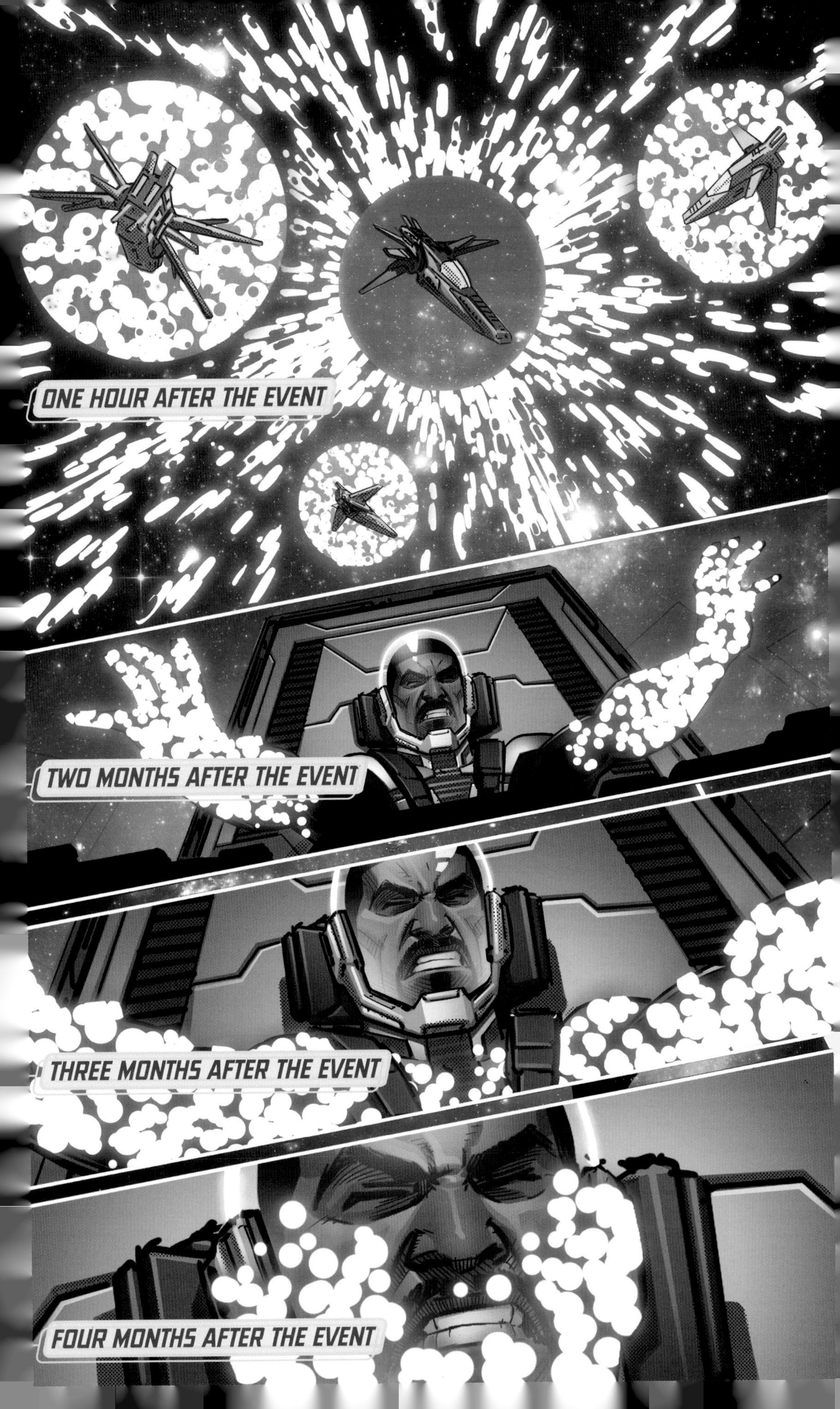
ONE HOUR AFTER THE EVENT
TWO MONTHS AFTER THE EVENT
THREE MONTHS AFTER THE EVENT
FOUR MONTHS AFTER THE EVENT

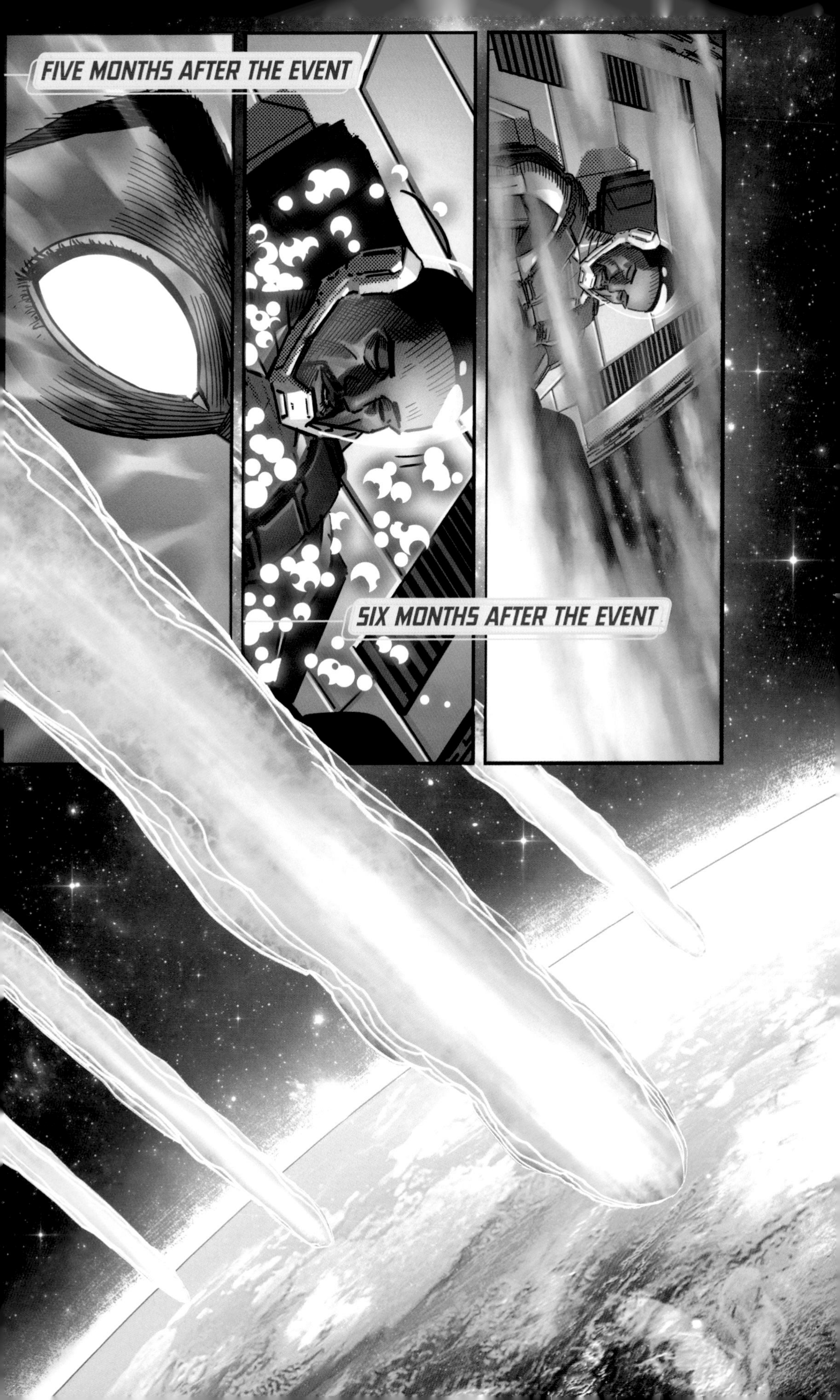
FIVE MONTHS AFTER THE EVENT
SIX MONTHS AFTER THE EVENT

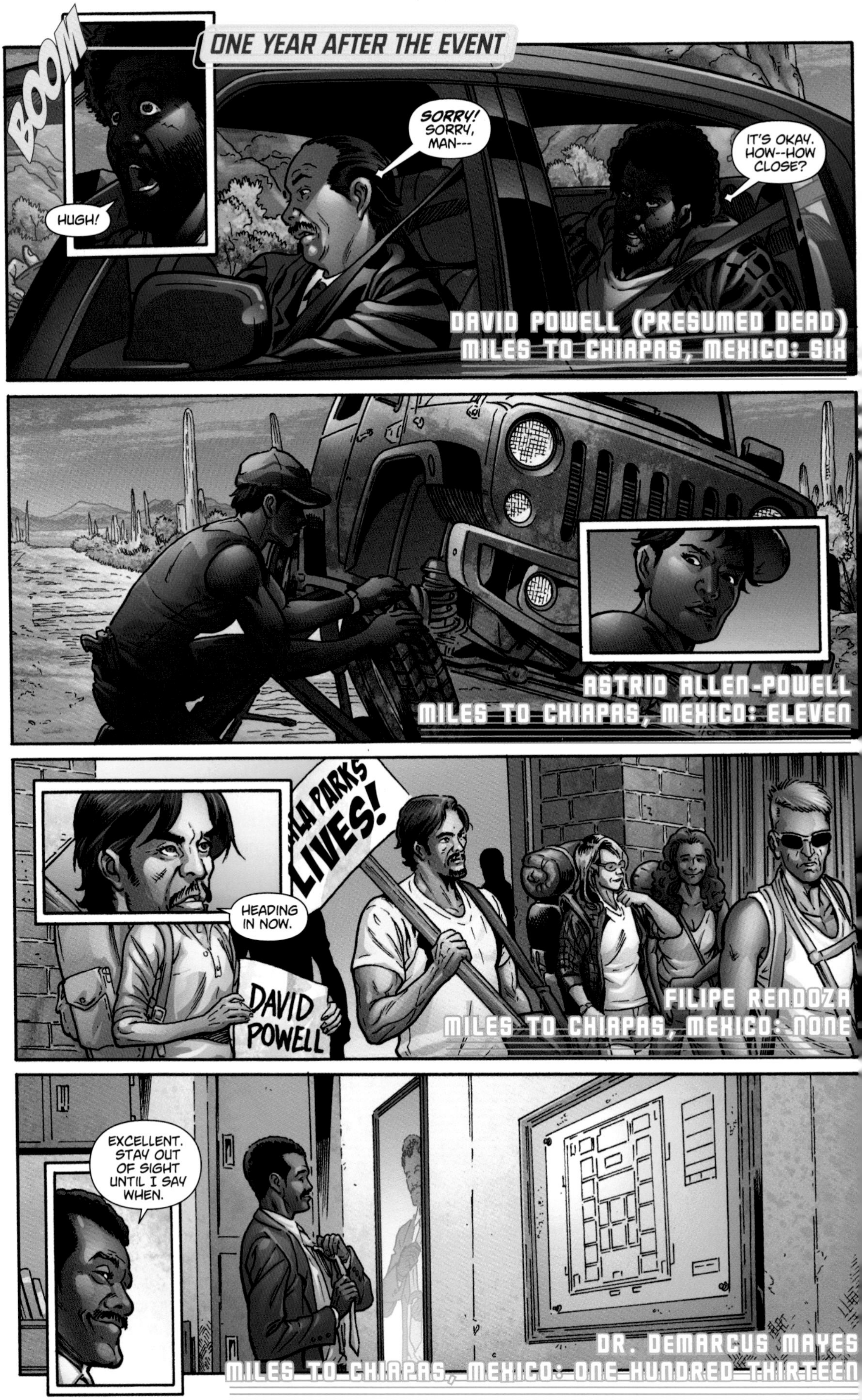
BOOM
ONE YEAR AFTER THE EVENT
HUGH!
SORRY! SORRY, MAN---
IT'S OKAY. HOW--HOW CLOSE?
DAVID POWELL (PRESUMED DEAD)
MILES TO CHIAPAS, MEXICO: SIX
ASTRID ALLEN-POWELL
MILES TO CHIAPAS, MEXICO: ELEVEN
HEADING IN NOW.
LA PARKS LIVES!
DAVID POWELL
FILIPE RENDOZA
MILES TO CHIAPAS, MEXICO: NONE
EXCELLENT. STAY OUT OF SIGHT UNTIL I SAY WHEN.
DR. DEMARCUS MAYES
MILES TO CHIAPAS, MEXICO: ONE HUNDRED THIRTEEN

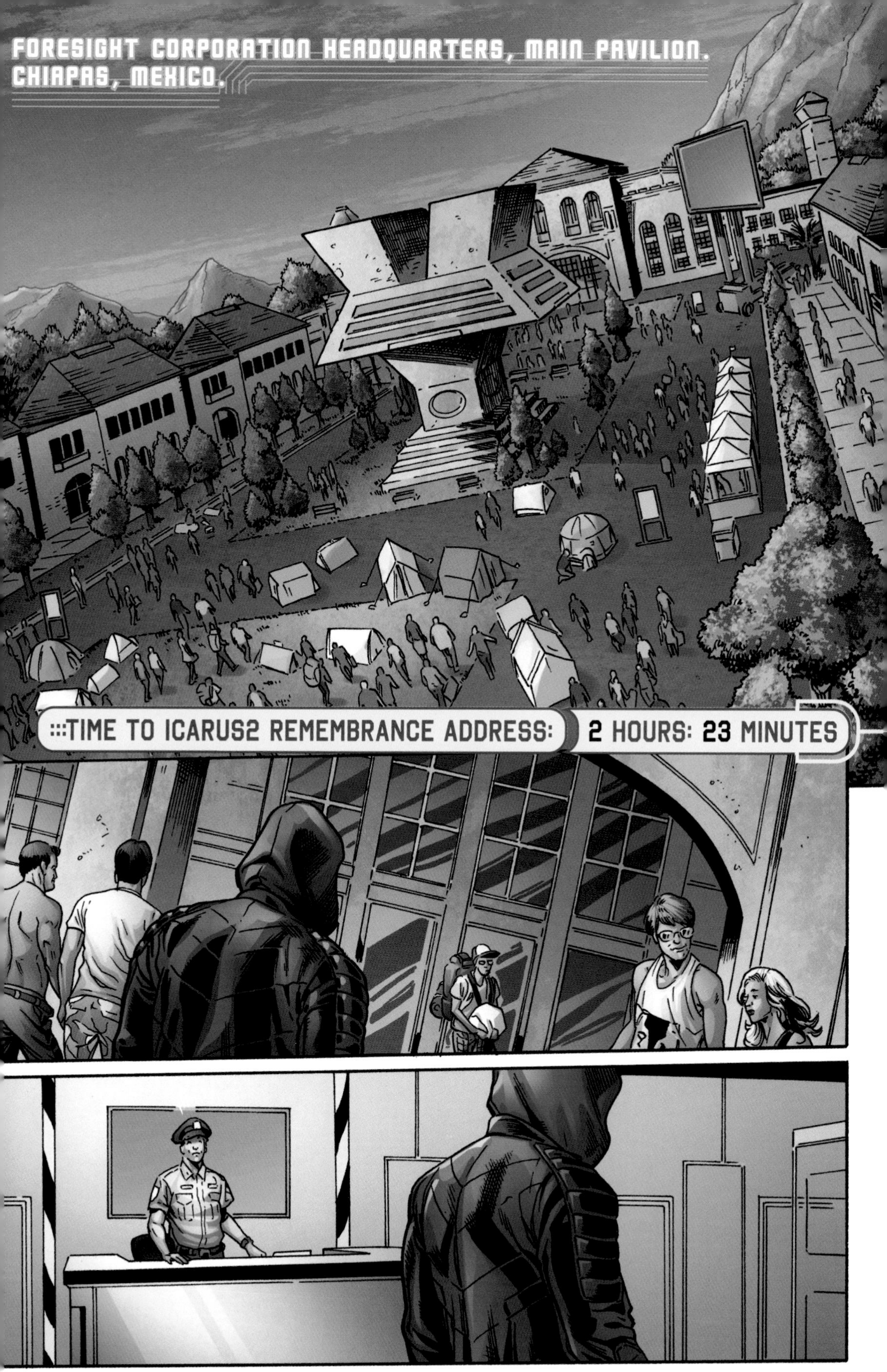
FORESIGHT CORPORATION HEADQUARTERS, MAIN PAVILION.
CHIAPAS, MEXICO.
:::TIME TO ICARUS2 REMEMBRANCE ADDRESS:
2 HOURS: 23 MINUTES

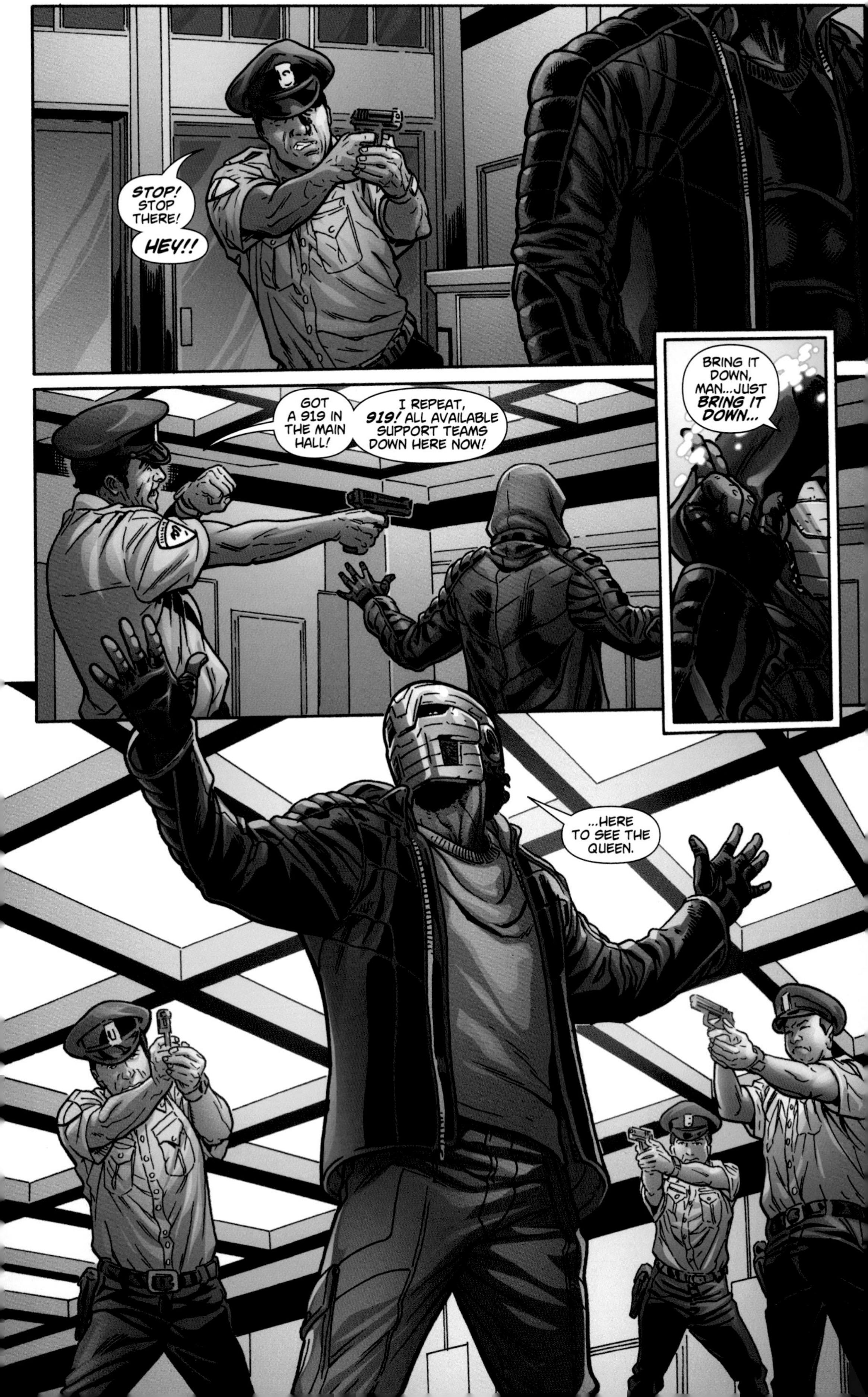
STOP! STOP THERE!
HEY!!
GOT A 919 IN THE MAIN HALL!
I REPEAT, 919! ALL AVAILABLE SUPPORT TEAMS DOWN HERE NOW!
BRING IT DOWN, MAN...JUST BRING IT DOWN...
...HERE TO SEE THE QUEEN.

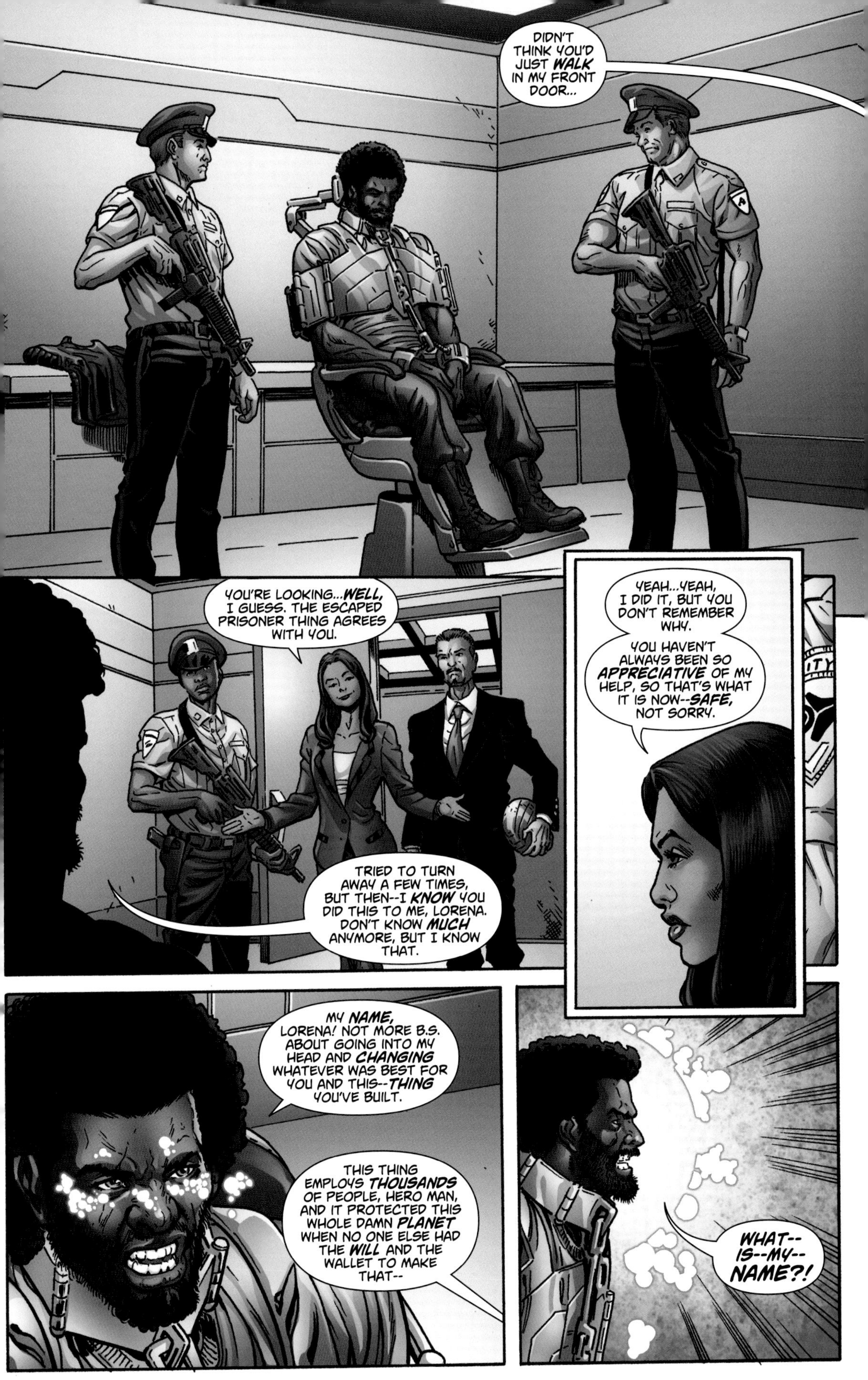
DIDN'T THINK YOU'D JUST WALK IN MY FRONT DOOR...
YOU'RE LOOKING...WELL, I GUESS. THE ESCAPED PRISONER THING AGREES WITH YOU.
TRIED TO TURN AWAY A FEW TIMES, BUT THEN--I KNOW YOU DID THIS TO ME, LORENA. DON'T KNOW MUCH ANYMORE, BUT I KNOW THAT.
YEAH...YEAH, I DID IT, BUT YOU DON'T REMEMBER WHY.
YOU HAVEN'T ALWAYS BEEN SO APPRECIATIVE OF MY HELP, SO THAT'S WHAT IT IS NOW--SAFE, NOT SORRY.
MY NAME, LORENA! NOT MORE B.S. ABOUT GOING INTO MY HEAD AND CHANGING WHATEVER WAS BEST FOR YOU AND THIS--THING YOU'VE BUILT.
THIS THING EMPLOYS THOUSANDS OF PEOPLE, HERO MAN, AND IT PROTECTED THIS WHOLE DAMN PLANET WHEN NO ONE ELSE HAD THE WILL AND THE WALLET TO MAKE THAT--
WHAT--IS--MY--NAME?!

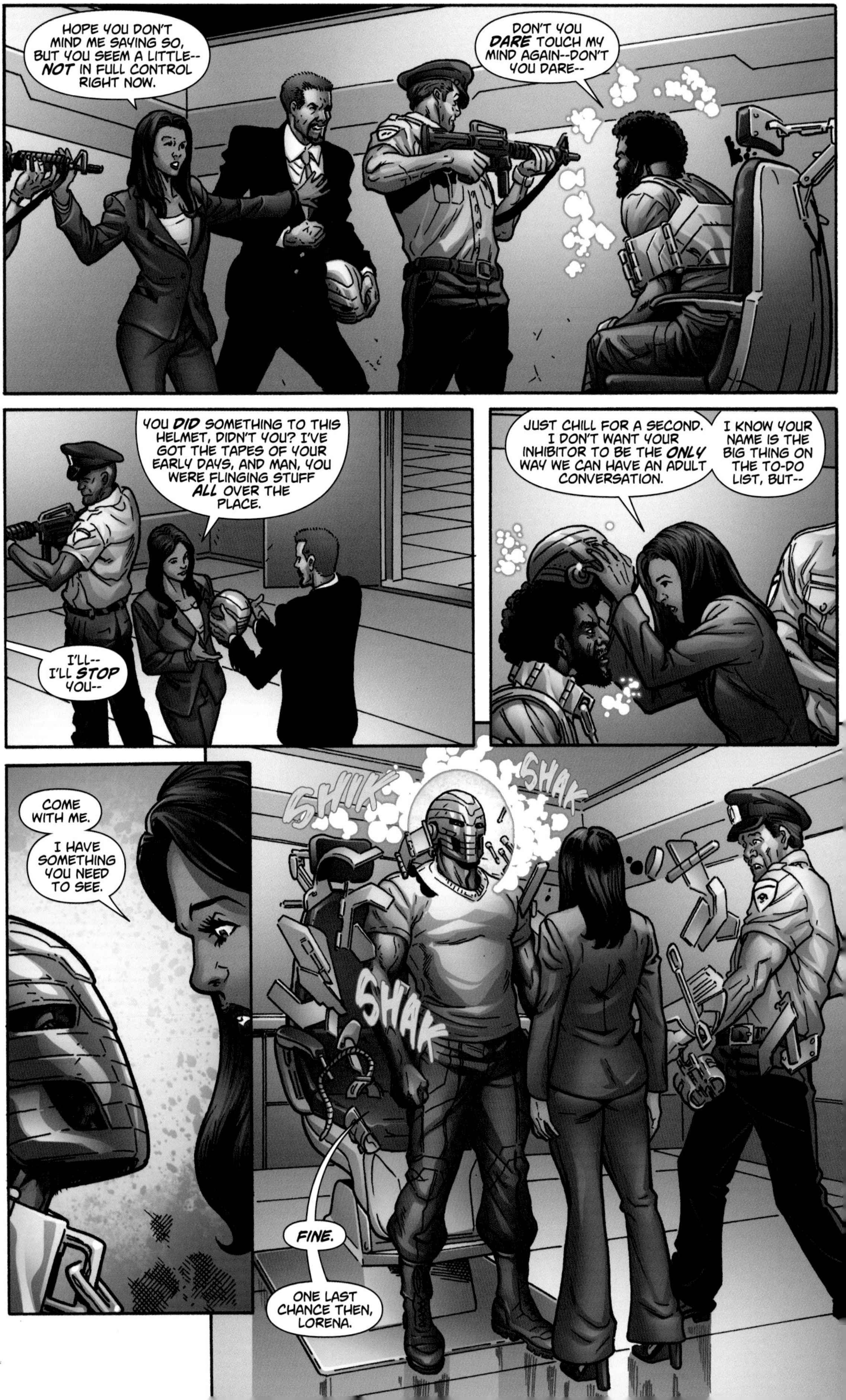
HOPE YOU DON'T MIND ME SAYING SO, BUT YOU SEEM A LITTLE-- NOT IN FULL CONTROL RIGHT NOW.
DON'T YOU DARE TOUCH MY MIND AGAIN--DON'T YOU DARE--
YOU DID SOMETHING TO THIS HELMET, DIDN'T YOU? I'VE GOT THE TAPES OF YOUR EARLY DAYS, AND MAN, YOU WERE FLINGING STUFF ALL OVER THE PLACE.
I'LL-- I'LL STOP YOU--
JUST CHILL FOR A SECOND. I DON'T WANT YOUR INHIBITOR TO BE THE ONLY WAY WE CAN HAVE AN ADULT CONVERSATION.
I KNOW YOUR NAME IS THE BIG THING ON THE TO-DO LIST, BUT--
COME WITH ME.
I HAVE SOMETHING YOU NEED TO SEE.
SHIIK
SHAK
SHAK
FINE.
ONE LAST CHANCE THEN, LORENA.

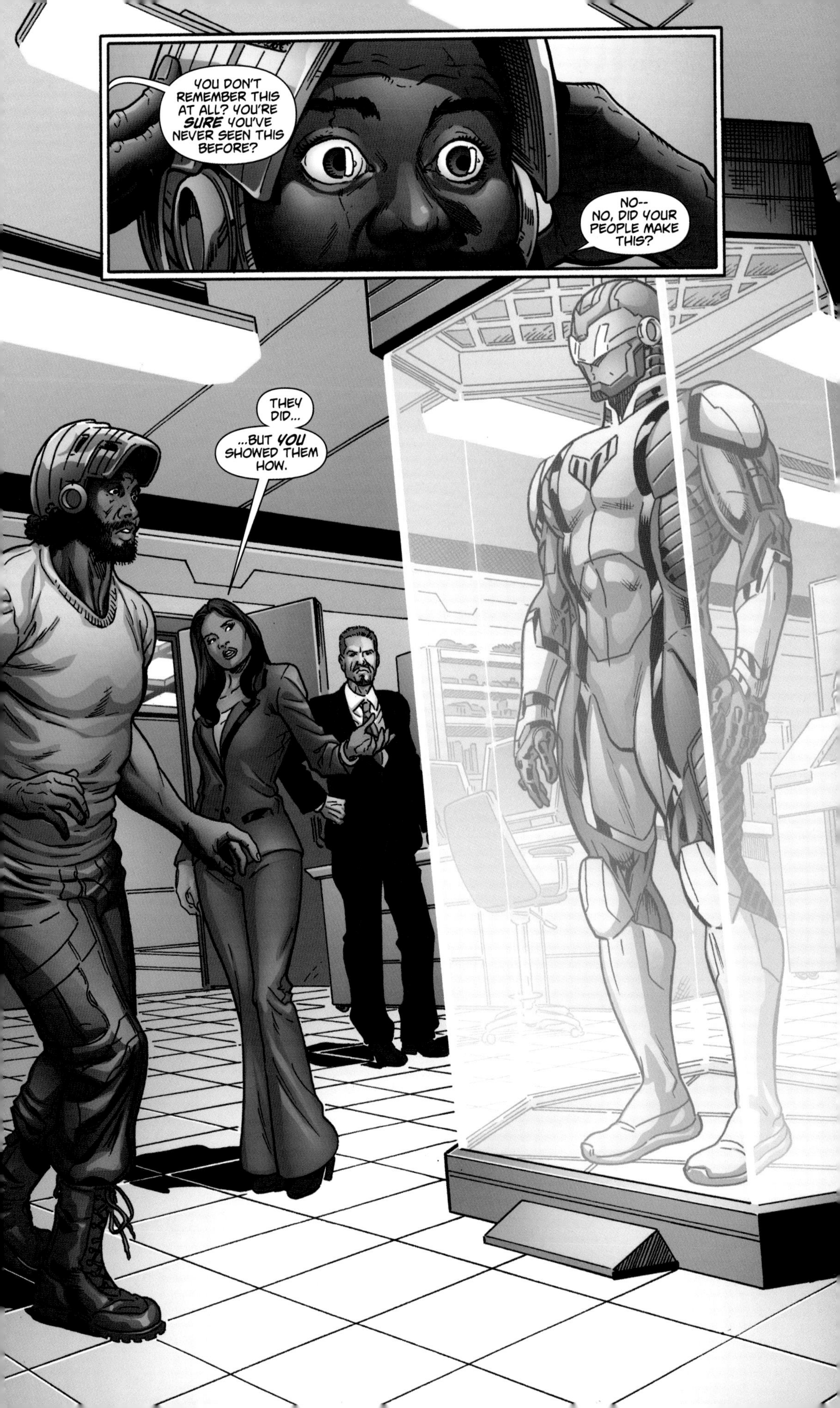
YOU DON'T REMEMBER THIS AT ALL? YOU'RE SURE YOU'VE NEVER SEEN THIS BEFORE?
NO-- NO, DID YOUR PEOPLE MAKE THIS?
THEY DID...
...BUT YOU SHOWED THEM HOW.

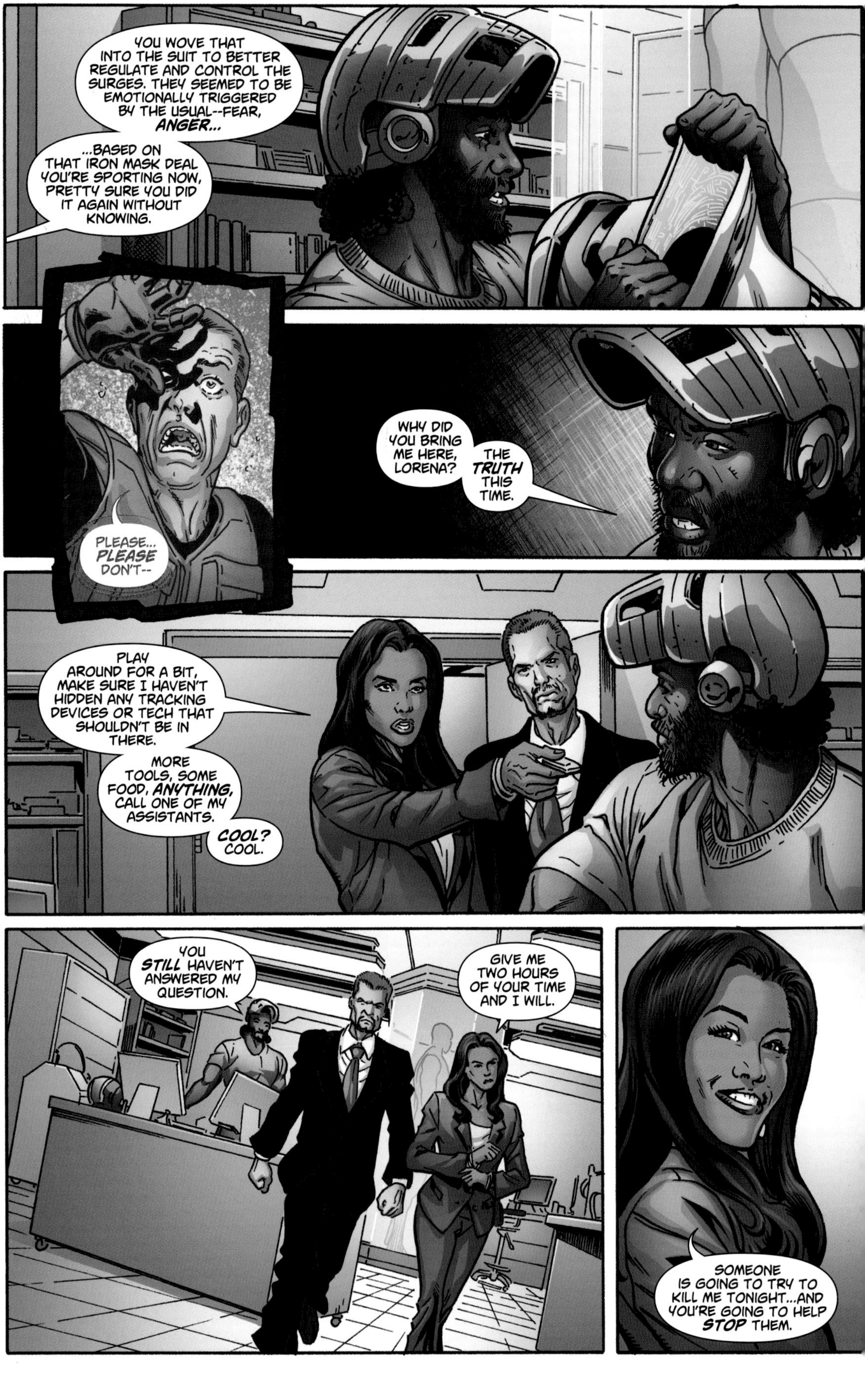
YOU WOVE THAT INTO THE SUIT TO BETTER REGULATE AND CONTROL THE SURGES. THEY SEEMED TO BE EMOTIONALLY TRIGGERED BY THE USUAL--FEAR, ANGER...
...BASED ON THAT IRON MASK DEAL YOU'RE SPORTING NOW, PRETTY SURE YOU DID IT AGAIN WITHOUT KNOWING.
PLEASE... PLEASE DON'T--
WHY DID YOU BRING ME HERE, LORENA?
THE TRUTH THIS TIME.
PLAY AROUND FOR A BIT, MAKE SURE I HAVEN'T HIDDEN ANY TRACKING DEVICES OR TECH THAT SHOULDN'T BE IN THERE.
MORE TOOLS, SOME FOOD, ANYTHING, CALL ONE OF MY ASSISTANTS.
COOL? COOL.
YOU STILL HAVEN'T ANSWERED MY QUESTION.
GIVE ME TWO HOURS OF YOUR TIME AND I WILL.
SOMEONE IS GOING TO TRY TO KILL ME TONIGHT...AND YOU'RE GOING TO HELP STOP THEM.

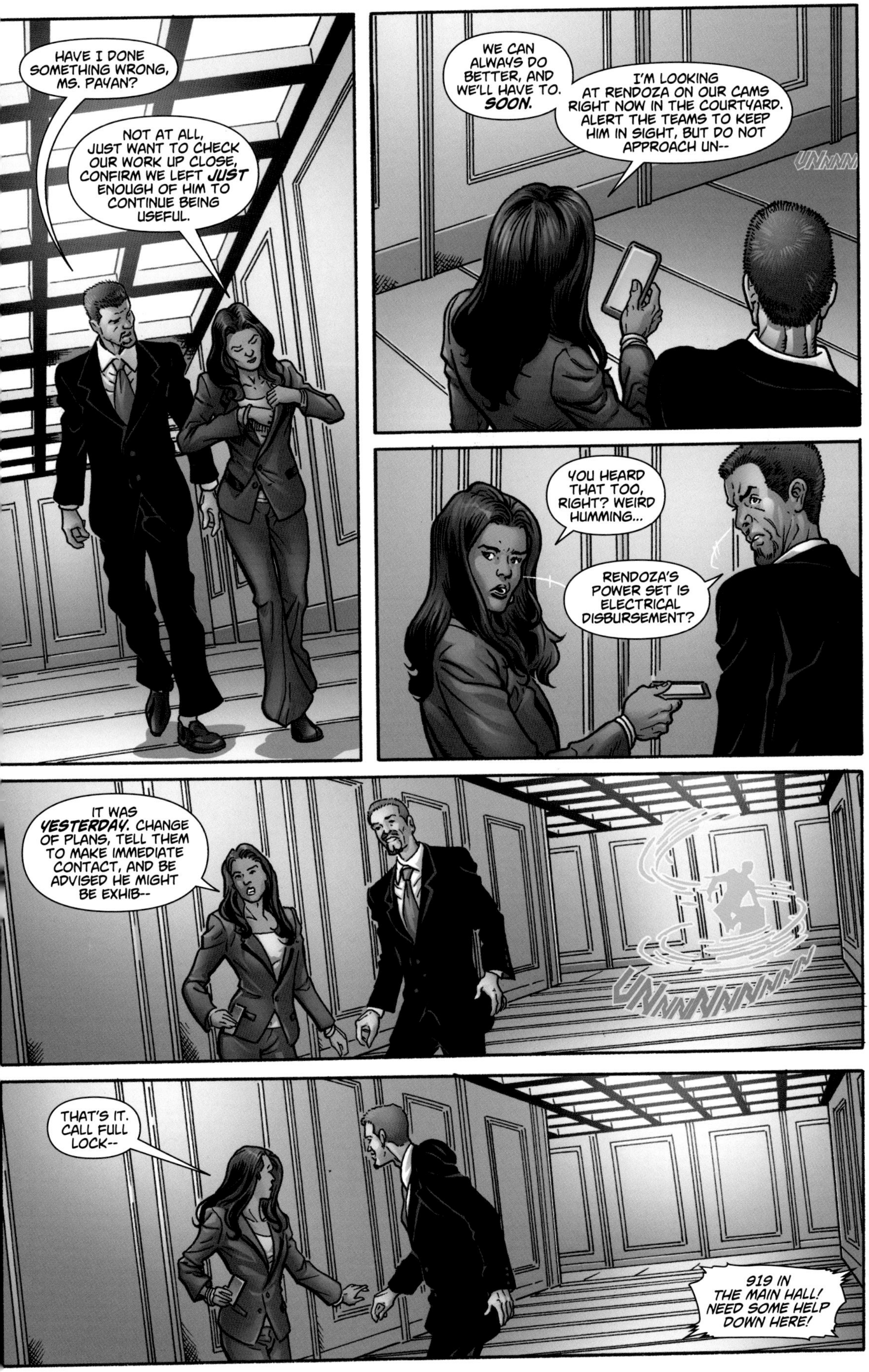
HAVE I DONE SOMETHING WRONG, MS. PAYAN?
NOT AT ALL, JUST WANT TO CHECK OUR WORK UP CLOSE, CONFIRM WE LEFT JUST ENOUGH OF HIM TO CONTINUE BEING USEFUL.
WE CAN ALWAYS DO BETTER, AND WE'LL HAVE TO. SOON.
I'M LOOKING AT RENDOZA ON OUR CAMS RIGHT NOW IN THE COURTYARD. ALERT THE TEAMS TO KEEP HIM IN SIGHT, BUT DO NOT APPROACH UN--
UNNNN
YOU HEARD THAT TOO, RIGHT? WEIRD HUMMING...
RENDOZA'S POWER SET IS ELECTRICAL DISBURSEMENT?
IT WAS YESTERDAY. CHANGE OF PLANS, TELL THEM TO MAKE IMMEDIATE CONTACT, AND BE ADVISED HE MIGHT BE EXHIB--
UNNNNNNNNNN
THAT'S IT. CALL FULL LOCK--
919 IN THE MAIN HALL! NEED SOME HELP DOWN HERE!

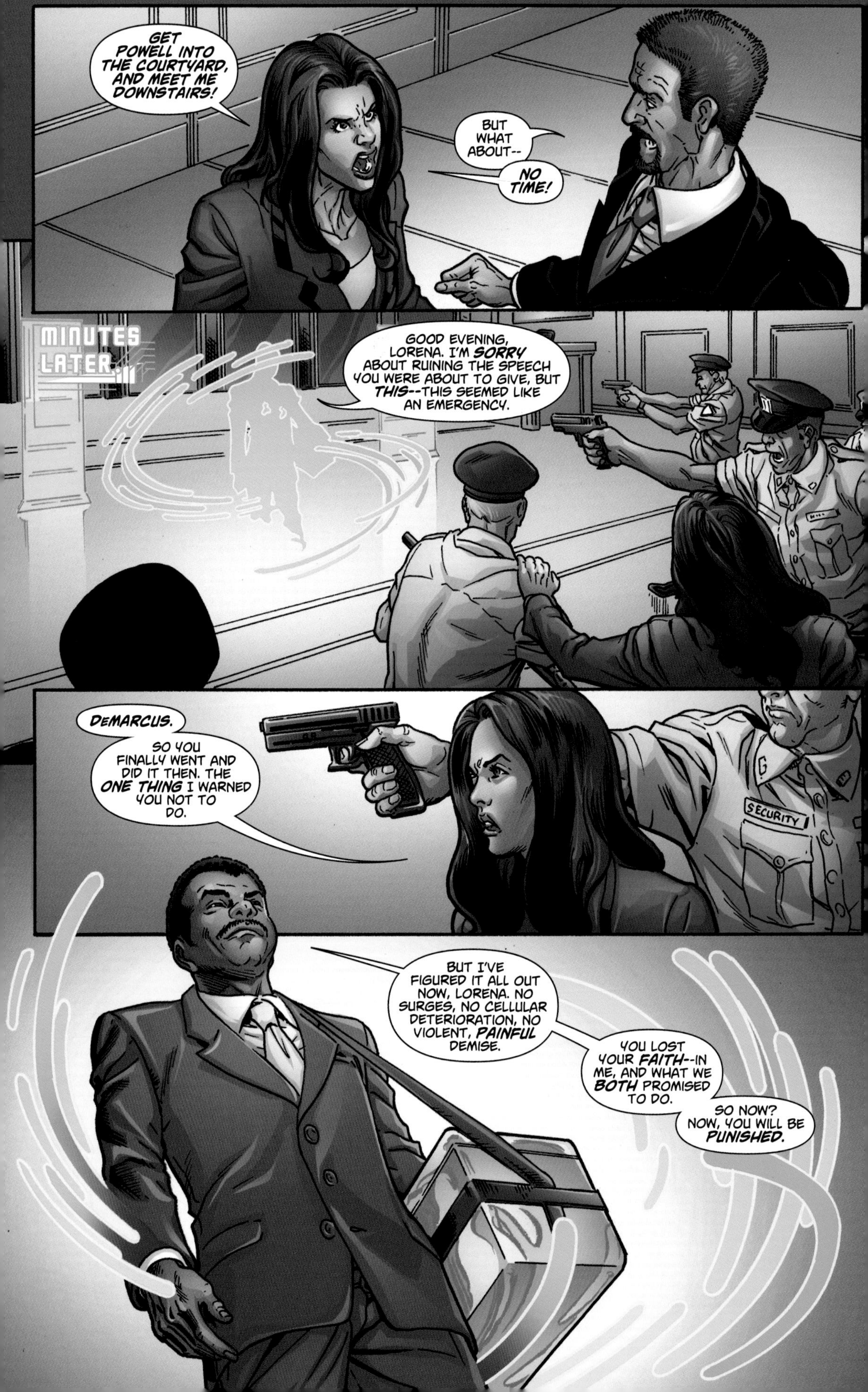
GET POWELL INTO THE COURTYARD, AND MEET ME DOWNSTAIRS!
BUT WHAT ABOUT--
NO TIME!
MINUTES LATER...
GOOD EVENING, LORENA. I'M SORRY ABOUT RUINING THE SPEECH YOU WERE ABOUT TO GIVE, BUT THIS--THIS SEEMED LIKE AN EMERGENCY.
DEMARCUS.
SO YOU FINALLY WENT AND DID IT THEN. THE ONE THING I WARNED YOU NOT TO DO.
SECURITY
BUT I'VE FIGURED IT ALL OUT NOW, LORENA. NO SURGES, NO CELLULAR DETERIORATION, NO VIOLENT, PAINFUL DEMISE.
YOU LOST YOUR FAITH--IN ME, AND WHAT WE BOTH PROMISED TO DO.
SO NOW? NOW, YOU WILL BE PUNISHED.

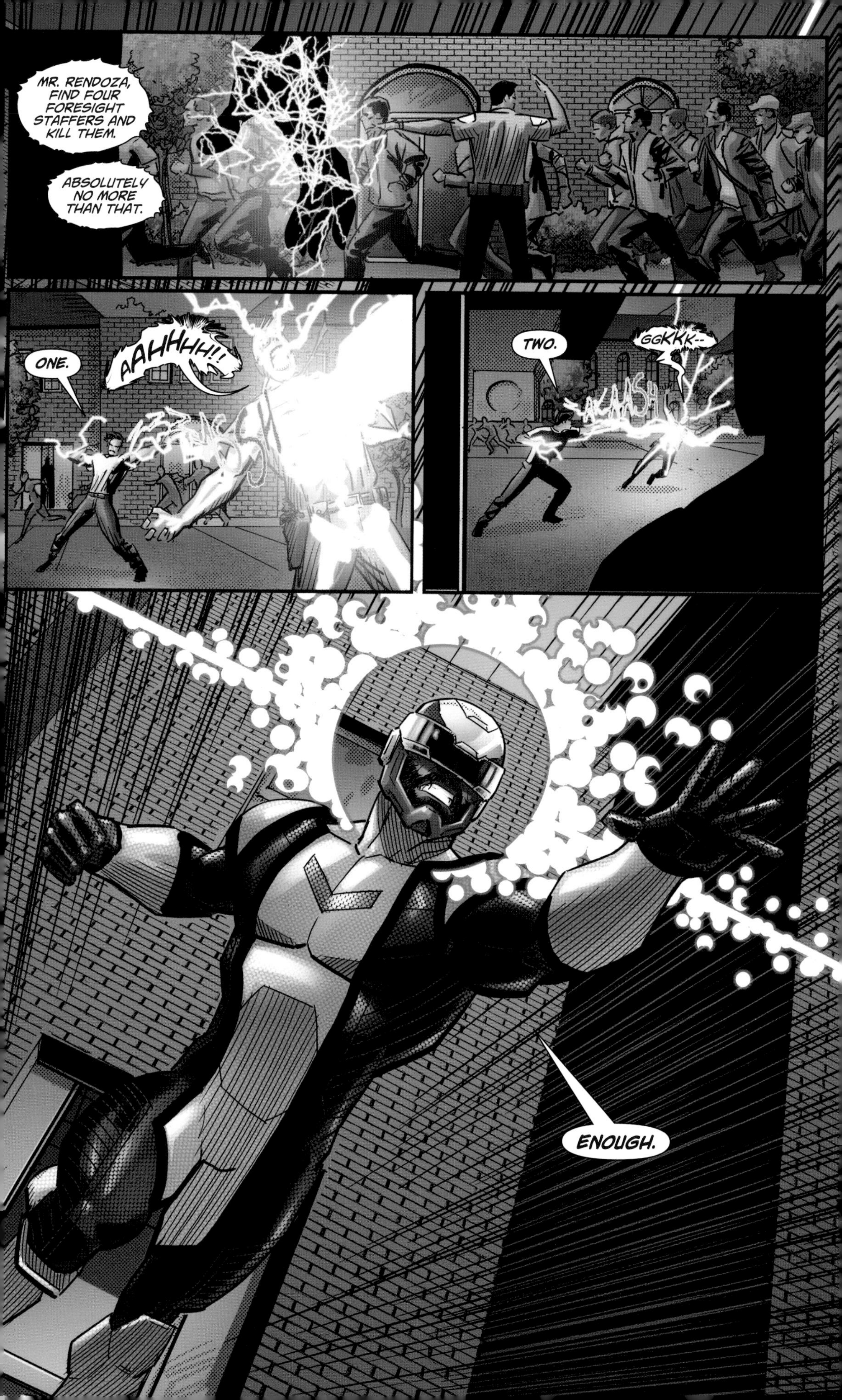
MR. RENDOZA, FIND FOUR FORESIGHT STAFFERS AND KILL THEM.
ABSOLUTELY NO MORE THAN THAT.
ONE.
AAHHHH!!
TWO.
GGKKK--
ENOUGH.

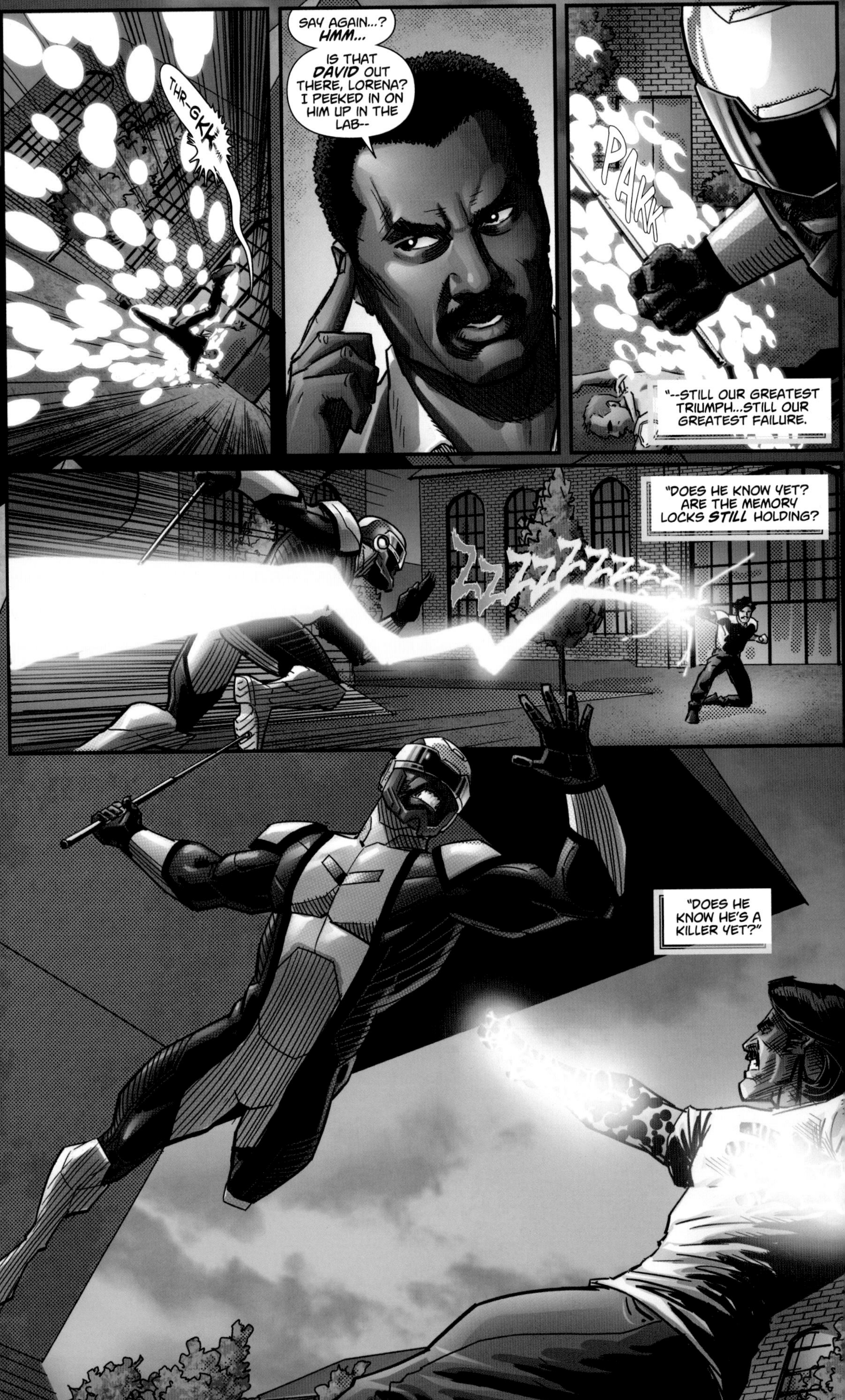
THR-GKK
SAY AGAIN...? HMM...
IS THAT DAVID OUT THERE, LORENA? I PEEKED IN ON HIM UP IN THE LAB--
PAKK
"--STILL OUR GREATEST TRIUMPH...STILL OUR GREATEST FAILURE.
"DOES HE KNOW YET? ARE THE MEMORY LOCKS STILL HOLDING?
ZZZZZZZZZ
"DOES HE KNOW HE'S A KILLER YET?"

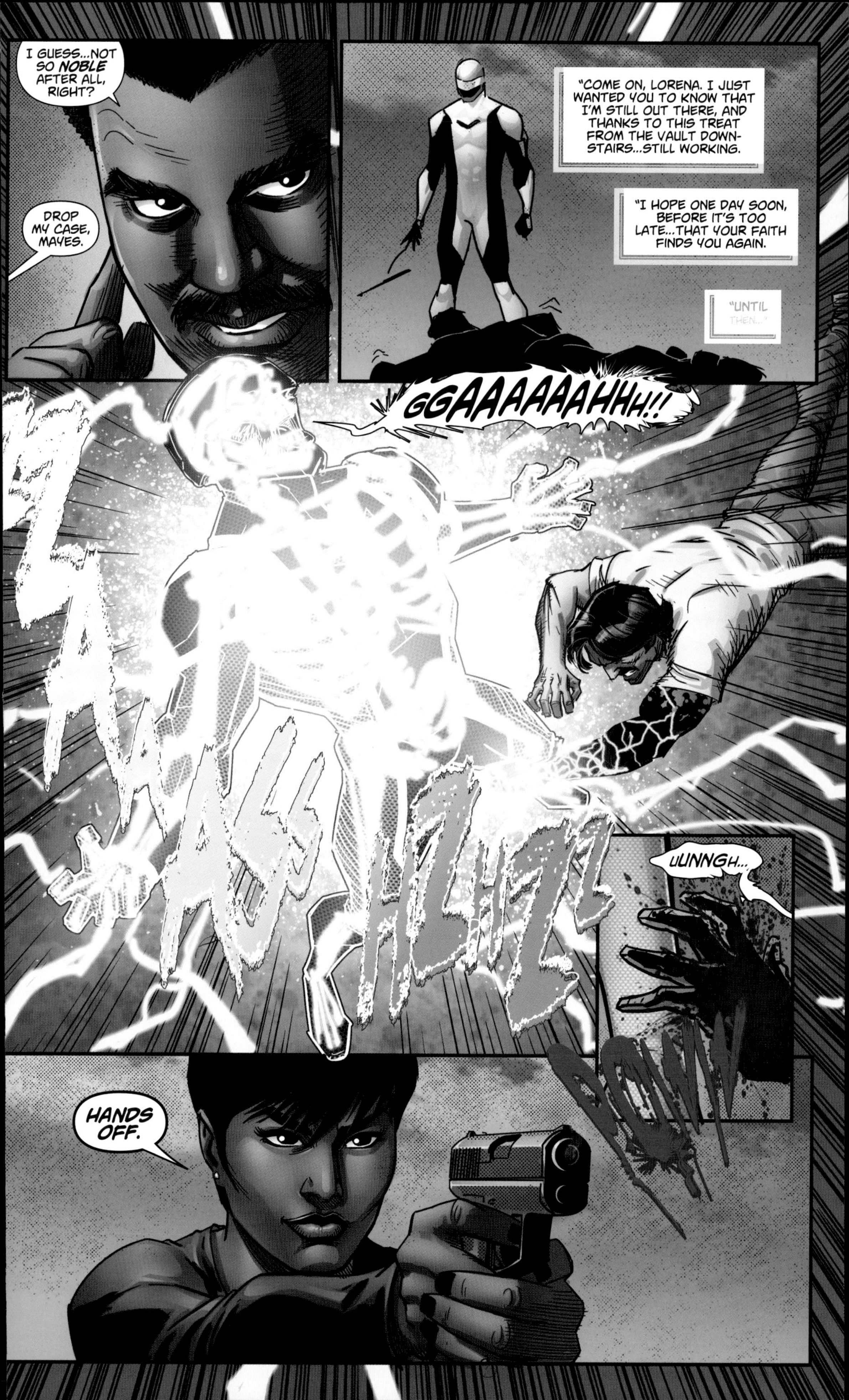
I GUESS...NOT SO **NOBLE** AFTER ALL, RIGHT?
DROP MY CASE, MAYES.
"COME ON, LORENA. I JUST WANTED YOU TO KNOW THAT I'M STILL OUT THERE, AND THANKS TO THIS TREAT FROM THE VAULT DOWN-STAIRS...STILL WORKING.
"I HOPE ONE DAY SOON, BEFORE IT'S TOO LATE...THAT YOUR FAITH FINDS YOU AGAIN.
"UNTIL THEN..."
GGAAAAAAAHHH!!
ZZAAASSHHZZHHZZ
UUNNGH...
BOOM
HANDS OFF.

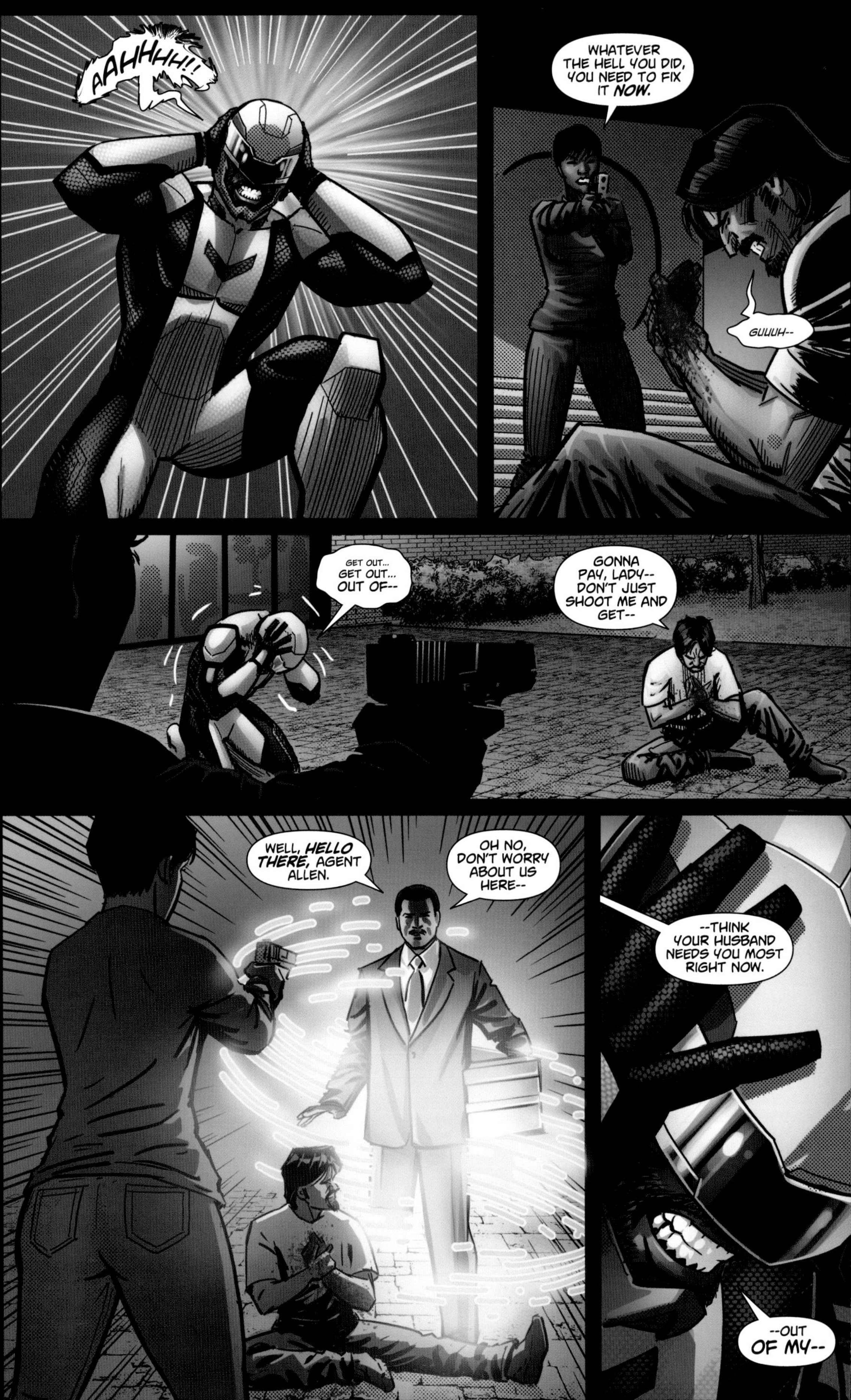
AAHHHH!!
WHATEVER THE HELL YOU DID, YOU NEED TO FIX IT NOW.
GUUUH--
GET OUT... GET OUT... OUT OF--
GONNA PAY, LADY-- DON'T JUST SHOOT ME AND GET--
WELL, HELLO THERE, AGENT ALLEN.
OH NO, DON'T WORRY ABOUT US HERE--
--THINK YOUR HUSBAND NEEDS YOU MOST RIGHT NOW.
--OUT OF MY--

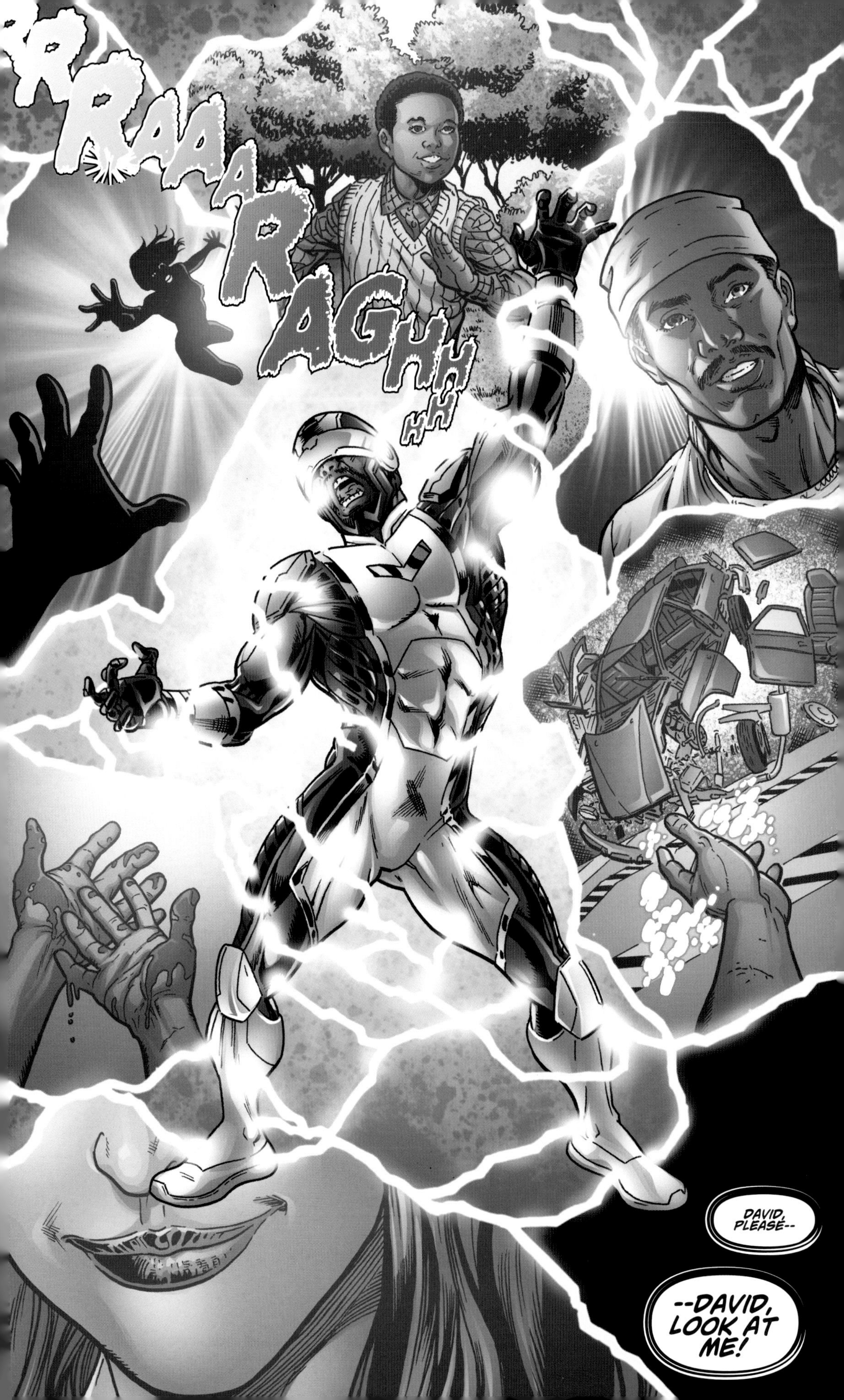
RRRAAAARRAGHHHH
DAVID, PLEASE--
--DAVID, LOOK AT ME!

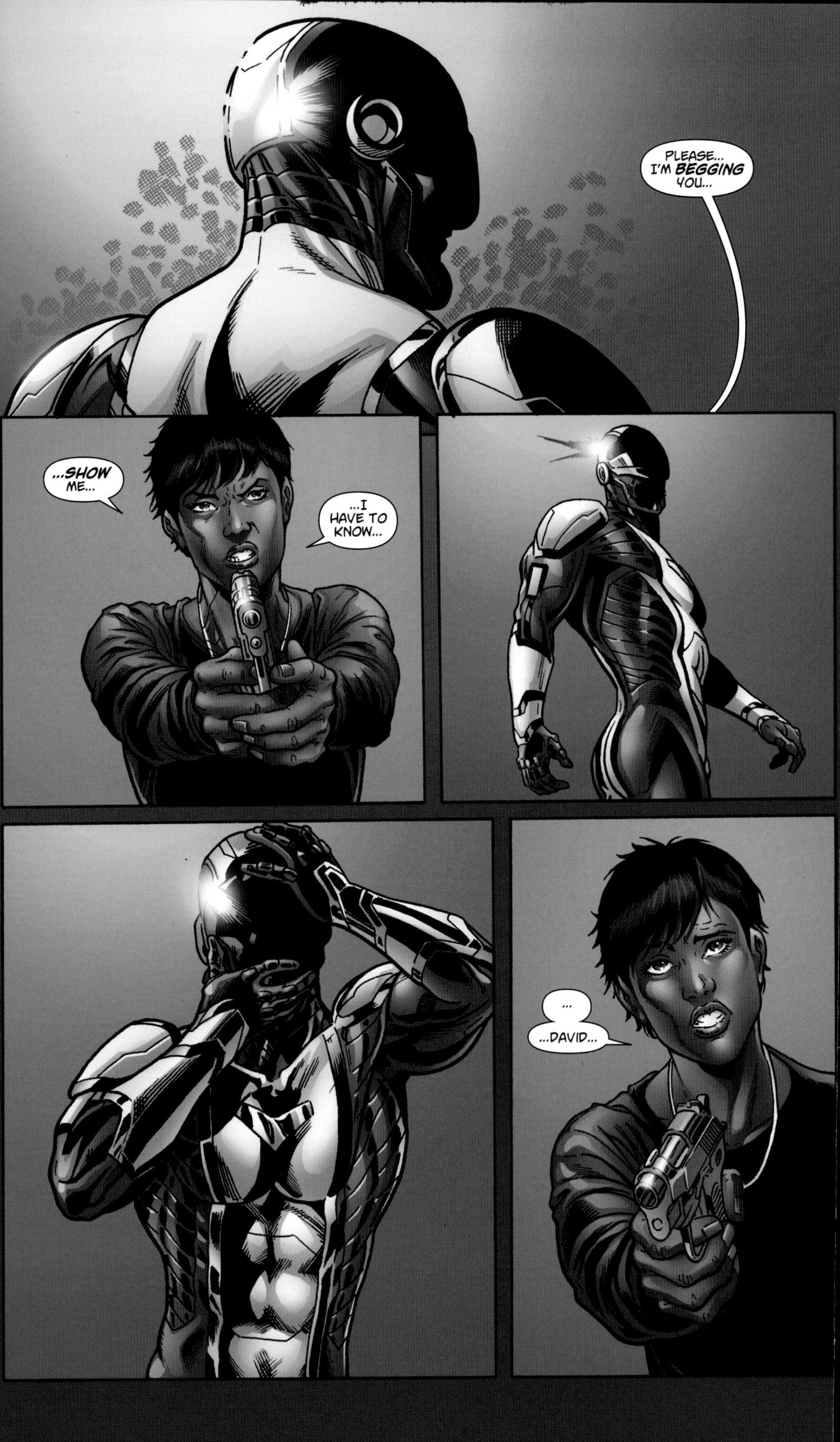
PLEASE... I'M BEGGING YOU...
...SHOW ME...
...I HAVE TO KNOW...
...
...DAVID...

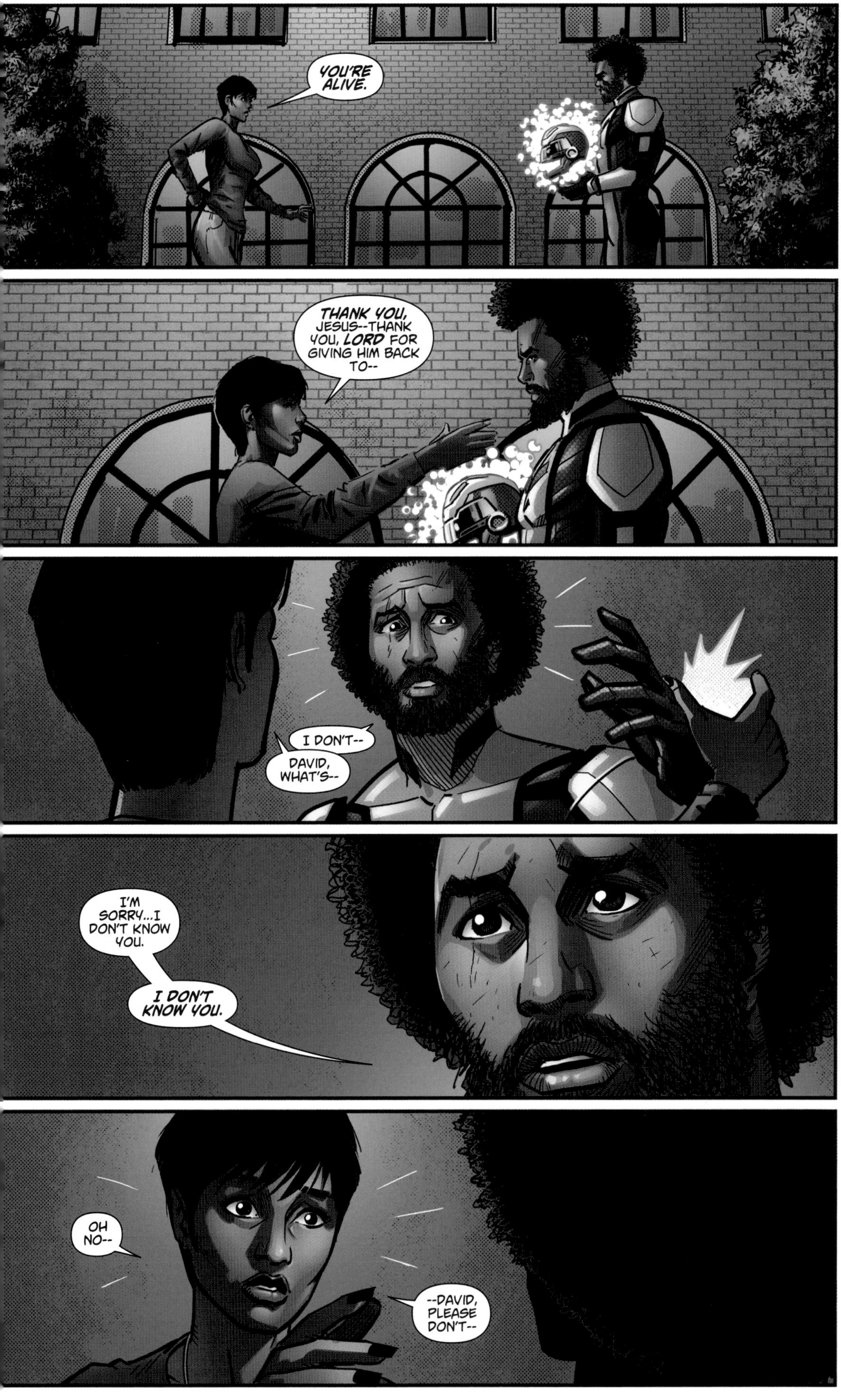
YOU'RE ALIVE.
THANK YOU, JESUS--THANK YOU, LORD FOR GIVING HIM BACK TO--
I DON'T--
DAVID, WHAT'S--
I'M SORRY...I DON'T KNOW YOU.
I DON'T KNOW YOU.
OH NO--
--DAVID, PLEASE DON'T--

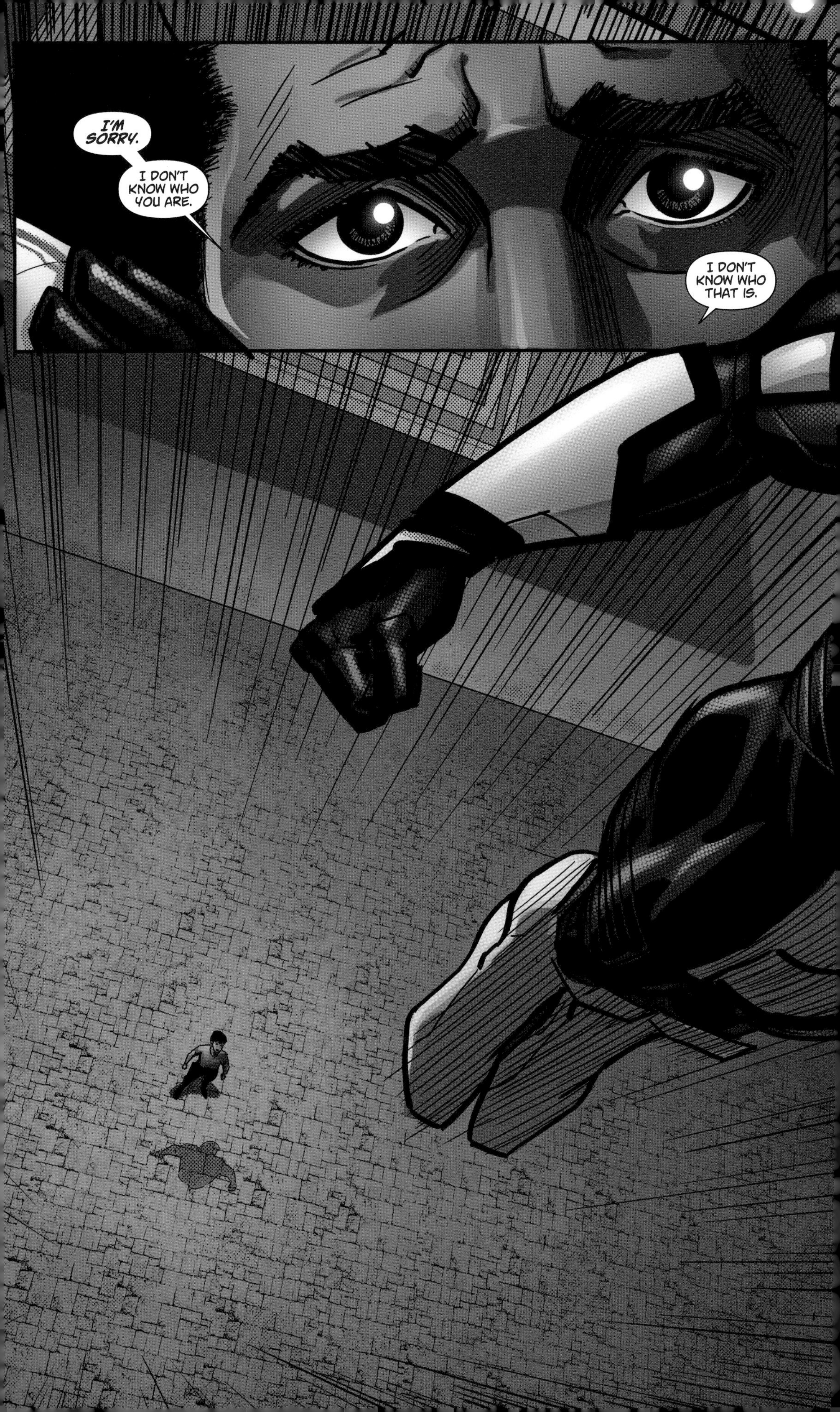
I'M SORRY.
I DON'T KNOW WHO YOU ARE.
I DON'T KNOW WHO THAT IS.

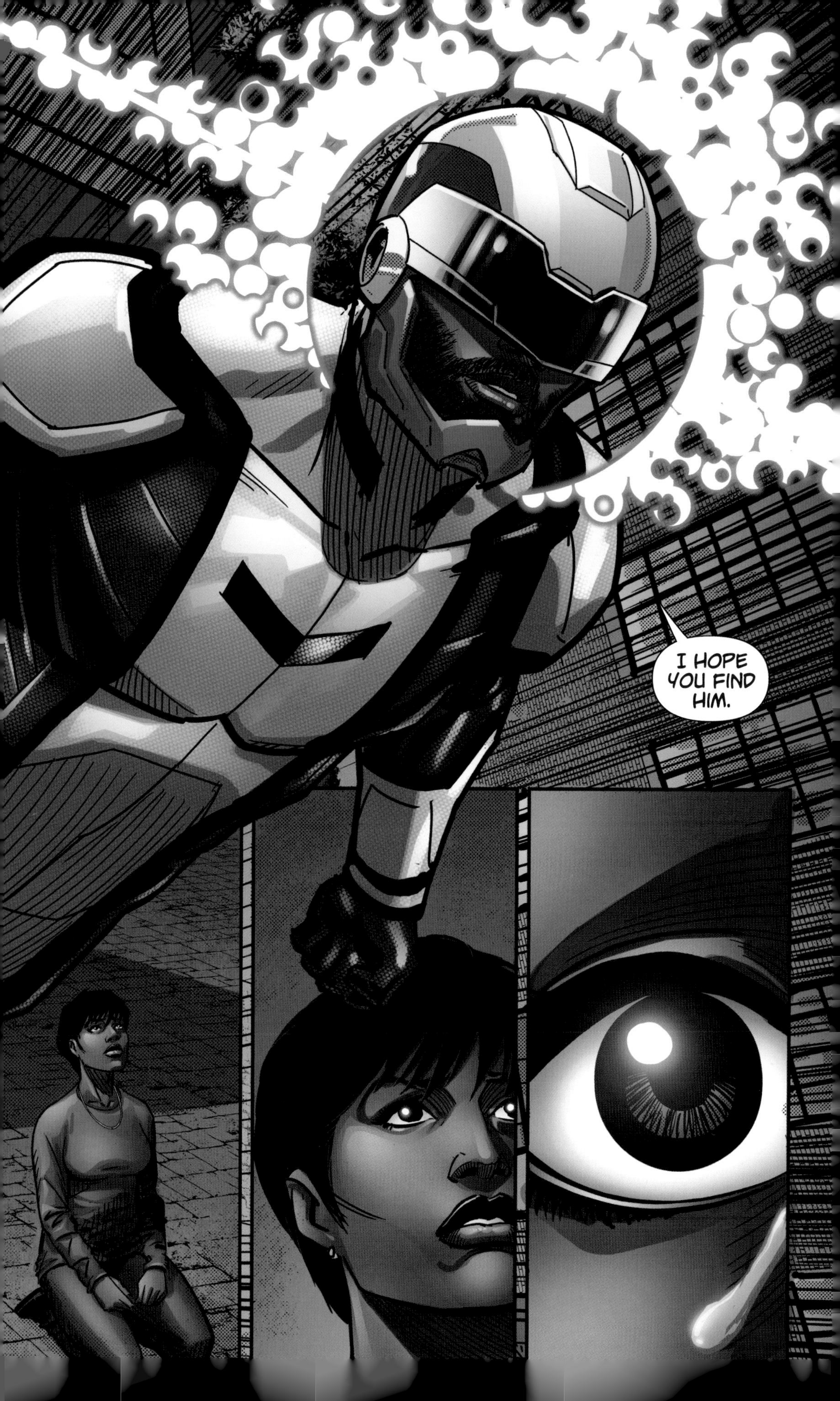
I HOPE YOU FIND HIM.

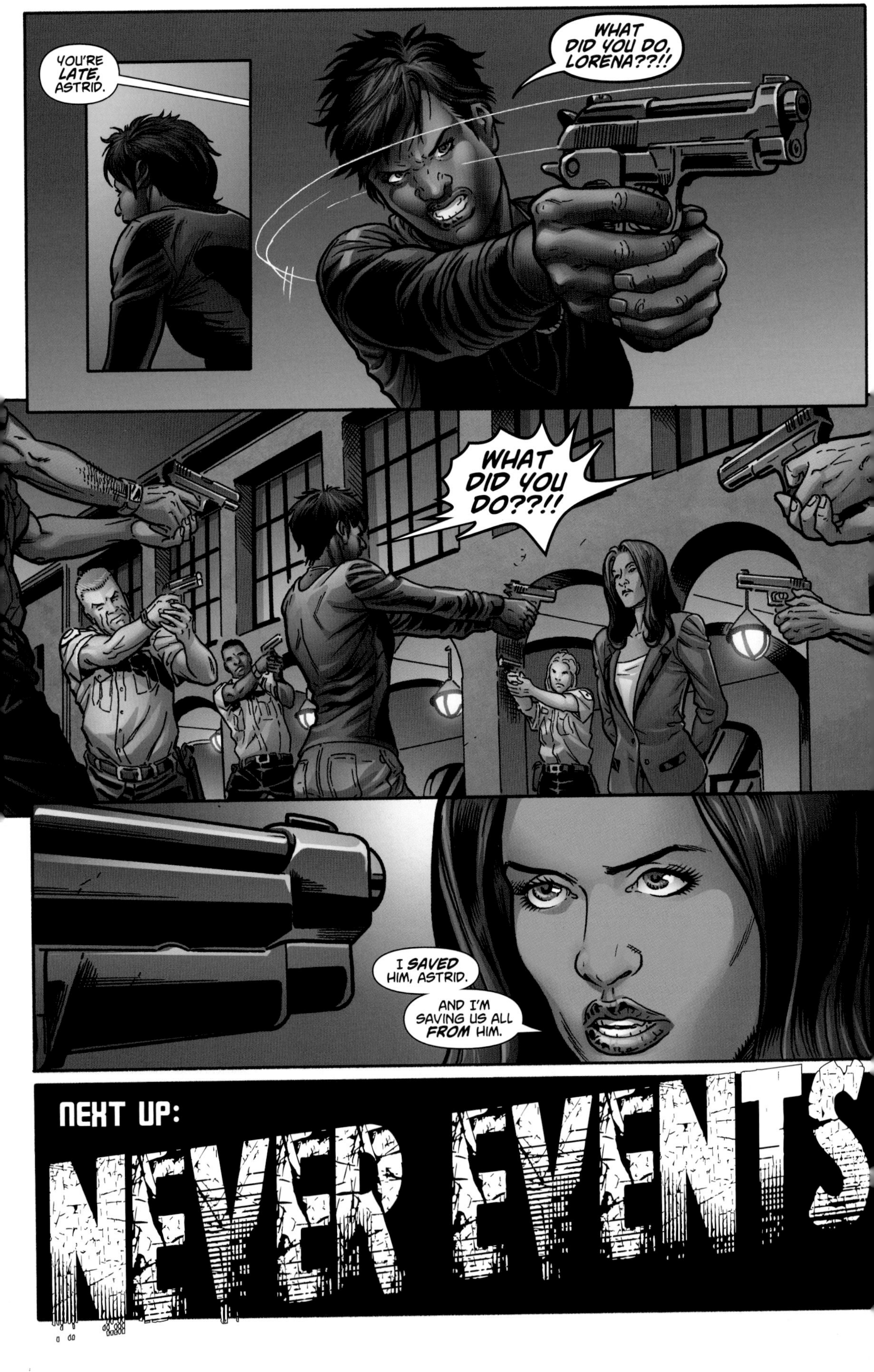

YOU'RE LATE, ASTRID.
WHAT DID YOU DO, LORENA??!!
WHAT DID YOU DO??!!
I SAVED HIM, ASTRID.
AND I'M SAVING US ALL FROM HIM.
NEXT UP:
NEVER EVENTS

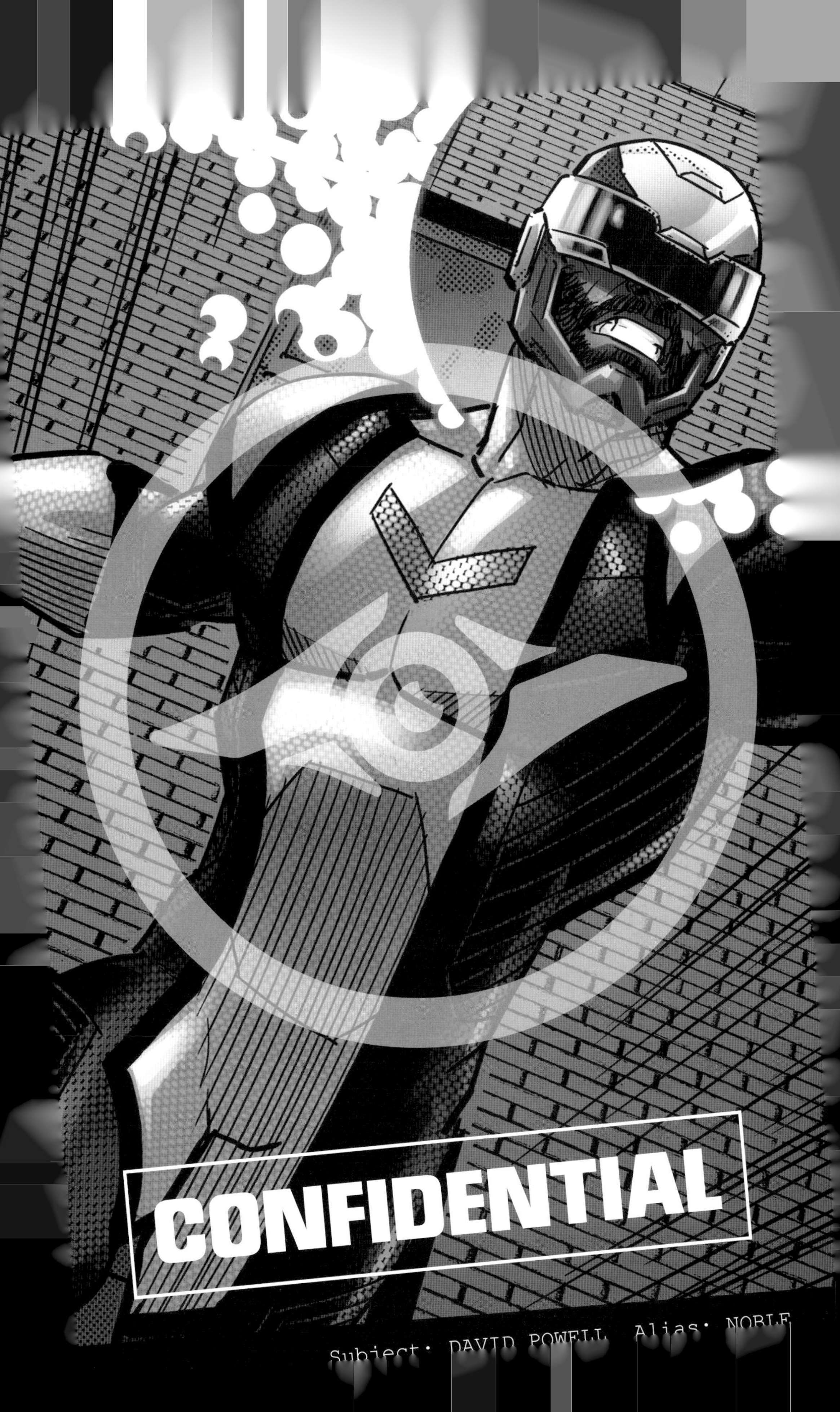
CONFIDENTIAL
Subject: DAVID POWELL Alias: NOBLE

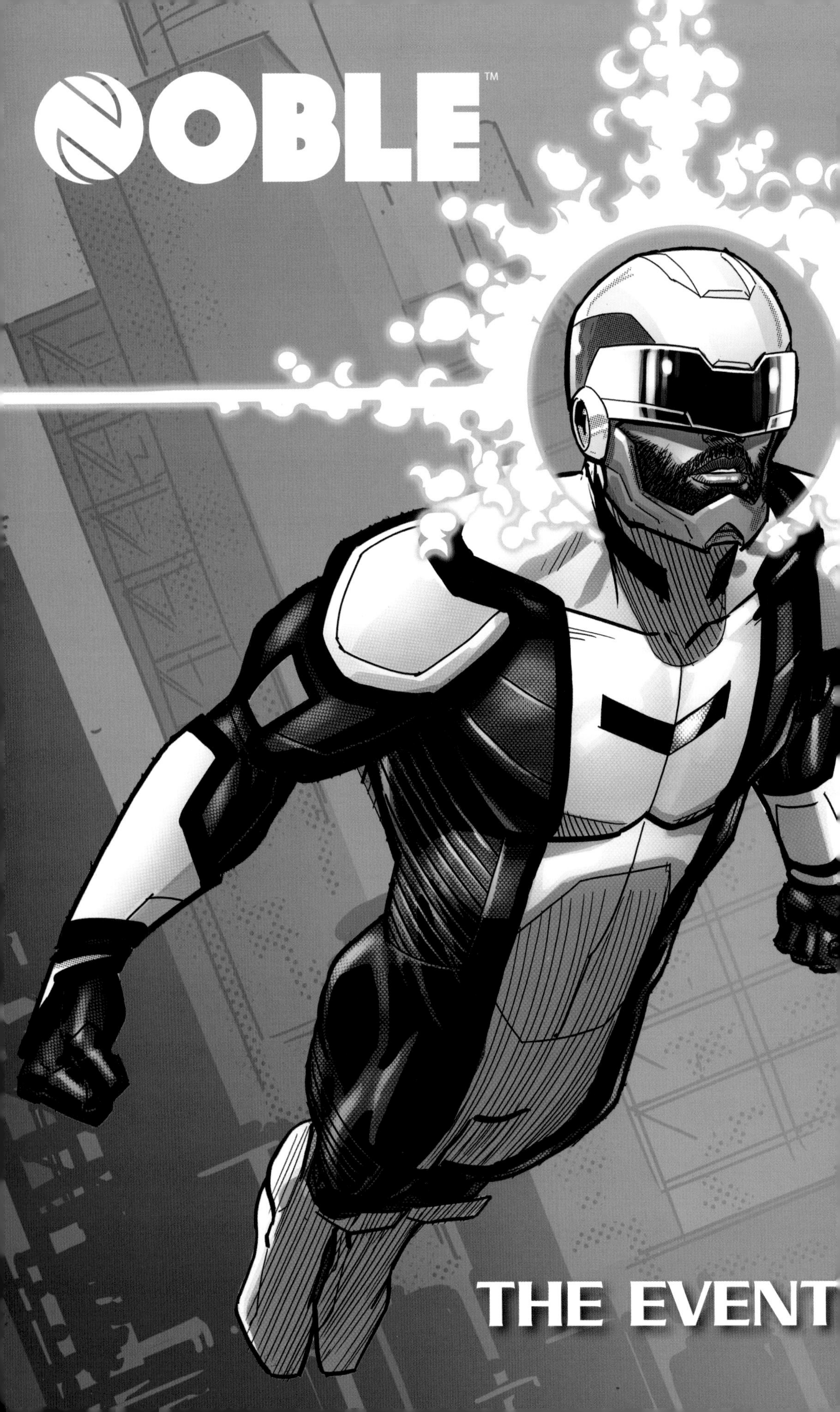
NOBLE™
THE EVENT

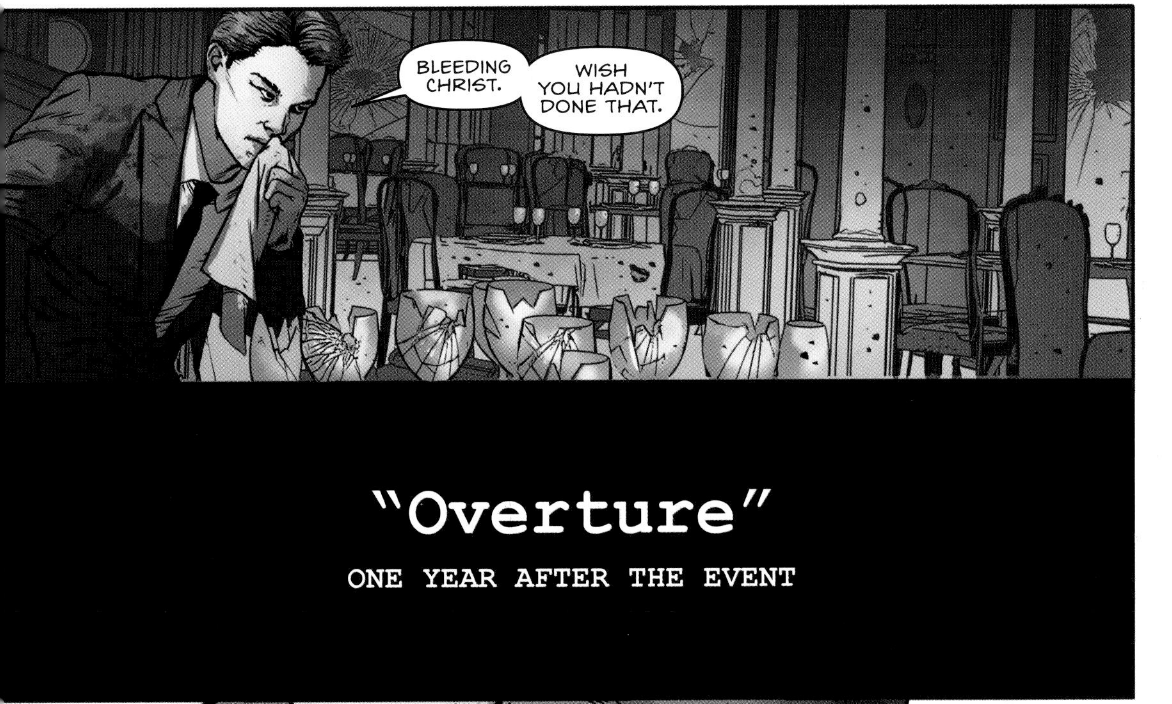
BLEEDING CHRIST.
WISH YOU HADN'T DONE THAT.

"Overture"

ONE YEAR AFTER THE EVENT

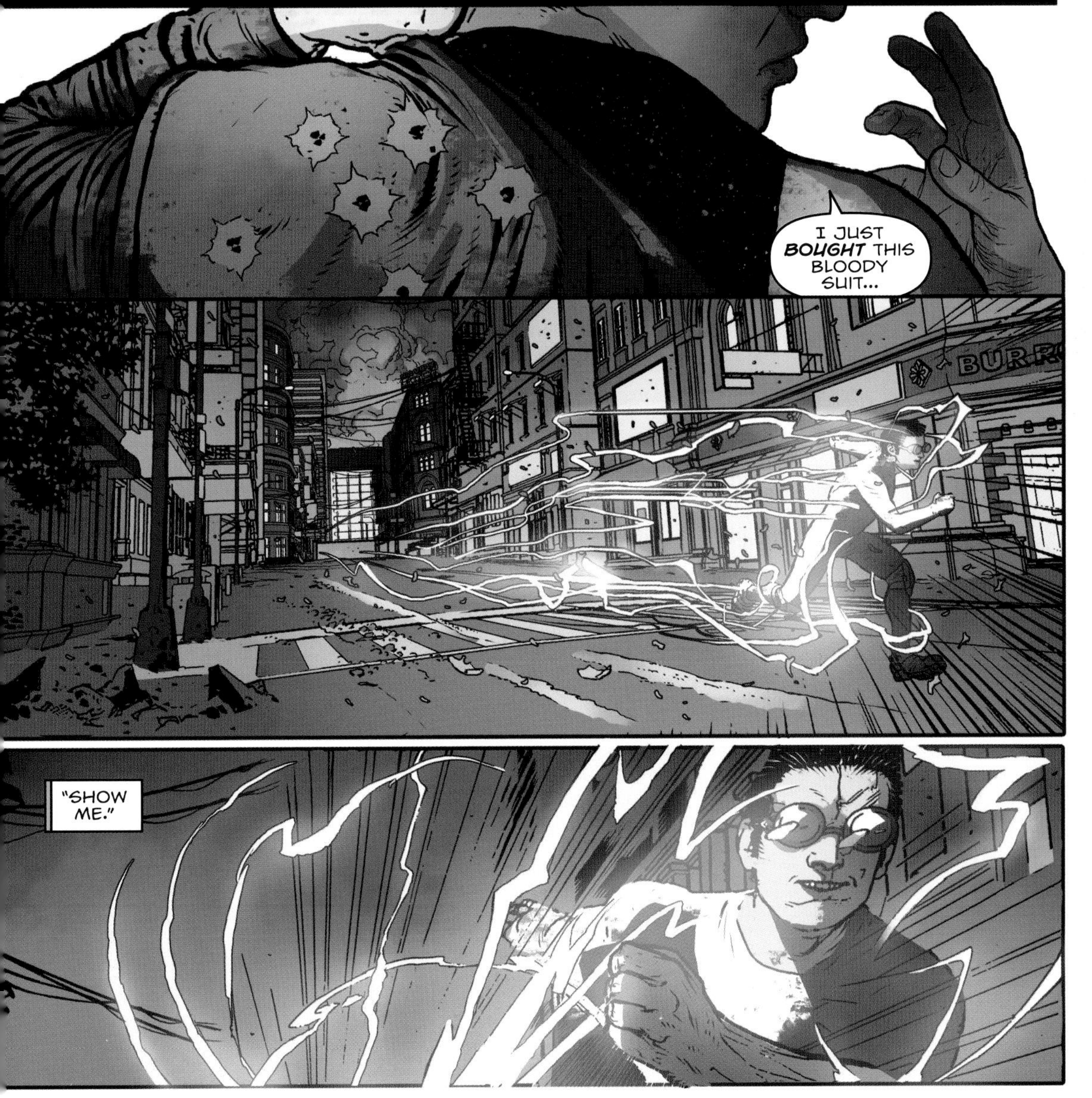
I JUST *BOUGHT* THIS BLOODY SUIT...
"SHOW ME."

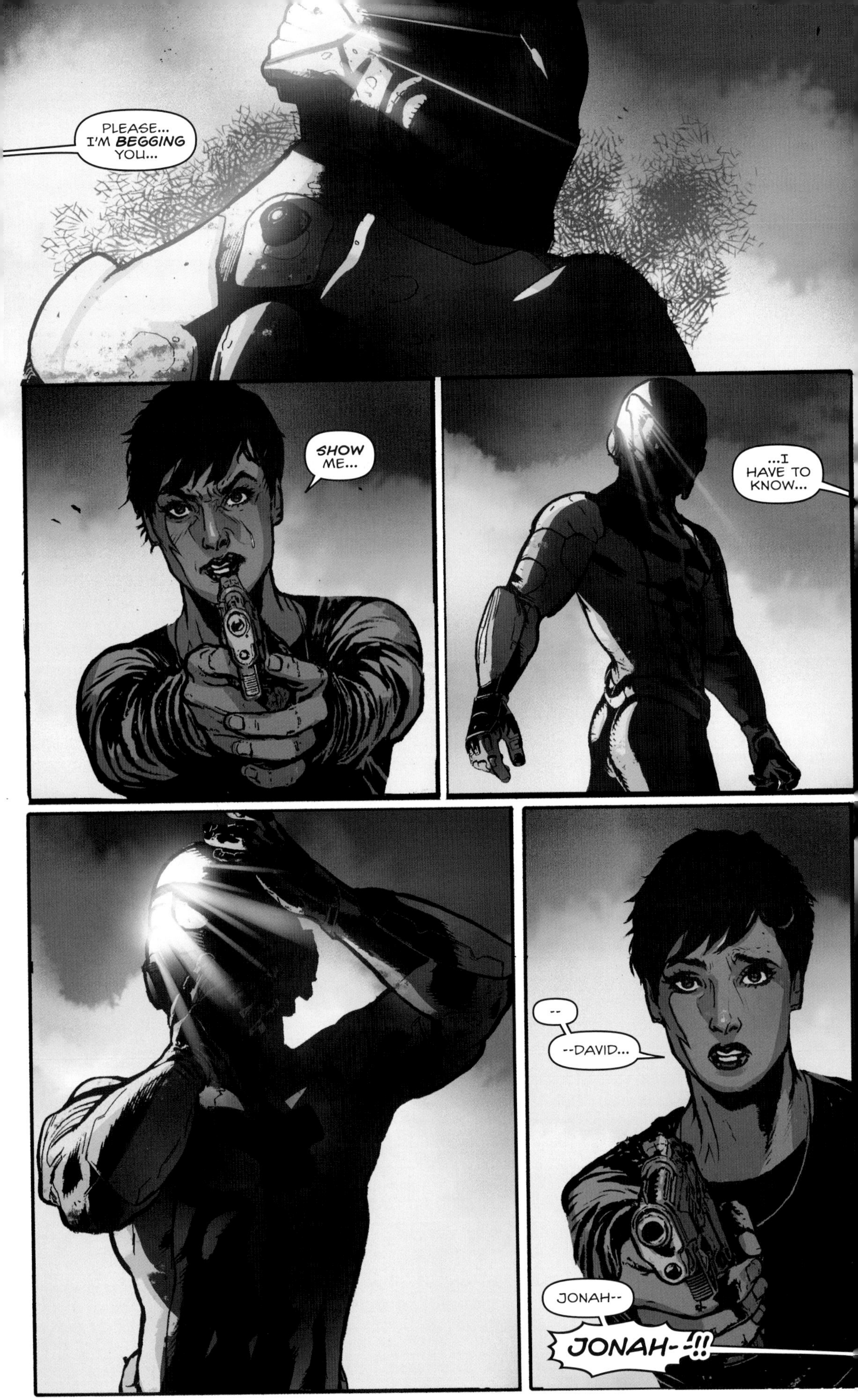
PLEASE... I'M BEGGING YOU...
SHOW ME...
...I HAVE TO KNOW...
--
--DAVID...
JONAH--
JONAH--!!

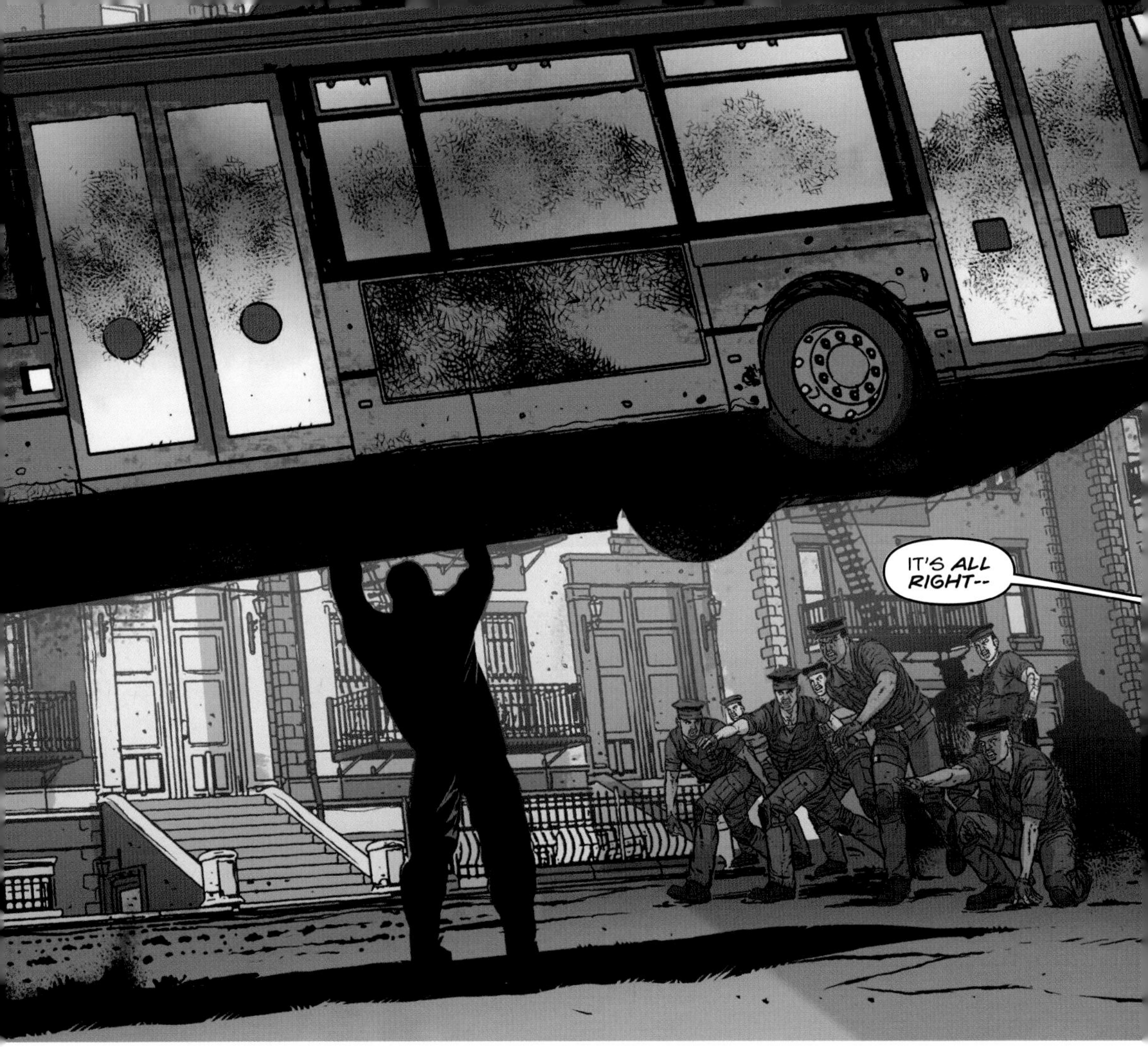
IT'S ALL RIGHT--

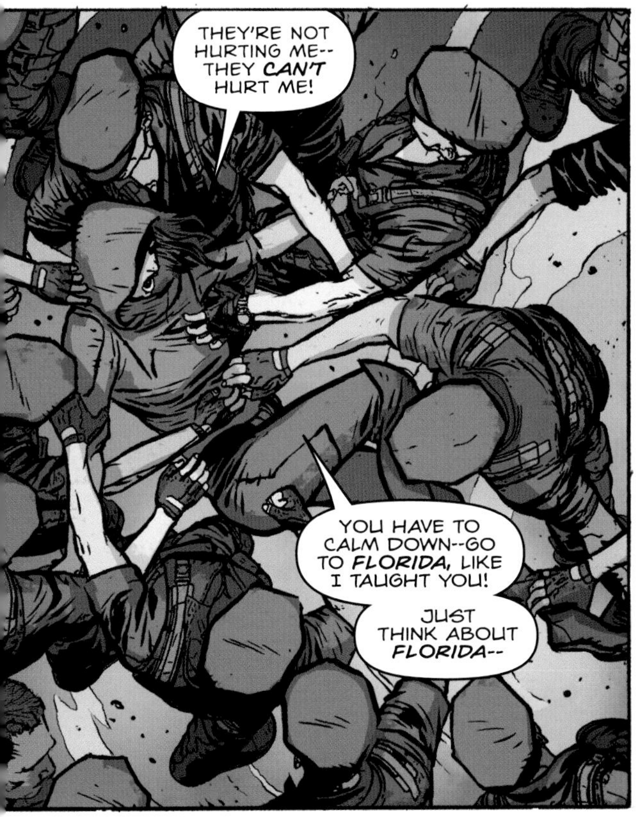
THEY'RE NOT HURTING ME-- THEY CAN'T HURT ME!
YOU HAVE TO CALM DOWN--GO TO FLORIDA, LIKE I TAUGHT YOU!
JUST THINK ABOUT FLORIDA--

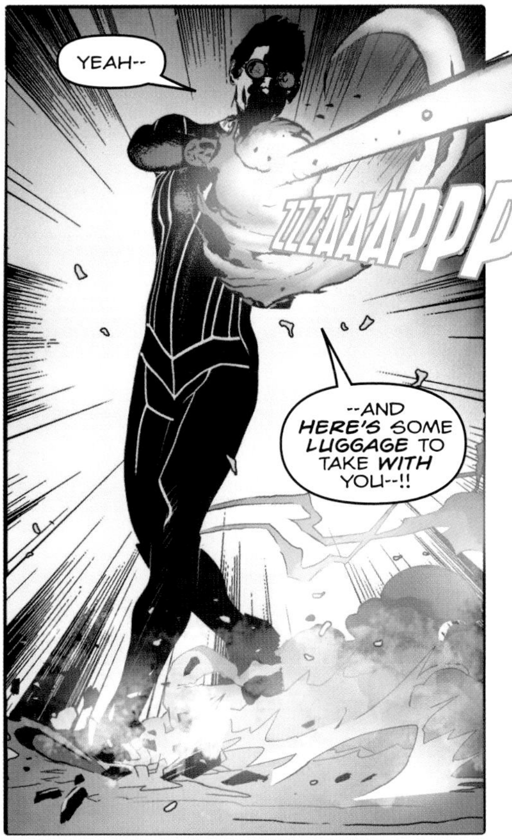
YEAH--
ZZZAAAPPP
--AND HERE'S SOME LUGGAGE TO TAKE WITH YOU--!!

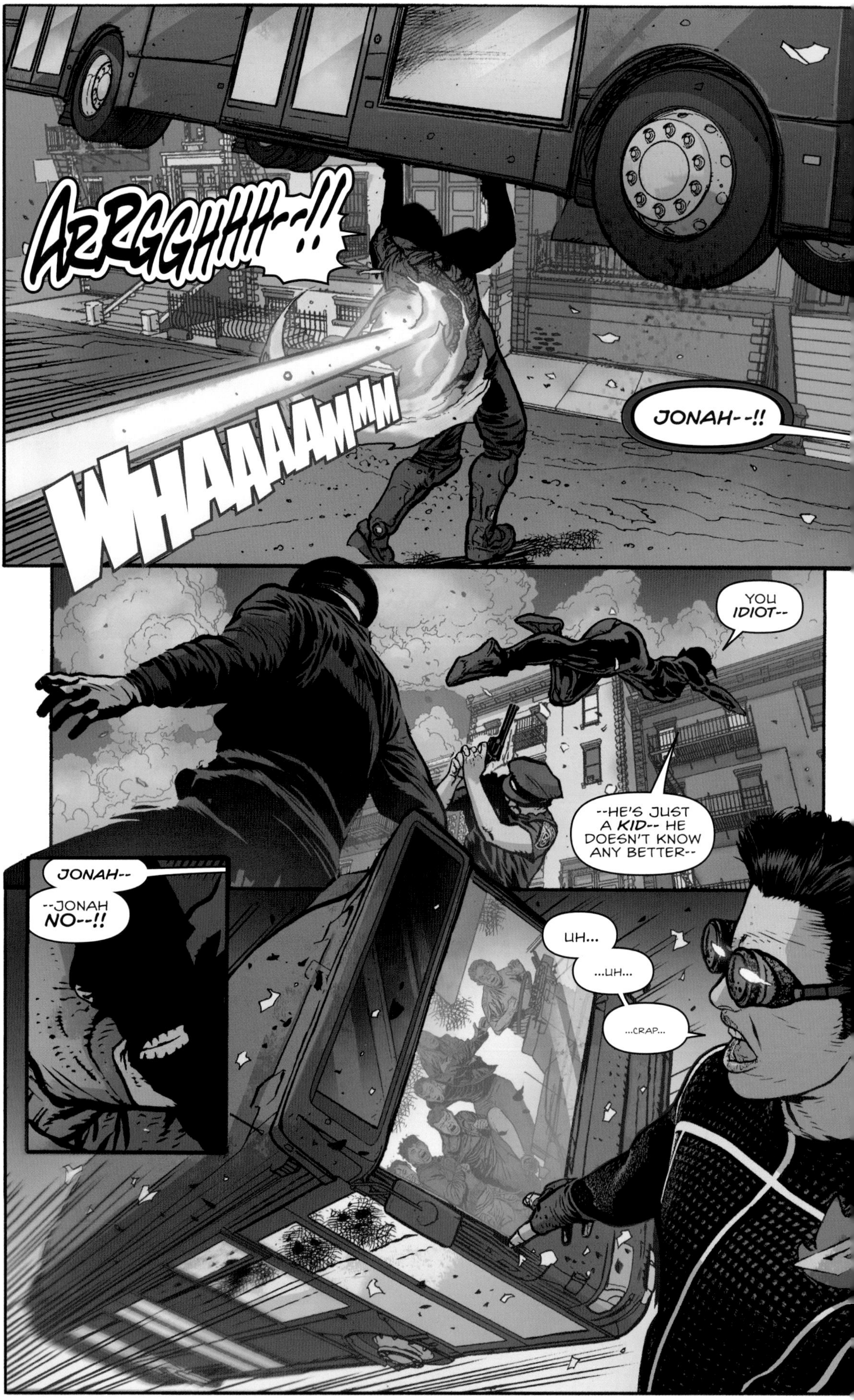
ARRGGHHH--!!
WHAAAAAMMM
JONAH--!!
YOU IDIOT--
--HE'S JUST A KID-- HE DOESN'T KNOW ANY BETTER--
JONAH--
--JONAH NO--!!
UH...
...UH...
...CRAP...

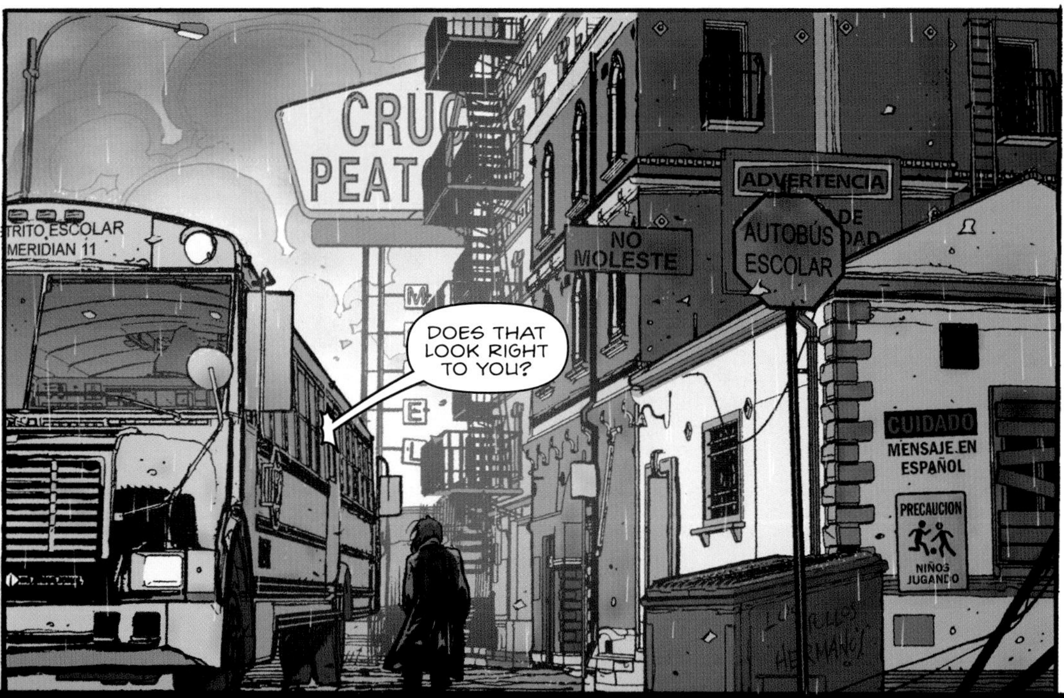
CRUC
PEAT
TRITO ESCOLAR
MERIDIAN 11
ADVERTENCIA
NO MOLESTE
AUTOBÚS ESCOLAR
CUIDADO
MENSAJE EN ESPAÑOL
PRECAUCION
NIÑOS JUGANDO
DOES THAT LOOK RIGHT TO YOU?

"La Dama en El Autobús"

ONE WEEK BEFORE THE EVENT

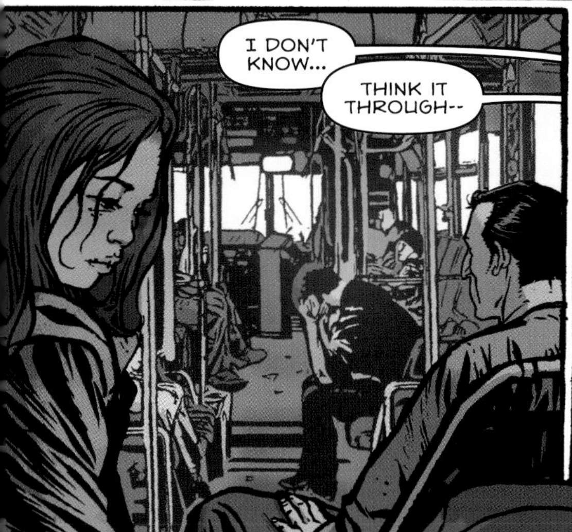
I DON'T KNOW...
THINK IT THROUGH--

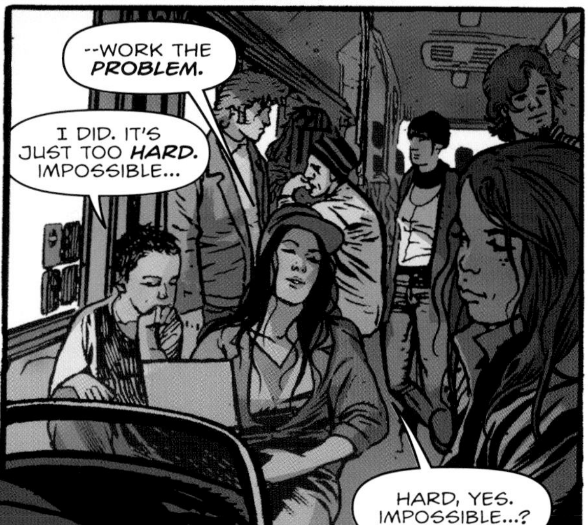
--WORK THE ***PROBLEM.***
I DID. IT'S JUST TOO ***HARD.*** IMPOSSIBLE...
HARD, YES. IMPOSSIBLE...?

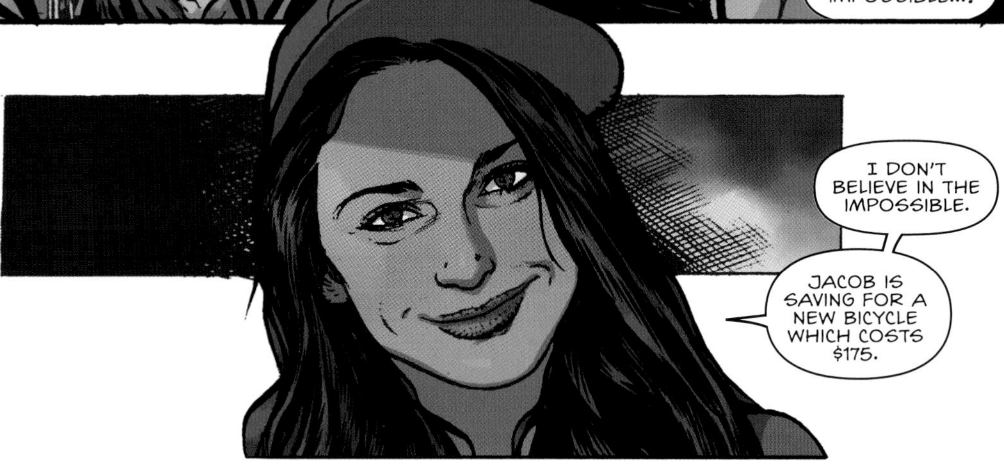
I DON'T BELIEVE IN THE IMPOSSIBLE.
JACOB IS SAVING FOR A NEW BICYCLE WHICH COSTS $175.

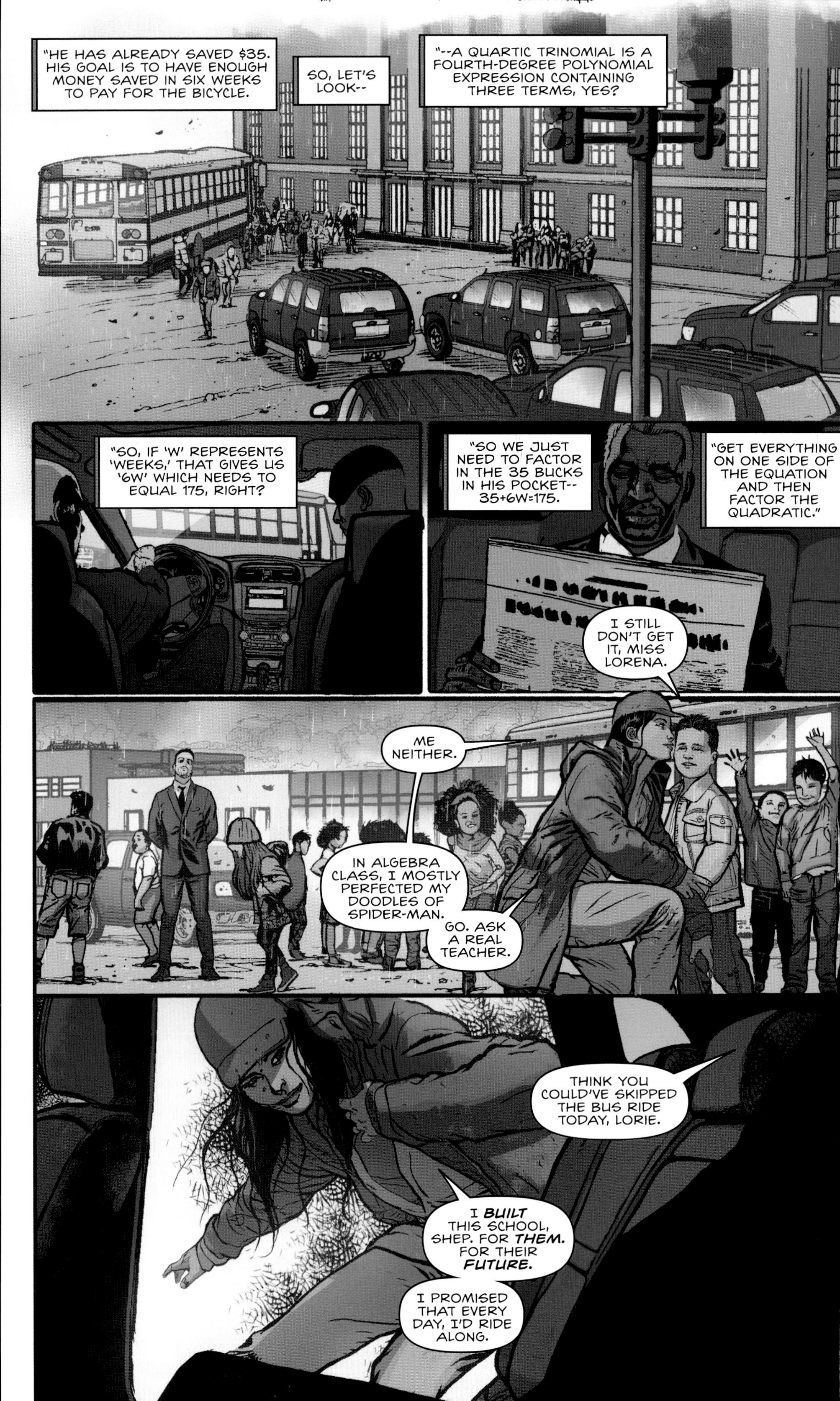
"HE HAS ALREADY SAVED $35. HIS GOAL IS TO HAVE ENOUGH MONEY SAVED IN SIX WEEKS TO PAY FOR THE BICYCLE.
SO, LET'S LOOK--
"--A QUARTIC TRINOMIAL IS A FOURTH-DEGREE POLYNOMIAL EXPRESSION CONTAINING THREE TERMS, YES?
"SO, IF 'W' REPRESENTS 'WEEKS,' THAT GIVES US '6W' WHICH NEEDS TO EQUAL 175, RIGHT?
"SO WE JUST NEED TO FACTOR IN THE 35 BUCKS IN HIS POCKET-- 35+6W=175.
"GET EVERYTHING ON ONE SIDE OF THE EQUATION AND THEN FACTOR THE QUADRATIC."
I STILL DON'T GET IT, MISS LORENA.
ME NEITHER.
IN ALGEBRA CLASS, I MOSTLY PERFECTED MY DOODLES OF SPIDER-MAN.
GO. ASK A REAL TEACHER.
THINK YOU COULD'VE SKIPPED THE BUS RIDE TODAY, LORIE.
I *BUILT* THIS SCHOOL, SHEP. FOR *THEM.* FOR THEIR *FUTURE.*
I PROMISED THAT EVERY DAY, I'D RIDE ALONG.

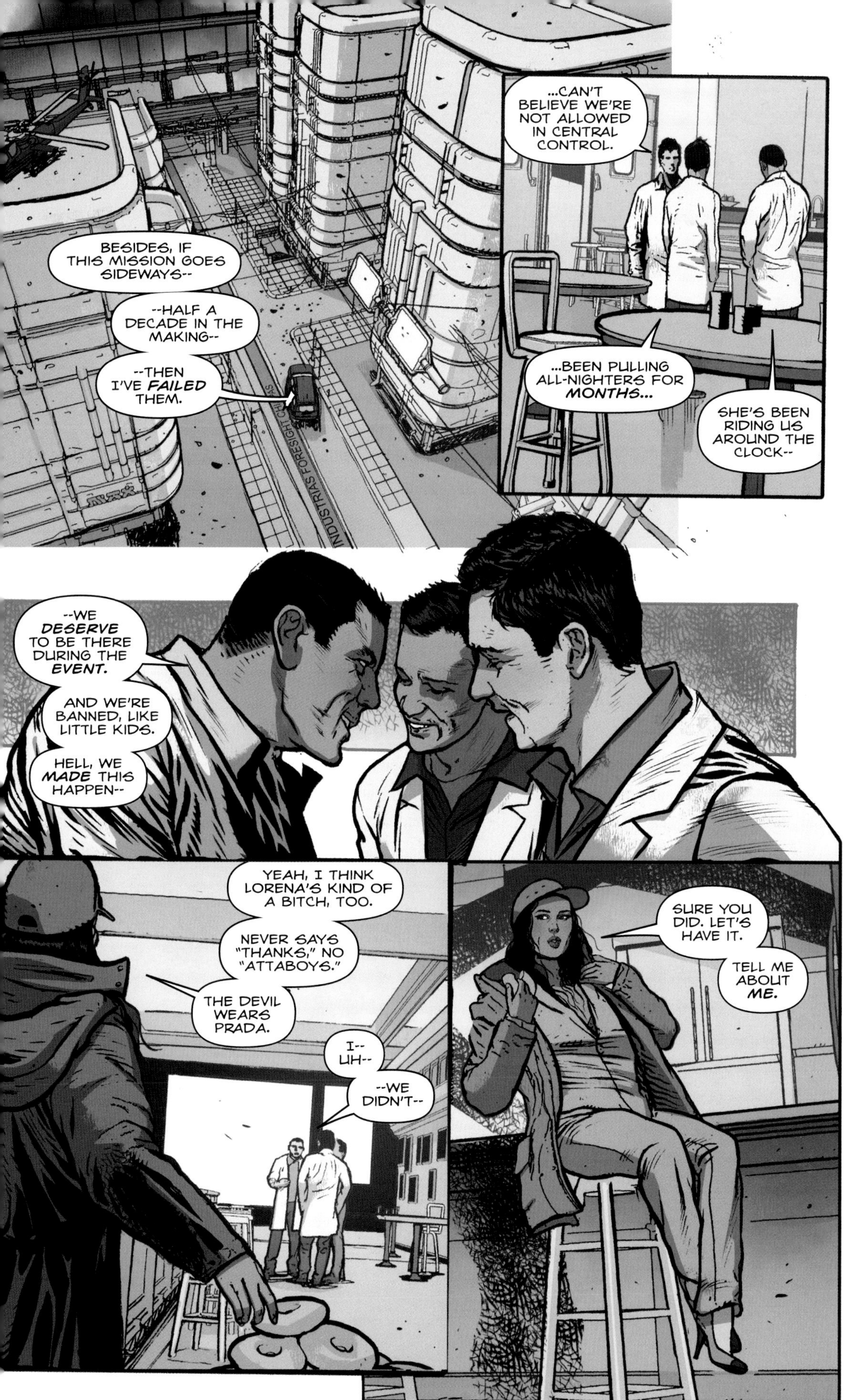
BESIDES, IF THIS MISSION GOES SIDEWAYS--
--HALF A DECADE IN THE MAKING--
--THEN I'VE *FAILED* THEM.
INDUSTRIAS FORESIGHT CHILAS
...CAN'T BELIEVE WE'RE NOT ALLOWED IN CENTRAL CONTROL.
...BEEN PULLING ALL-NIGHTERS FOR *MONTHS*...
SHE'S BEEN RIDING US AROUND THE CLOCK--
--WE *DESERVE* TO BE THERE DURING THE *EVENT.*
AND WE'RE BANNED, LIKE LITTLE KIDS.
HELL, WE *MADE* THIS HAPPEN--
YEAH, I THINK LORENA'S KIND OF A BITCH, TOO.
NEVER SAYS "THANKS," NO "ATTABOYS."
THE DEVIL WEARS PRADA.
I-- UH--
--WE DIDN'T--
SURE YOU DID. LET'S HAVE IT.
TELL ME ABOUT *ME.*

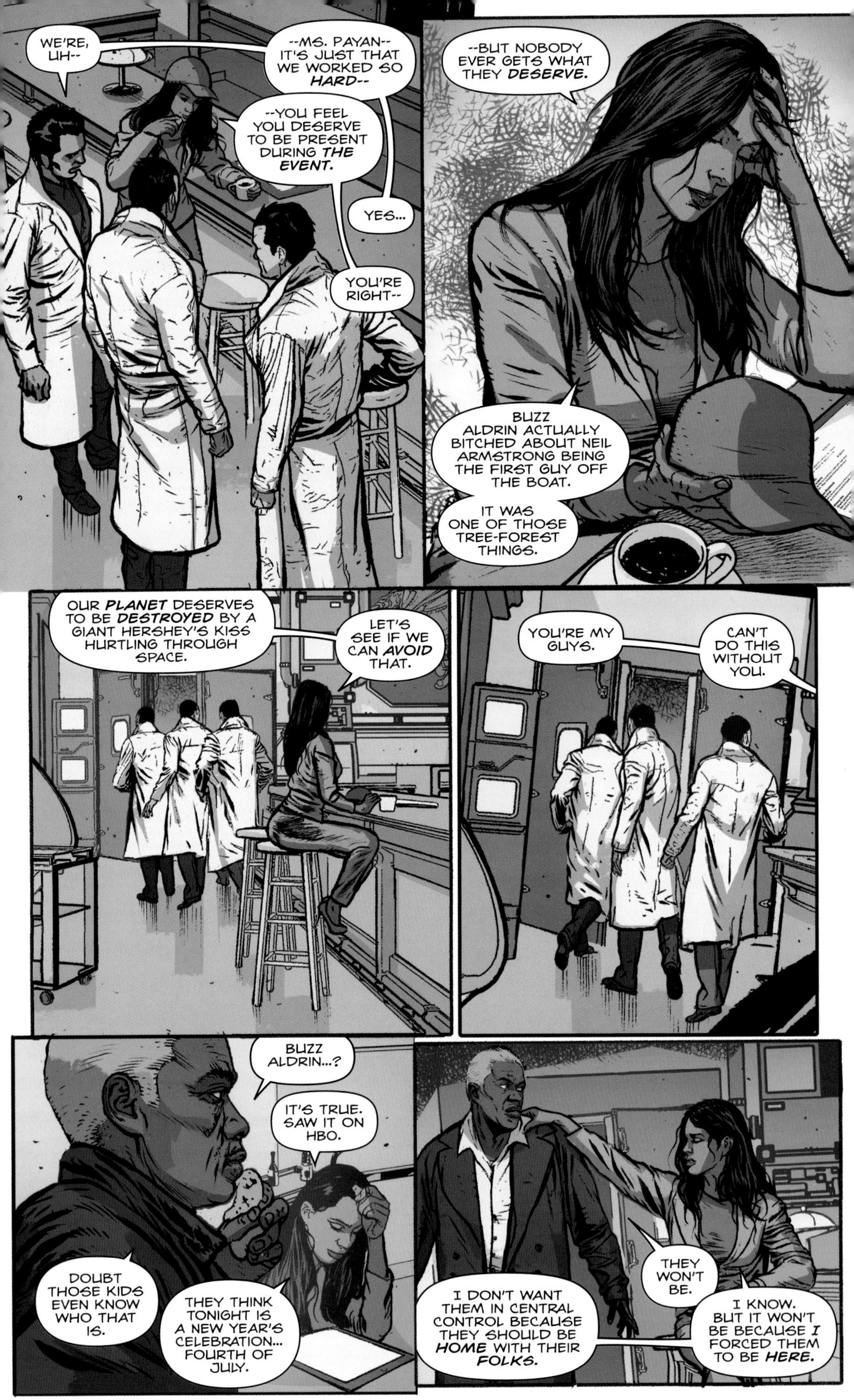

WE'RE, UH--
--MS. PAYAN-- IT'S JUST THAT WE WORKED SO *HARD*--
--YOU FEEL YOU DESERVE TO BE PRESENT DURING *THE EVENT.*
YES...
YOU'RE RIGHT--
--BUT NOBODY EVER GETS WHAT THEY *DESERVE.*
BUZZ ALDRIN ACTUALLY BITCHED ABOUT NEIL ARMSTRONG BEING THE FIRST GUY OFF THE BOAT.
IT WAS ONE OF THOSE TREE-FOREST THINGS.
OUR *PLANET* DESERVES TO BE *DESTROYED* BY A GIANT HERSHEY'S KISS HURTLING THROUGH SPACE.
LET'S SEE IF WE CAN *AVOID* THAT.
YOU'RE MY GUYS.
CAN'T DO THIS WITHOUT YOU.
BUZZ ALDRIN...?
IT'S TRUE. SAW IT ON HBO.
DOUBT THOSE KIDS EVEN KNOW WHO THAT IS.
THEY THINK TONIGHT IS A NEW YEAR'S CELEBRATION... FOURTH OF JULY.
I DON'T WANT THEM IN CENTRAL CONTROL BECAUSE THEY SHOULD BE *HOME* WITH THEIR *FOLKS.*
THEY WON'T BE.
I KNOW. BUT IT WON'T BE BECAUSE *I* FORCED THEM TO BE *HERE.*

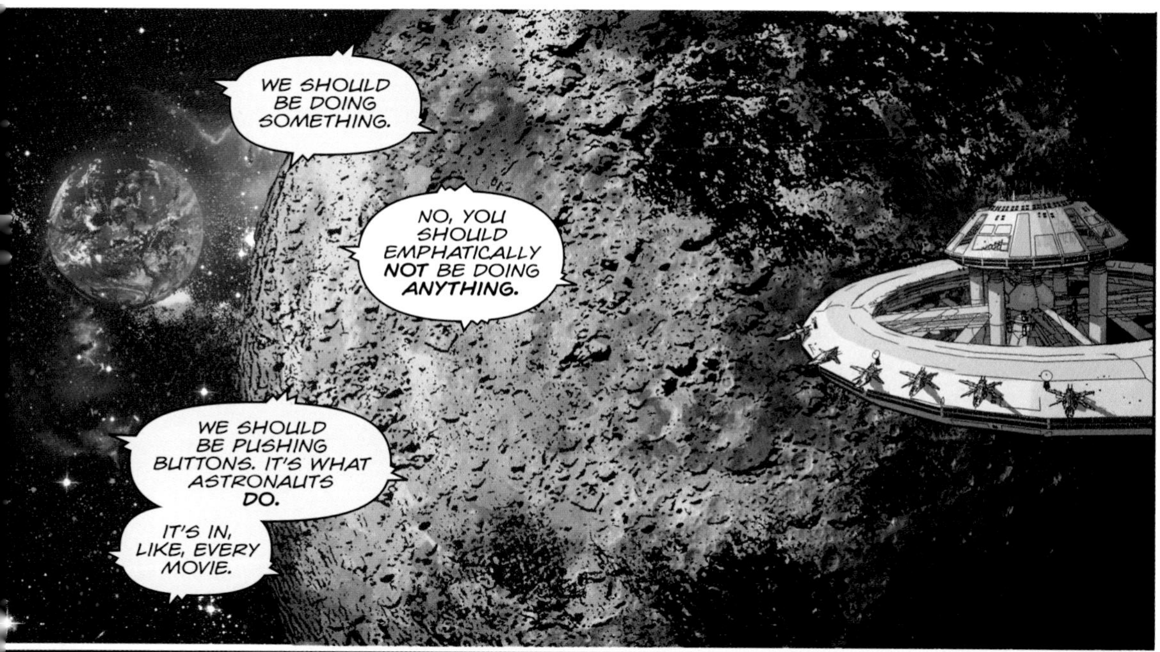
WE SHOULD BE DOING SOMETHING.
NO, YOU SHOULD EMPHATICALLY NOT BE DOING ANYTHING.
WE SHOULD BE PUSHING BUTTONS. IT'S WHAT ASTRONAUTS DO.
IT'S IN, LIKE, EVERY MOVIE.

"Monkeys"

FORESIGHT AMERICO LUNAR PLATFORM
ONE WEEK BEFORE THE EVENT

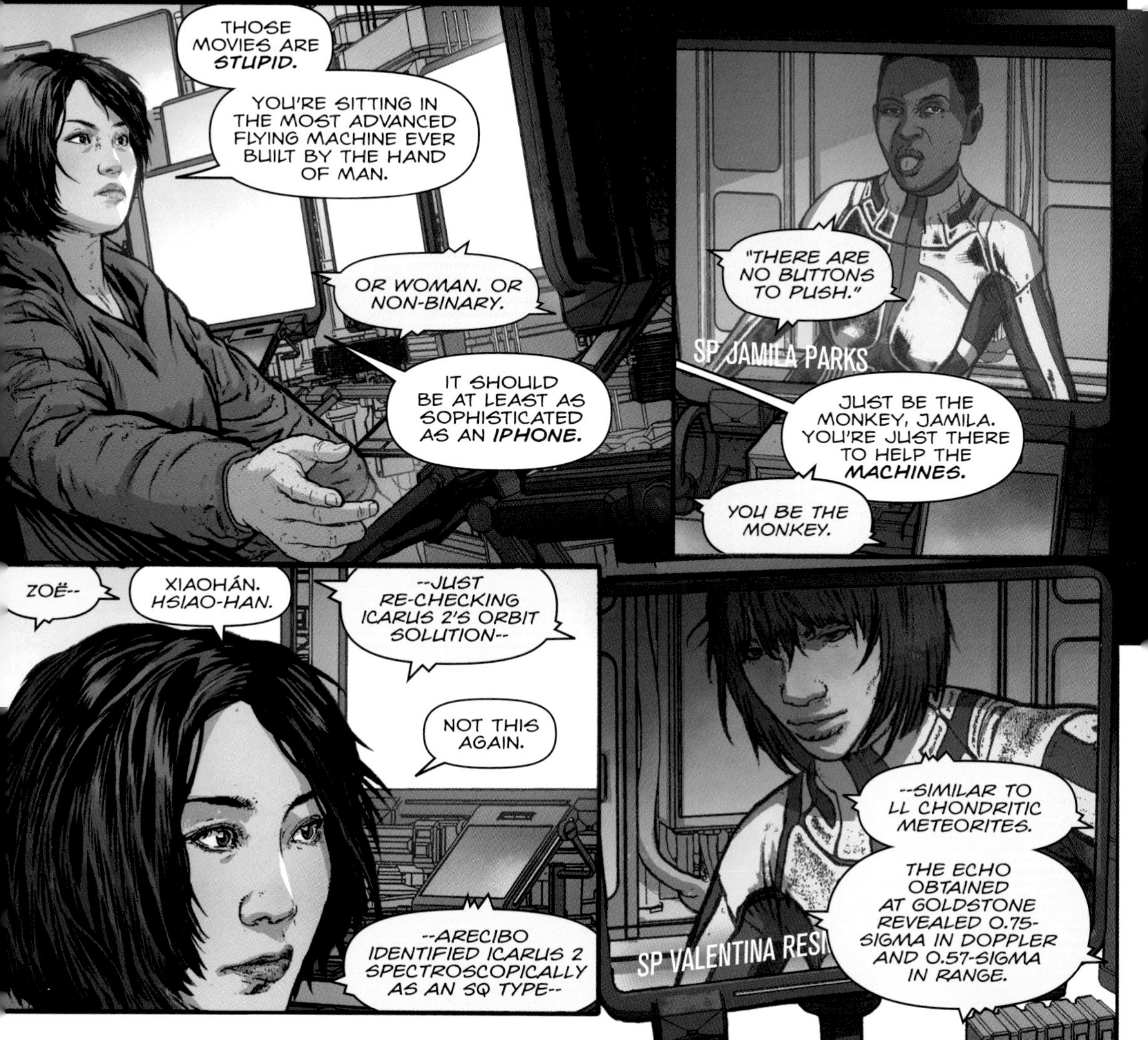
THOSE MOVIES ARE STUPID.
YOU'RE SITTING IN THE MOST ADVANCED FLYING MACHINE EVER BUILT BY THE HAND OF MAN.
OR WOMAN. OR NON-BINARY.
IT SHOULD BE AT LEAST AS SOPHISTICATED AS AN IPHONE.
"THERE ARE NO BUTTONS TO PUSH."
SP JAMILA PARKS
JUST BE THE MONKEY, JAMILA. YOU'RE JUST THERE TO HELP THE MACHINES.
YOU BE THE MONKEY.
ZOË--
XIAOHÁN. HSIAO-HAN.
--JUST RE-CHECKING ICARUS 2'S ORBIT SOLUTION--
NOT THIS AGAIN.
--ARECIBO IDENTIFIED ICARUS 2 SPECTROSCOPICALLY AS AN SQ TYPE--
--SIMILAR TO LL CHONDRITIC METEORITES.
THE ECHO OBTAINED AT GOLDSTONE REVEALED 0.75-SIGMA IN DOPPLER AND 0.57-SIGMA IN RANGE.
SP VALENTINA RES

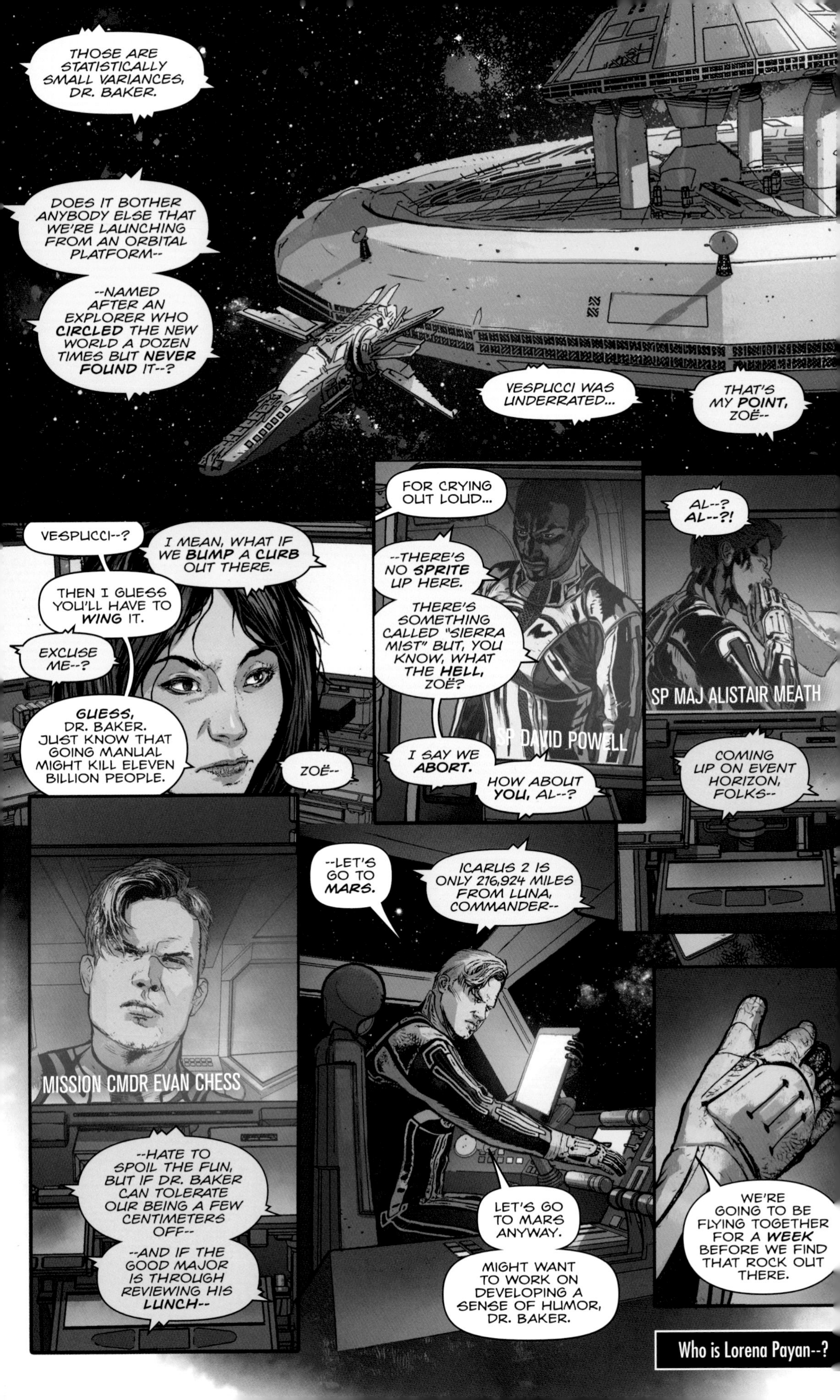
THOSE ARE STATISTICALLY SMALL VARIANCES, DR. BAKER.
DOES IT BOTHER ANYBODY ELSE THAT WE'RE LAUNCHING FROM AN ORBITAL PLATFORM--
--NAMED AFTER AN EXPLORER WHO CIRCLED THE NEW WORLD A DOZEN TIMES BUT NEVER FOUND IT--?
VESPUCCI WAS UNDERRATED...
THAT'S MY POINT, ZOË--
VESPUCCI--?
I MEAN, WHAT IF WE BUMP A CURB OUT THERE.
THEN I GUESS YOU'LL HAVE TO WING IT.
EXCUSE ME--?
GUESS, DR. BAKER. JUST KNOW THAT GOING MANUAL MIGHT KILL ELEVEN BILLION PEOPLE.
ZOË--
FOR CRYING OUT LOUD...
--THERE'S NO SPRITE UP HERE.
THERE'S SOMETHING CALLED "SIERRA MIST" BUT, YOU KNOW, WHAT THE HELL, ZOË?
SP DAVID POWELL
I SAY WE ABORT.
HOW ABOUT YOU, AL--?
AL--? AL--?!
SP MAJ ALISTAIR MEATH
COMING UP ON EVENT HORIZON, FOLKS--
MISSION CMDR EVAN CHESS
--HATE TO SPOIL THE FUN, BUT IF DR. BAKER CAN TOLERATE OUR BEING A FEW CENTIMETERS OFF--
--AND IF THE GOOD MAJOR IS THROUGH REVIEWING HIS LUNCH--
--LET'S GO TO MARS.
ICARUS 2 IS ONLY 216,924 MILES FROM LUNA, COMMANDER--
LET'S GO TO MARS ANYWAY.
MIGHT WANT TO WORK ON DEVELOPING A SENSE OF HUMOR, DR. BAKER.
WE'RE GOING TO BE FLYING TOGETHER FOR A WEEK BEFORE WE FIND THAT ROCK OUT THERE.
Who is Lorena Payan--?

GLOBAL NOW

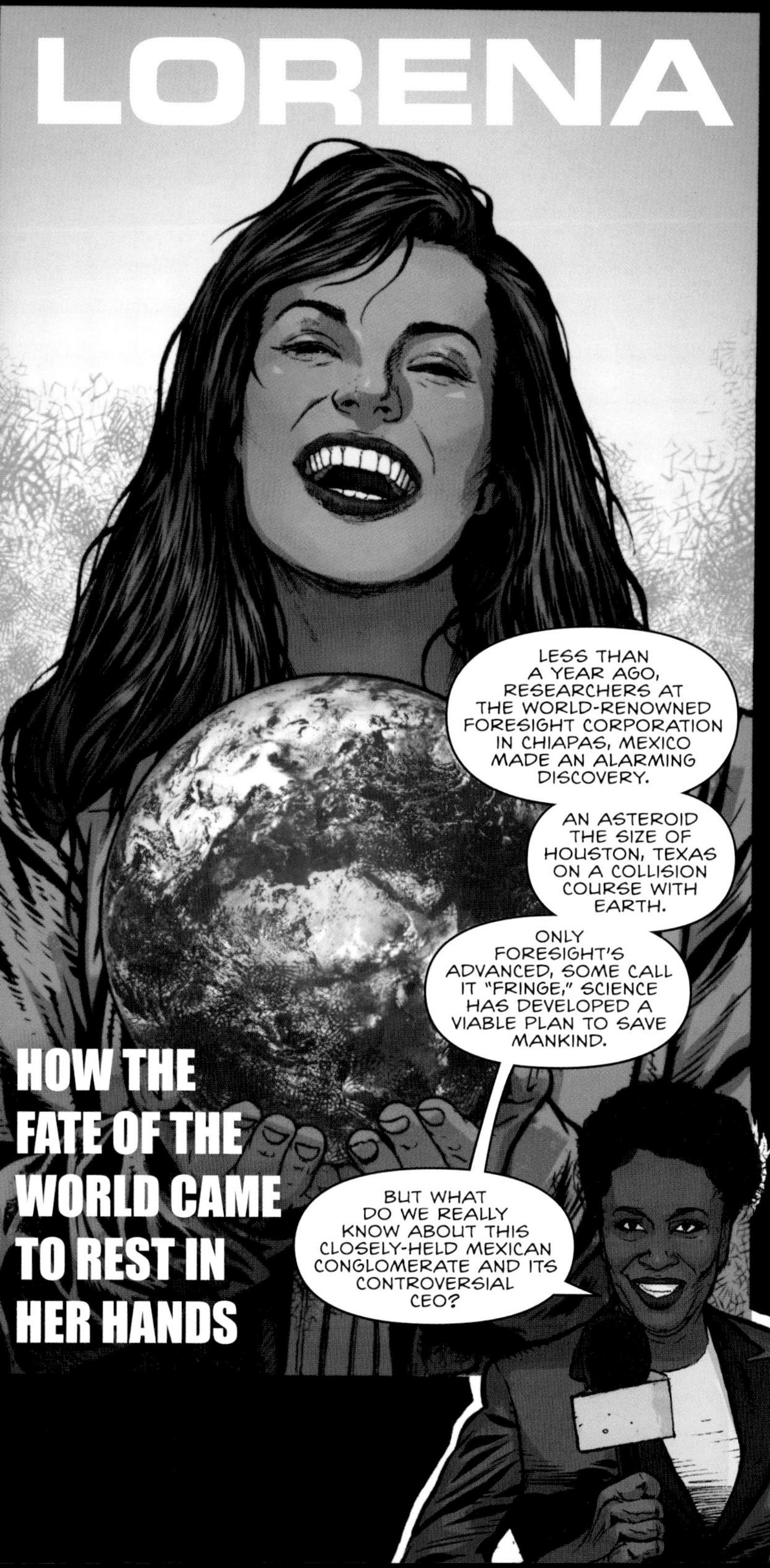
LORENA
LESS THAN A YEAR AGO, RESEARCHERS AT THE WORLD-RENOWNED FORESIGHT CORPORATION IN CHIAPAS, MEXICO MADE AN ALARMING DISCOVERY.
AN ASTEROID THE SIZE OF HOUSTON, TEXAS ON A COLLISION COURSE WITH EARTH.
ONLY FORESIGHT'S ADVANCED, SOME CALL IT "FRINGE," SCIENCE HAS DEVELOPED A VIABLE PLAN TO SAVE MANKIND.
BUT WHAT DO WE REALLY KNOW ABOUT THIS CLOSELY-HELD MEXICAN CONGLOMERATE AND ITS CONTROVERSIAL CEO?
HOW THE FATE OF THE WORLD CAME TO REST IN HER HANDS

In less than ten years, Lorena Payan built the Foresight Corporation into a global titan through innovations in aerospace development, space exploration, and so-called "fringe" science.

A native of the impoverished Mexican state of Chiapas, Payan lost her mother at age twelve. She and her brother Ramon were raised by their paternal grandmother Isabel, while their father Enrique Payan attended M.I.T. in the United States.

Payan's father founded the Foresight Corporation in Silicon Valley when she was a teenager, using wealth accumulated from his various business ventures in Mexico.

After immigrating to America, Payan studied under the tutelage of the eminent physicist, Dr. Parker "Shep" Bingham, who has served as her mentor and most trusted advisor.

While Payan lived in America with her father, her brother returned to Mexico, where Ramon Payan rose within the political structure. While Enrique Payan planted himself and his daughter in the ground of the American Dream, Lorena's brother chose to fight for his people back home, to work within the system to pull Mexico out of corruption and save it from the drug cartels.

Ramon Payan inherited the leadership of Foresight upon their father's death and relocated the corporation's central office to Chiapas. The Payan siblings hired a near 100% Mexican labor force in every section of the company and revolutionized the local economy while bringing global attention to the plight of Chiapas's indigenous tribes and social conflicts. Lorena Payan assumed control of Foresight after her brother was killed in a car bombing.

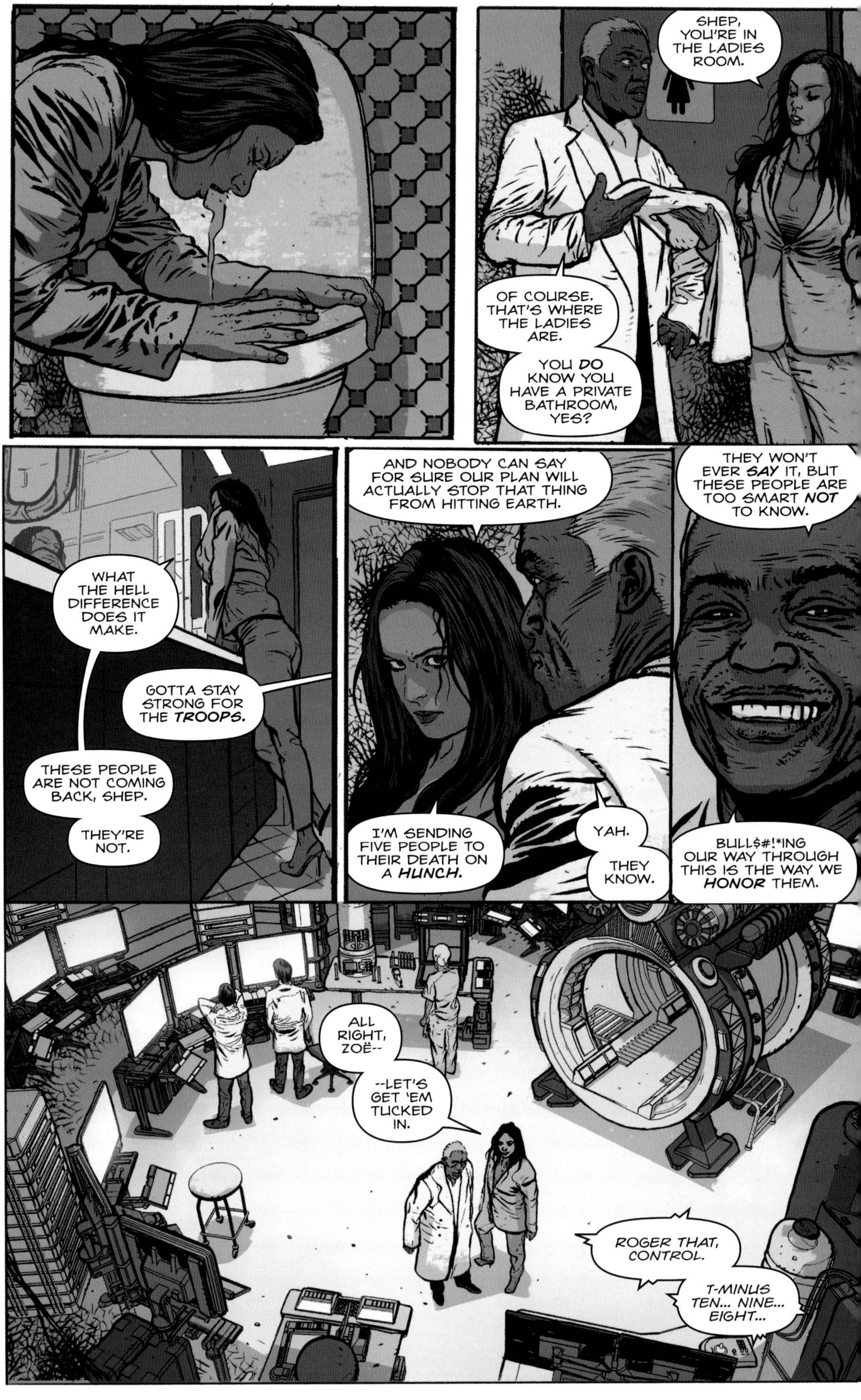
SHEP, YOU'RE IN THE LADIES ROOM.
OF COURSE. THAT'S WHERE THE LADIES ARE.
YOU DO KNOW YOU HAVE A PRIVATE BATHROOM, YES?
WHAT THE HELL DIFFERENCE DOES IT MAKE.
GOTTA STAY STRONG FOR THE TROOPS.
THESE PEOPLE ARE NOT COMING BACK, SHEP.
THEY'RE NOT.
AND NOBODY CAN SAY FOR SURE OUR PLAN WILL ACTUALLY STOP THAT THING FROM HITTING EARTH.
I'M SENDING FIVE PEOPLE TO THEIR DEATH ON A HUNCH.
YAH.
THEY KNOW.
THEY WON'T EVER SAY IT, BUT THESE PEOPLE ARE TOO SMART NOT TO KNOW.
BULL$#!*ING OUR WAY THROUGH THIS IS THE WAY WE HONOR THEM.
ALL RIGHT, ZOË--
--LET'S GET 'EM TUCKED IN.
ROGER THAT, CONTROL.
T-MINUS TEN... NINE... EIGHT...

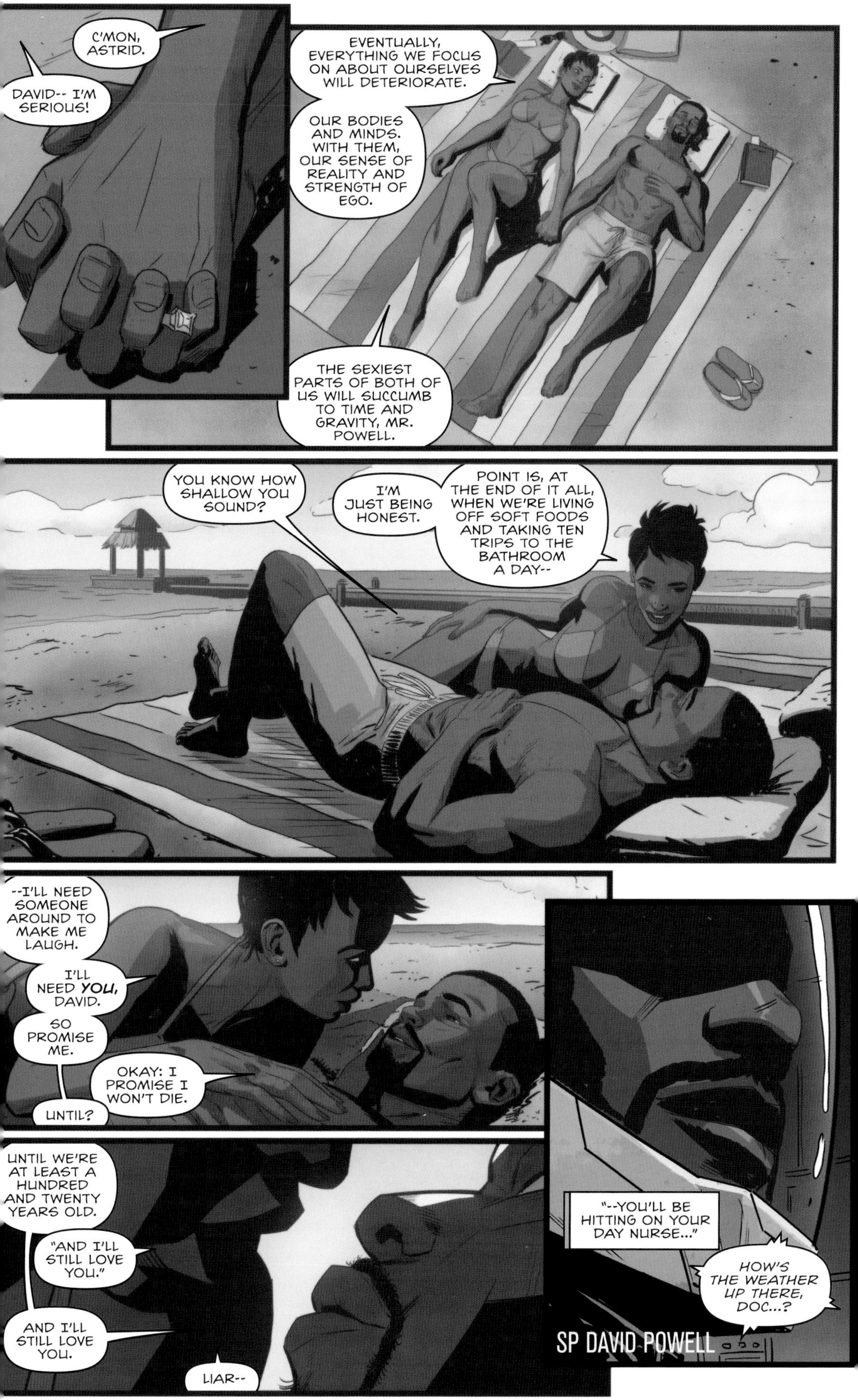
C'MON, ASTRID.
DAVID-- I'M SERIOUS!
EVENTUALLY, EVERYTHING WE FOCUS ON ABOUT OURSELVES WILL DETERIORATE.
OUR BODIES AND MINDS. WITH THEM, OUR SENSE OF REALITY AND STRENGTH OF EGO.
THE SEXIEST PARTS OF BOTH OF US WILL SUCCUMB TO TIME AND GRAVITY, MR. POWELL.
YOU KNOW HOW SHALLOW YOU SOUND?
I'M JUST BEING HONEST.
POINT IS, AT THE END OF IT ALL, WHEN WE'RE LIVING OFF SOFT FOODS AND TAKING TEN TRIPS TO THE BATHROOM A DAY--
--I'LL NEED SOMEONE AROUND TO MAKE ME LAUGH.
I'LL NEED *YOU,* DAVID.
SO PROMISE ME.
OKAY: I PROMISE I WON'T DIE.
UNTIL?
UNTIL WE'RE AT LEAST A HUNDRED AND TWENTY YEARS OLD.
"AND I'LL STILL LOVE YOU."
AND I'LL STILL LOVE YOU.
LIAR--
"--YOU'LL BE HITTING ON YOUR DAY NURSE..."
HOW'S THE WEATHER UP THERE, DOC...?
SP DAVID POWELL

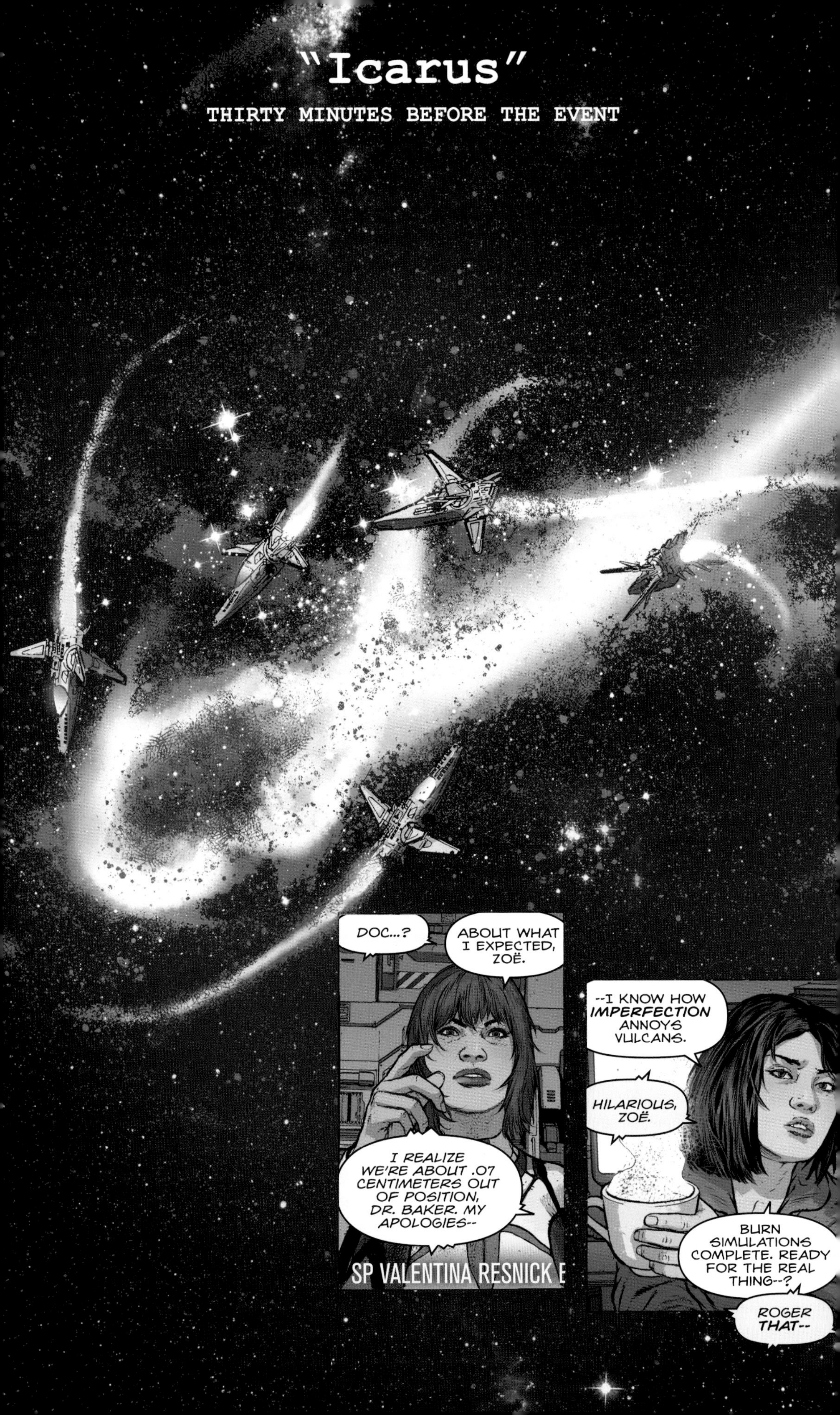
"Icarus"
THIRTY MINUTES BEFORE THE EVENT
DOC...?
ABOUT WHAT I EXPECTED, ZOË.
I REALIZE WE'RE ABOUT .07 CENTIMETERS OUT OF POSITION, DR. BAKER. MY APOLOGIES--
SP VALENTINA RESNICK
--I KNOW HOW IMPERFECTION ANNOYS VULCANS.
HILARIOUS, ZOË.
BURN SIMULATIONS COMPLETE. READY FOR THE REAL THING--?
ROGER THAT--

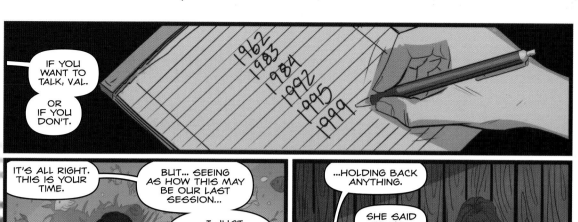

IF YOU WANT TO TALK, VAL.

OR IF YOU DON'T.

IT'S ALL RIGHT. THIS IS YOUR TIME.

BUT... SEEING AS HOW THIS MAY BE OUR LAST SESSION...

...I JUST WANT TO BE SURE YOU'RE NOT, FOR WHATEVER REASON...

...HOLDING BACK ANYTHING.

SHE SAID TO ME...

SHE *WHO*?

THE ONLY "WHO" THAT MATTERS HERE.

"YOU'RE THE ONLY PERSON I TRUST, OUT OF ALL THE SKILLED MINDS HERE, TO DO THIS THING," SHE TOLD ME.

KNOWING I HAVE NEVER DISAPPOINTED HER.

BECAUSE SHE AND I BOTH KNOW THE TRUTH, DOCTOR.

LIFE IS MADE UP OF A STRING OF ACCOMPLISHMENTS.

WHAT'S THIS?

THE YEARS.

THE YEARS WOMEN BEFORE ME DID AMAZING THINGS IN SPACE.

IF YOU ADD THEM ALL UP, THE NUMBER YOU'LL GET IS *ZERO*.

UNLESS I DO THE *IMPOSSIBLE*--

--AND PREVENT MY GIRLFRIEND, MY PARENTS, MY EX, YOU AND YOUR THREE HUNDRED DOLLAR HAIRCUT, AND EVERYONE ELSE...

"...FROM GOING THE WAY OF THE DINOSAUR."

SP VALENTINA RESNICK BAKER

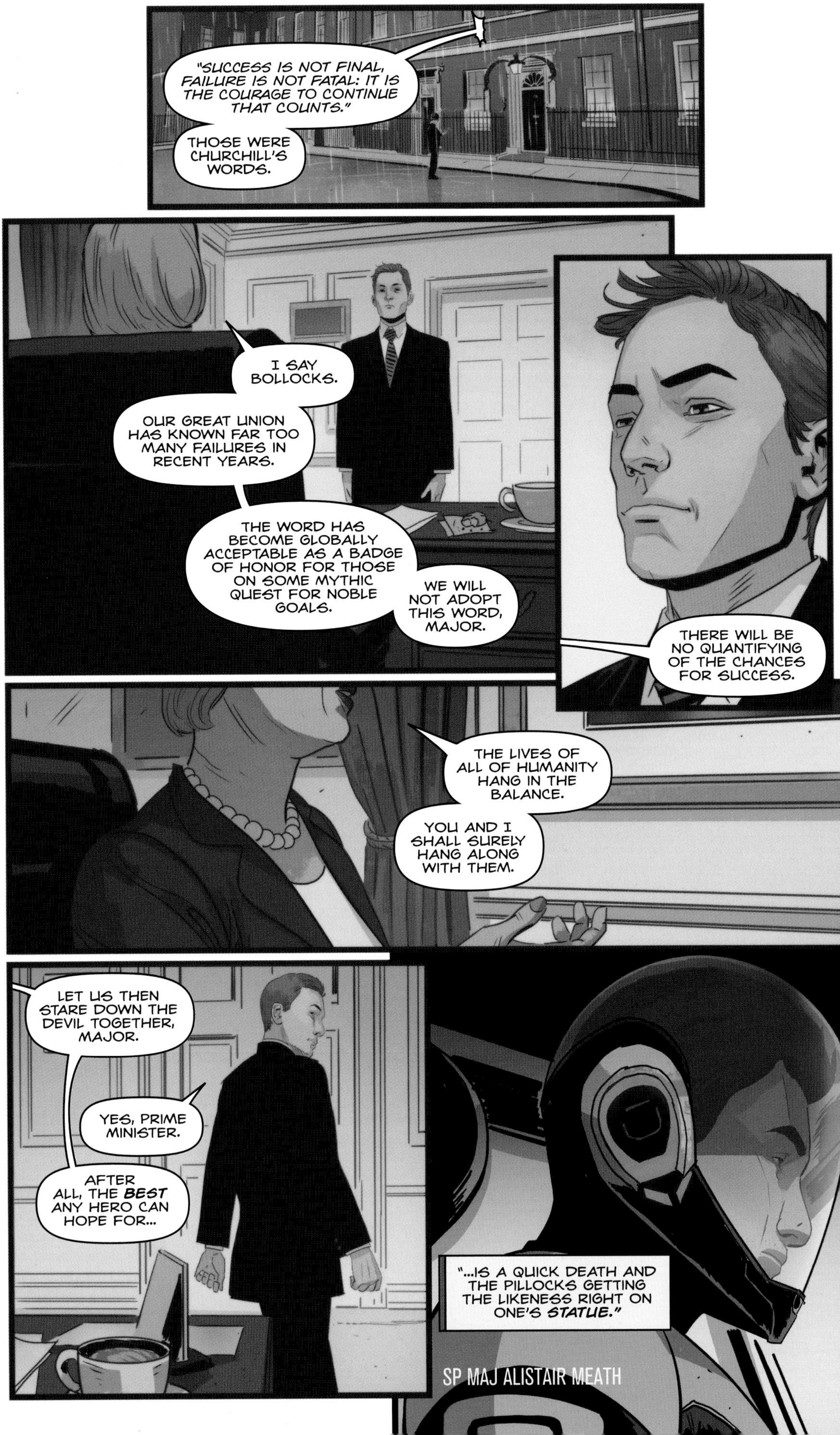
"SUCCESS IS NOT FINAL, FAILURE IS NOT FATAL: IT IS THE COURAGE TO CONTINUE THAT COUNTS."
THOSE WERE CHURCHILL'S WORDS.
I SAY BOLLOCKS.
OUR GREAT UNION HAS KNOWN FAR TOO MANY FAILURES IN RECENT YEARS.
THE WORD HAS BECOME GLOBALLY ACCEPTABLE AS A BADGE OF HONOR FOR THOSE ON SOME MYTHIC QUEST FOR NOBLE GOALS.
WE WILL NOT ADOPT THIS WORD, MAJOR.
THERE WILL BE NO QUANTIFYING OF THE CHANCES FOR SUCCESS.
THE LIVES OF ALL OF HUMANITY HANG IN THE BALANCE.
YOU AND I SHALL SURELY HANG ALONG WITH THEM.
LET US THEN STARE DOWN THE DEVIL TOGETHER, MAJOR.
YES, PRIME MINISTER.
AFTER ALL, THE ***BEST*** ANY HERO CAN HOPE FOR...
"...IS A QUICK DEATH AND THE PILLOCKS GETTING THE LIKENESS RIGHT ON ONE'S ***STATUE.***"
SP MAJ ALISTAIR MEATH

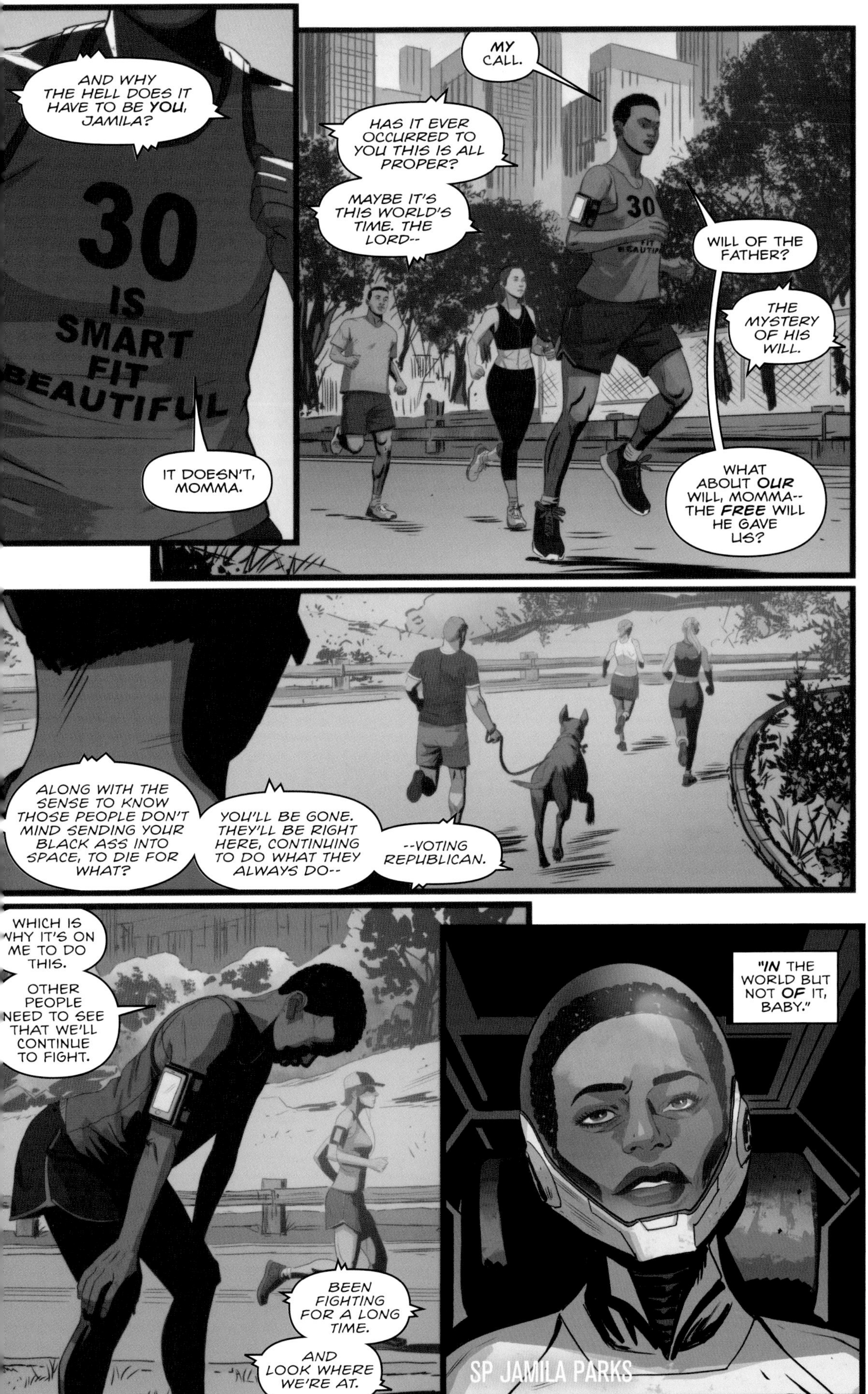

AND WHY THE HELL DOES IT HAVE TO BE YOU, JAMILA?
30 IS SMART FIT BEAUTIFUL
IT DOESN'T, MOMMA.
MY CALL.
HAS IT EVER OCCURRED TO YOU THIS IS ALL PROPER?
MAYBE IT'S THIS WORLD'S TIME. THE LORD--
WILL OF THE FATHER?
THE MYSTERY OF HIS WILL.
WHAT ABOUT OUR WILL, MOMMA-- THE FREE WILL HE GAVE US?
ALONG WITH THE SENSE TO KNOW THOSE PEOPLE DON'T MIND SENDING YOUR BLACK ASS INTO SPACE, TO DIE FOR WHAT?
YOU'LL BE GONE. THEY'LL BE RIGHT HERE, CONTINUING TO DO WHAT THEY ALWAYS DO--
--VOTING REPUBLICAN.
WHICH IS WHY IT'S ON ME TO DO THIS.
OTHER PEOPLE NEED TO SEE THAT WE'LL CONTINUE TO FIGHT.
BEEN FIGHTING FOR A LONG TIME.
AND LOOK WHERE WE'RE AT.
"IN THE WORLD BUT NOT OF IT, BABY."
SP JAMILA PARKS

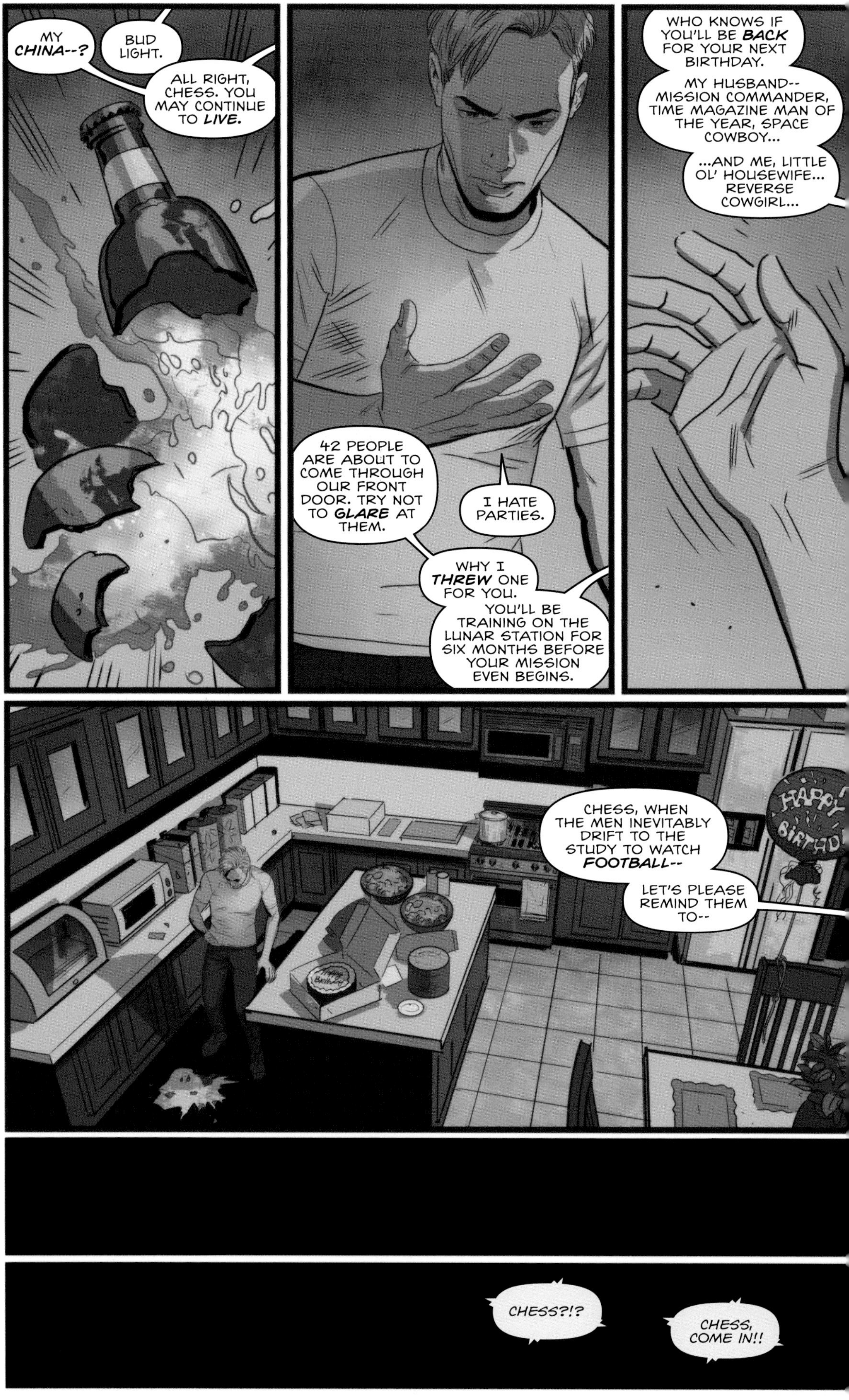
MY CHINA--?
BUD LIGHT.
ALL RIGHT, CHESS. YOU MAY CONTINUE TO LIVE.
42 PEOPLE ARE ABOUT TO COME THROUGH OUR FRONT DOOR. TRY NOT TO GLARE AT THEM.
I HATE PARTIES.
WHY I THREW ONE FOR YOU.
YOU'LL BE TRAINING ON THE LUNAR STATION FOR SIX MONTHS BEFORE YOUR MISSION EVEN BEGINS.
WHO KNOWS IF YOU'LL BE BACK FOR YOUR NEXT BIRTHDAY.
MY HUSBAND-- MISSION COMMANDER, TIME MAGAZINE MAN OF THE YEAR, SPACE COWBOY...
...AND ME, LITTLE OL' HOUSEWIFE... REVERSE COWGIRL...
HAPPY BIRTHD
CHESS, WHEN THE MEN INEVITABLY DRIFT TO THE STUDY TO WATCH FOOTBALL--
LET'S PLEASE REMIND THEM TO--
CHESS?!?
CHESS, COME IN!!

"Eleven Billion"

SIXTY SECONDS BEFORE THE EVENT

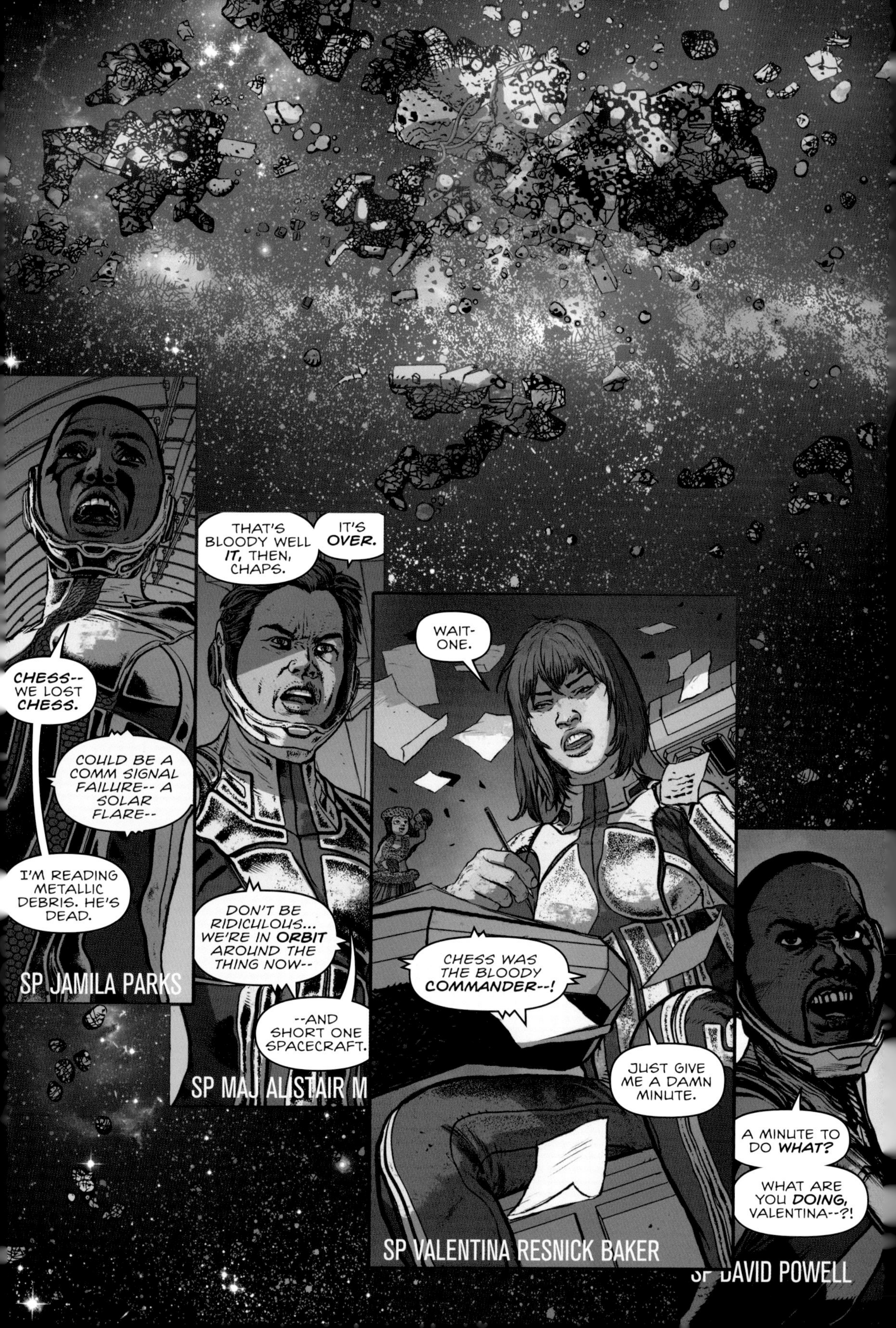
CHESS-- WE LOST CHESS.
COULD BE A COMM SIGNAL FAILURE-- A SOLAR FLARE--
I'M READING METALLIC DEBRIS. HE'S DEAD.
SP JAMILA PARKS
THAT'S BLOODY WELL IT, THEN, CHAPS.
IT'S OVER.
DON'T BE RIDICULOUS... WE'RE IN ORBIT AROUND THE THING NOW--
--AND SHORT ONE SPACECRAFT.
SP MAJ ALISTAIR M
WAIT-ONE.
CHESS WAS THE BLOODY COMMANDER--!
JUST GIVE ME A DAMN MINUTE.
SP VALENTINA RESNICK BAKER
A MINUTE TO DO WHAT?
WHAT ARE YOU DOING, VALENTINA--?!
SP DAVID POWELL

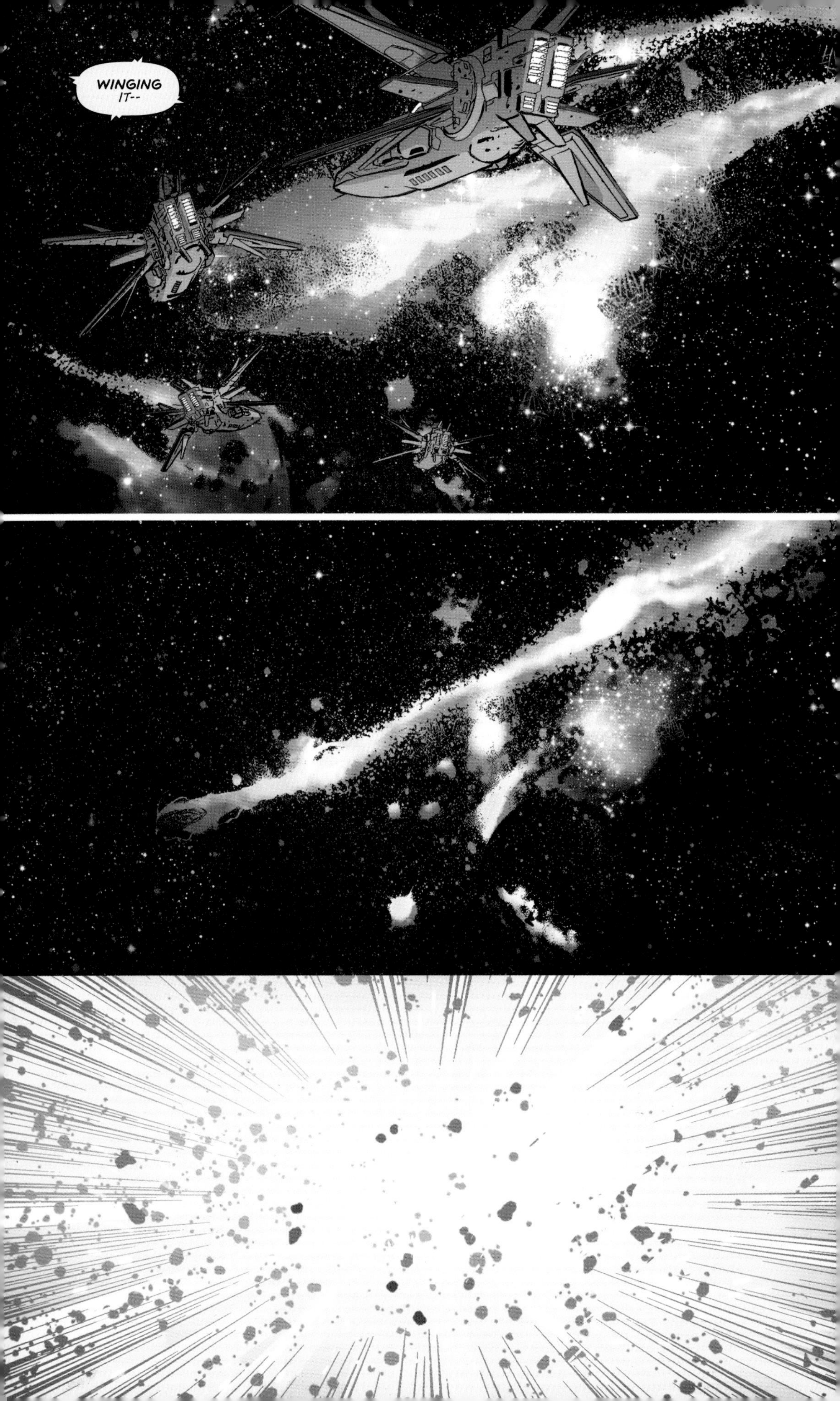
WINGING IT--

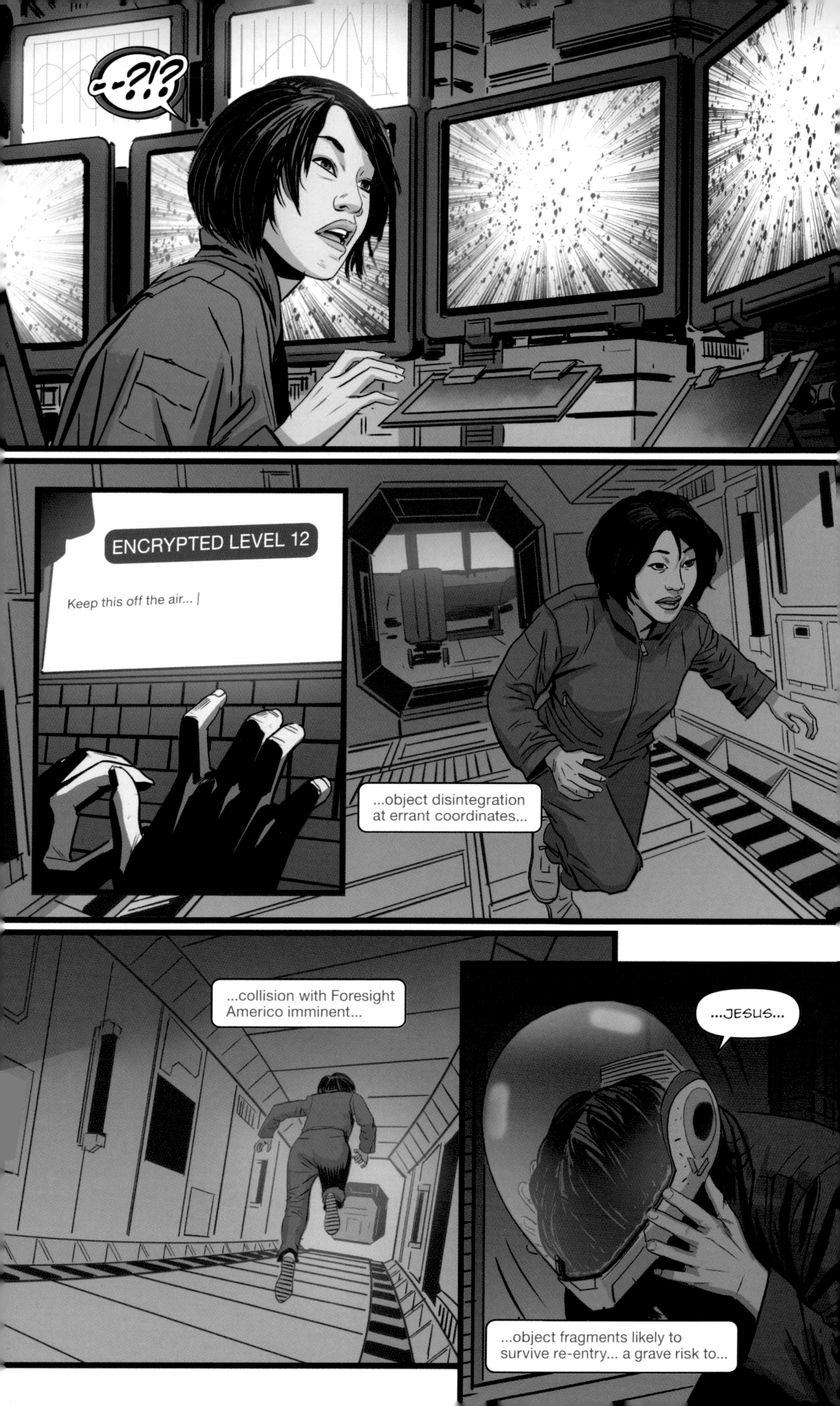
--?!?
ENCRYPTED LEVEL 12
Keep this off the air... |
...object disintegration at errant coordinates...
...collision with Foresight Americo imminent...
...JESUS...
...object fragments likely to survive re-entry... a grave risk to...

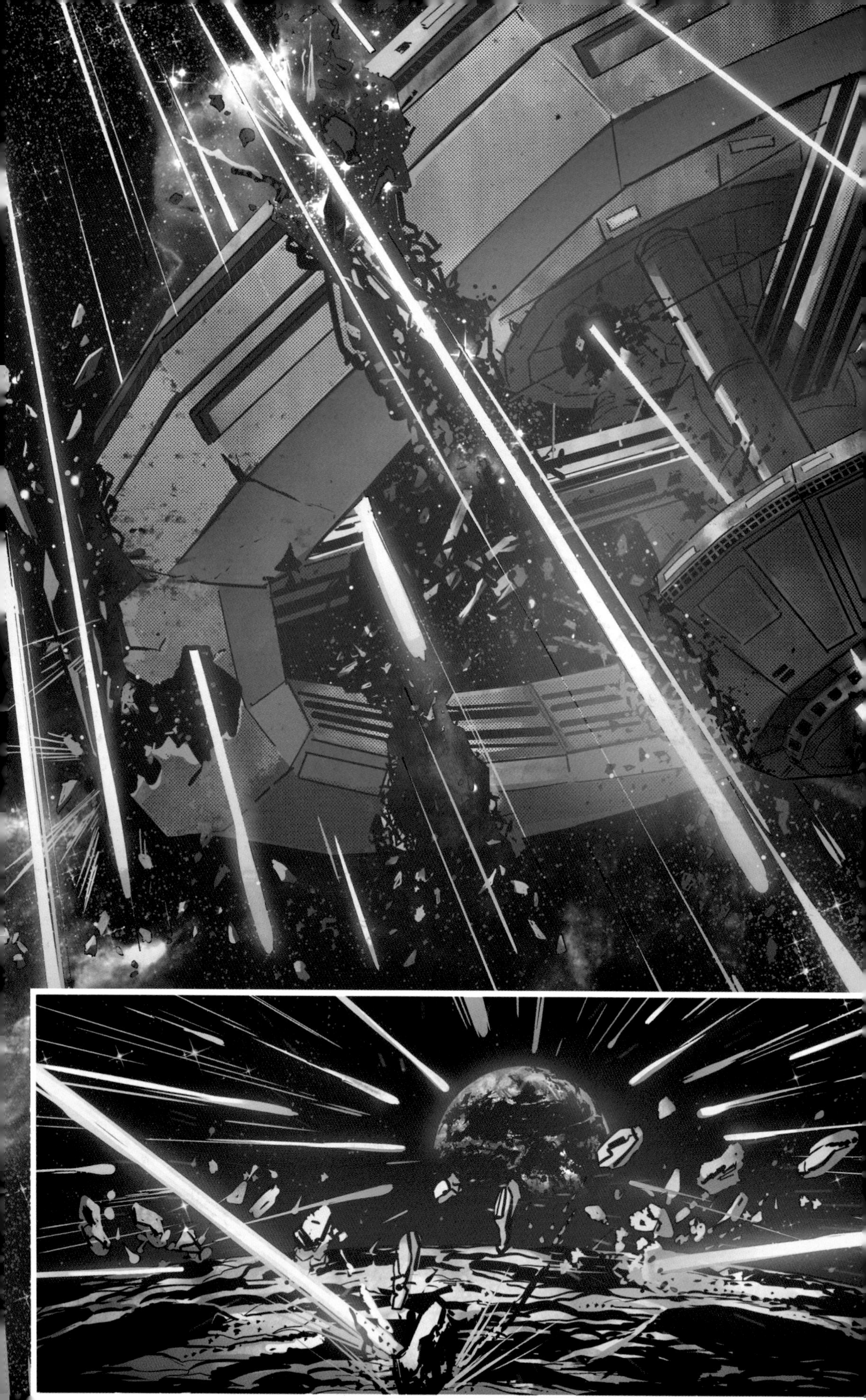

"The Beginning"

THE EVENT

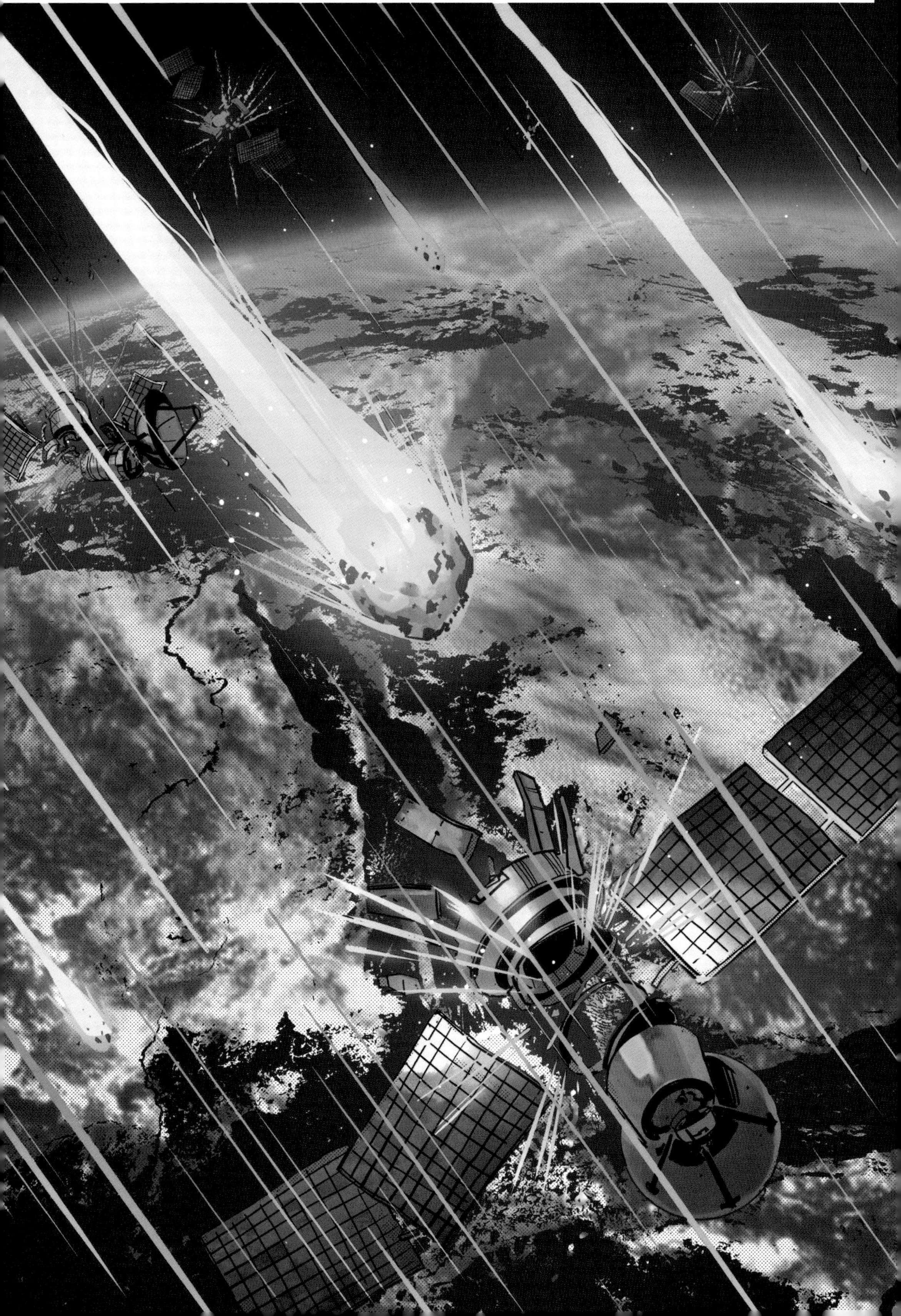

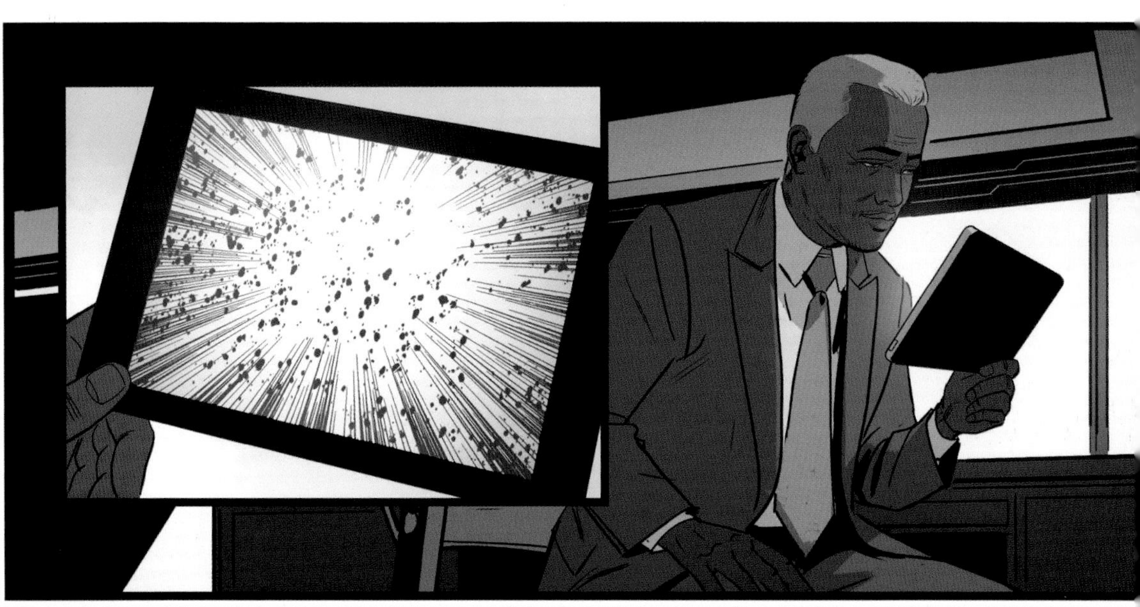

"Clouds"

TWO WEEKS AFTER THE EVENT

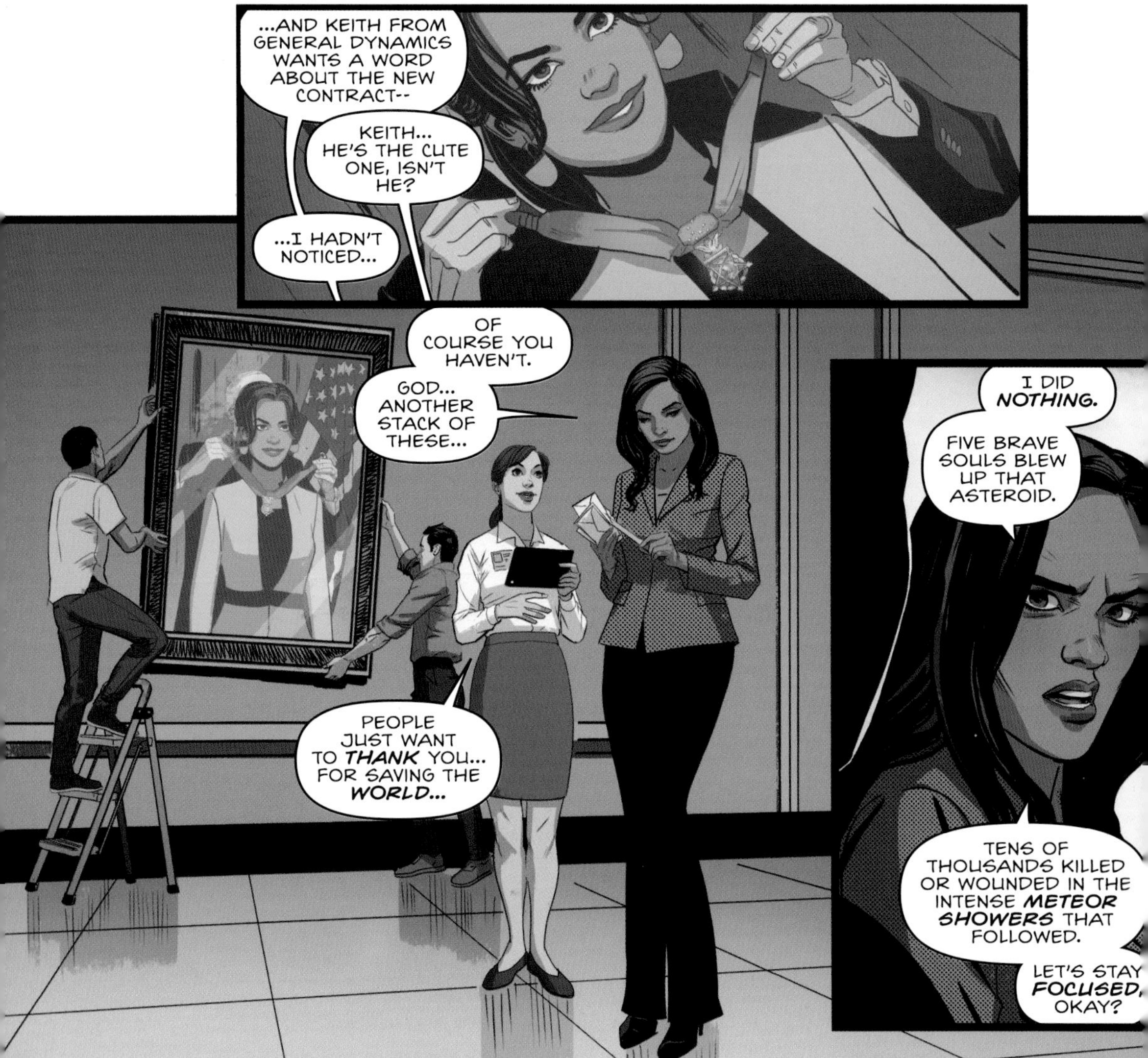

...AND KEITH FROM GENERAL DYNAMICS WANTS A WORD ABOUT THE NEW CONTRACT--
KEITH... HE'S THE CUTE ONE, ISN'T HE?
...I HADN'T NOTICED...
OF COURSE YOU HAVEN'T.
GOD... ANOTHER STACK OF THESE...
PEOPLE JUST WANT TO THANK YOU... FOR SAVING THE WORLD...
I DID NOTHING.
FIVE BRAVE SOULS BLEW UP THAT ASTEROID.
TENS OF THOUSANDS KILLED OR WOUNDED IN THE INTENSE METEOR SHOWERS THAT FOLLOWED.
LET'S STAY FOCUSED, OKAY?

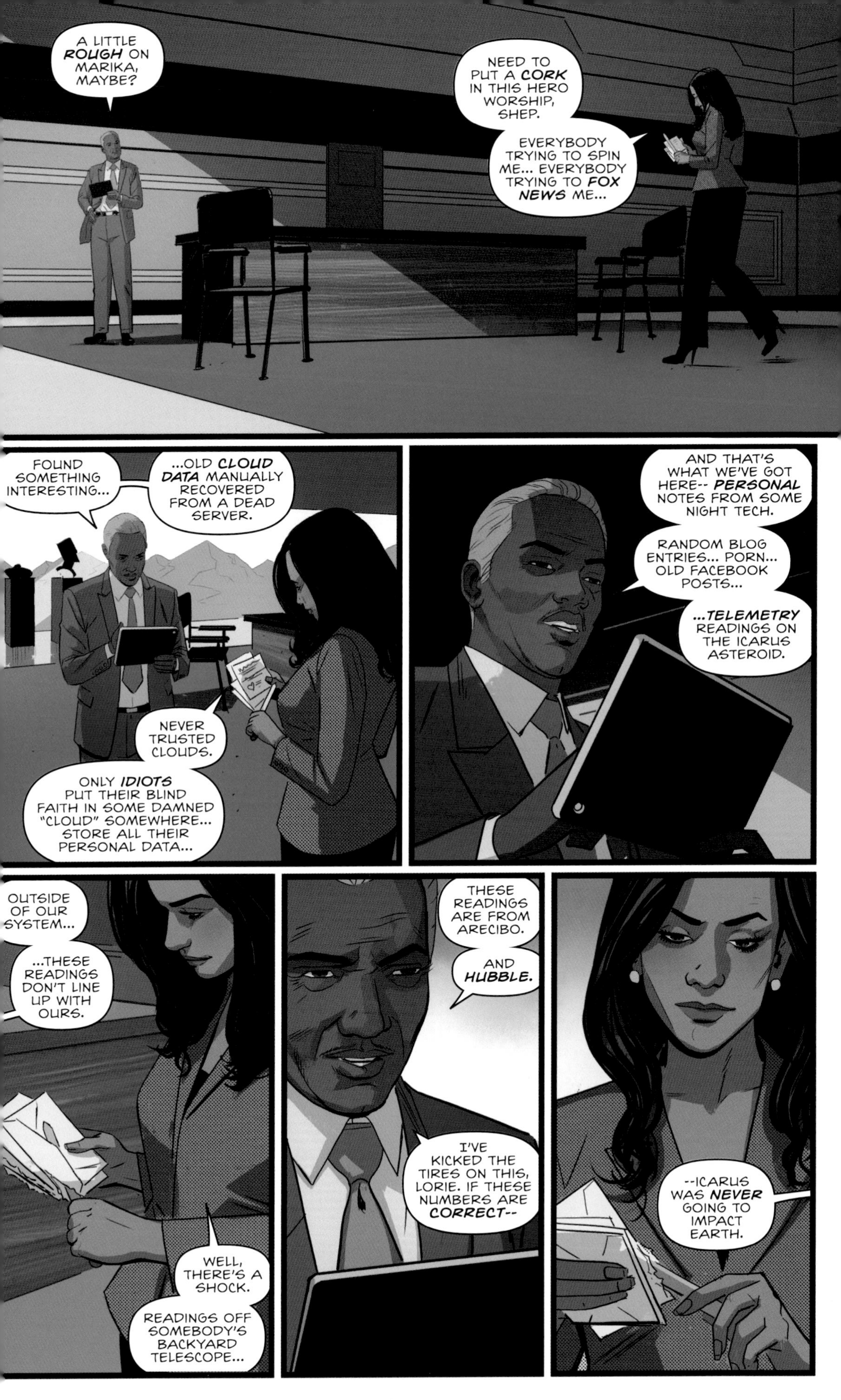
A LITTLE ROUGH ON MARIKA, MAYBE?
NEED TO PUT A CORK IN THIS HERO WORSHIP, SHEP.
EVERYBODY TRYING TO SPIN ME... EVERYBODY TRYING TO FOX NEWS ME...
FOUND SOMETHING INTERESTING...
...OLD CLOUD DATA MANUALLY RECOVERED FROM A DEAD SERVER.
NEVER TRUSTED CLOUDS.
ONLY IDIOTS PUT THEIR BLIND FAITH IN SOME DAMNED "CLOUD" SOMEWHERE... STORE ALL THEIR PERSONAL DATA...
AND THAT'S WHAT WE'VE GOT HERE-- PERSONAL NOTES FROM SOME NIGHT TECH.
RANDOM BLOG ENTRIES... PORN... OLD FACEBOOK POSTS...
...TELEMETRY READINGS ON THE ICARUS ASTEROID.
OUTSIDE OF OUR SYSTEM...
...THESE READINGS DON'T LINE UP WITH OURS.
WELL, THERE'S A SHOCK.
READINGS OFF SOMEBODY'S BACKYARD TELESCOPE...
THESE READINGS ARE FROM ARECIBO.
AND HUBBLE.
I'VE KICKED THE TIRES ON THIS, LORIE. IF THESE NUMBERS ARE CORRECT--
--ICARUS WAS NEVER GOING TO IMPACT EARTH.

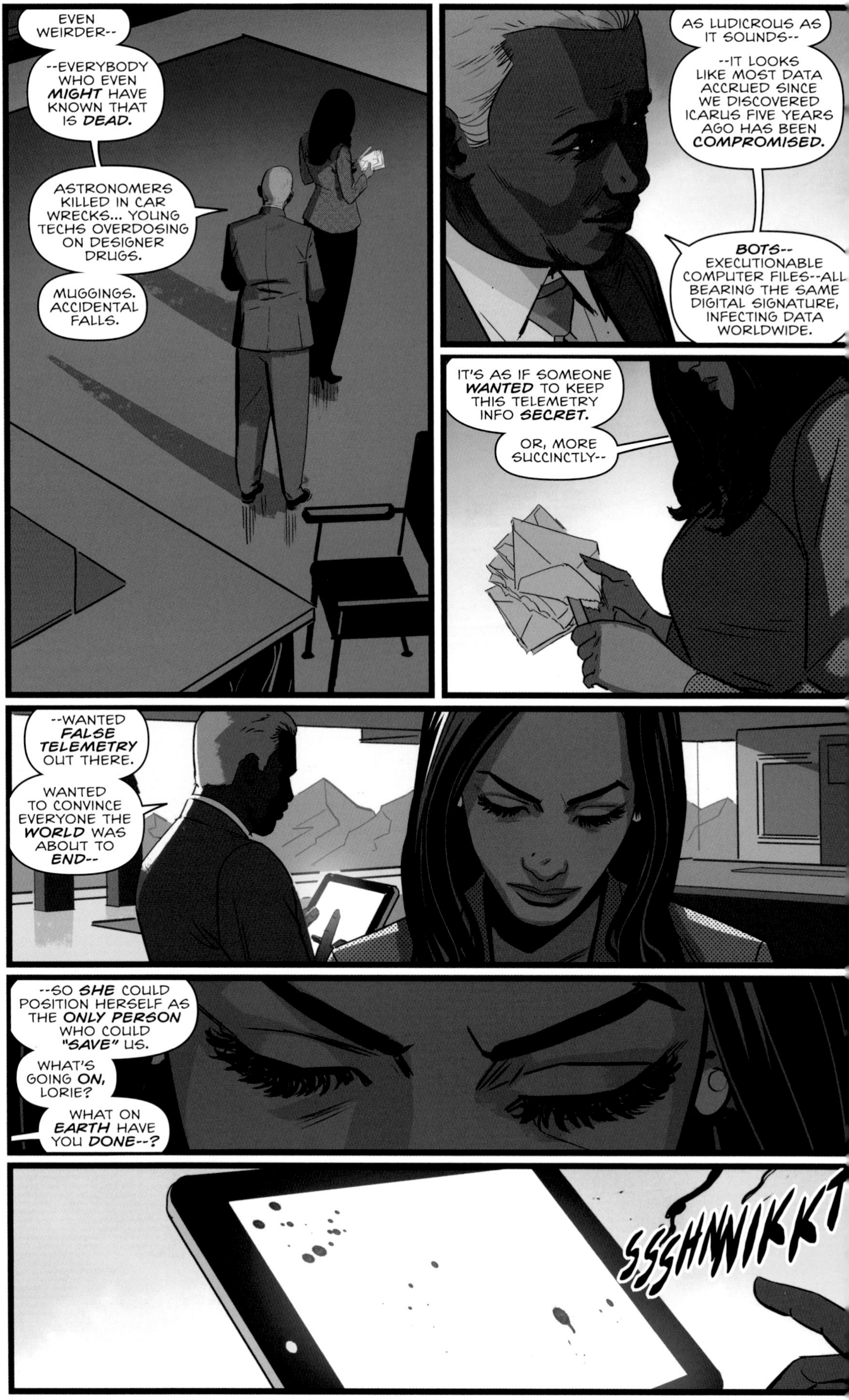
EVEN WEIRDER--
--EVERYBODY WHO EVEN MIGHT HAVE KNOWN THAT IS DEAD.
ASTRONOMERS KILLED IN CAR WRECKS... YOUNG TECHS OVERDOSING ON DESIGNER DRUGS.
MUGGINGS. ACCIDENTAL FALLS.
AS LUDICROUS AS IT SOUNDS--
--IT LOOKS LIKE MOST DATA ACCRUED SINCE WE DISCOVERED ICARUS FIVE YEARS AGO HAS BEEN COMPROMISED.
BOTS-- EXECUTIONABLE COMPUTER FILES--ALL BEARING THE SAME DIGITAL SIGNATURE, INFECTING DATA WORLDWIDE.
IT'S AS IF SOMEONE WANTED TO KEEP THIS TELEMETRY INFO SECRET.
OR, MORE SUCCINCTLY--
--WANTED FALSE TELEMETRY OUT THERE.
WANTED TO CONVINCE EVERYONE THE WORLD WAS ABOUT TO END--
--SO SHE COULD POSITION HERSELF AS THE ONLY PERSON WHO COULD "SAVE" US.
WHAT'S GOING ON, LORIE?
WHAT ON EARTH HAVE YOU DONE--?
SSSHNIKKT

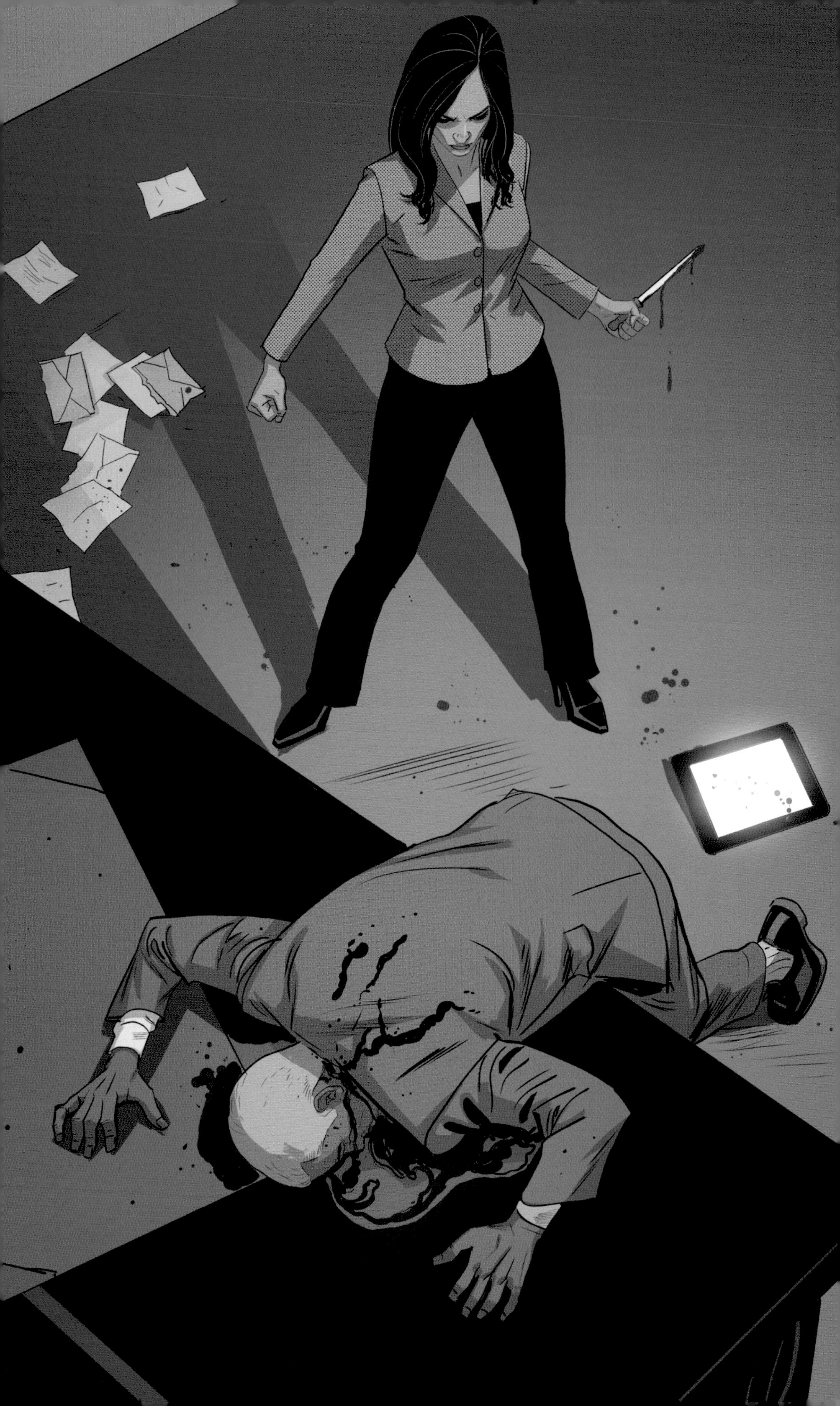

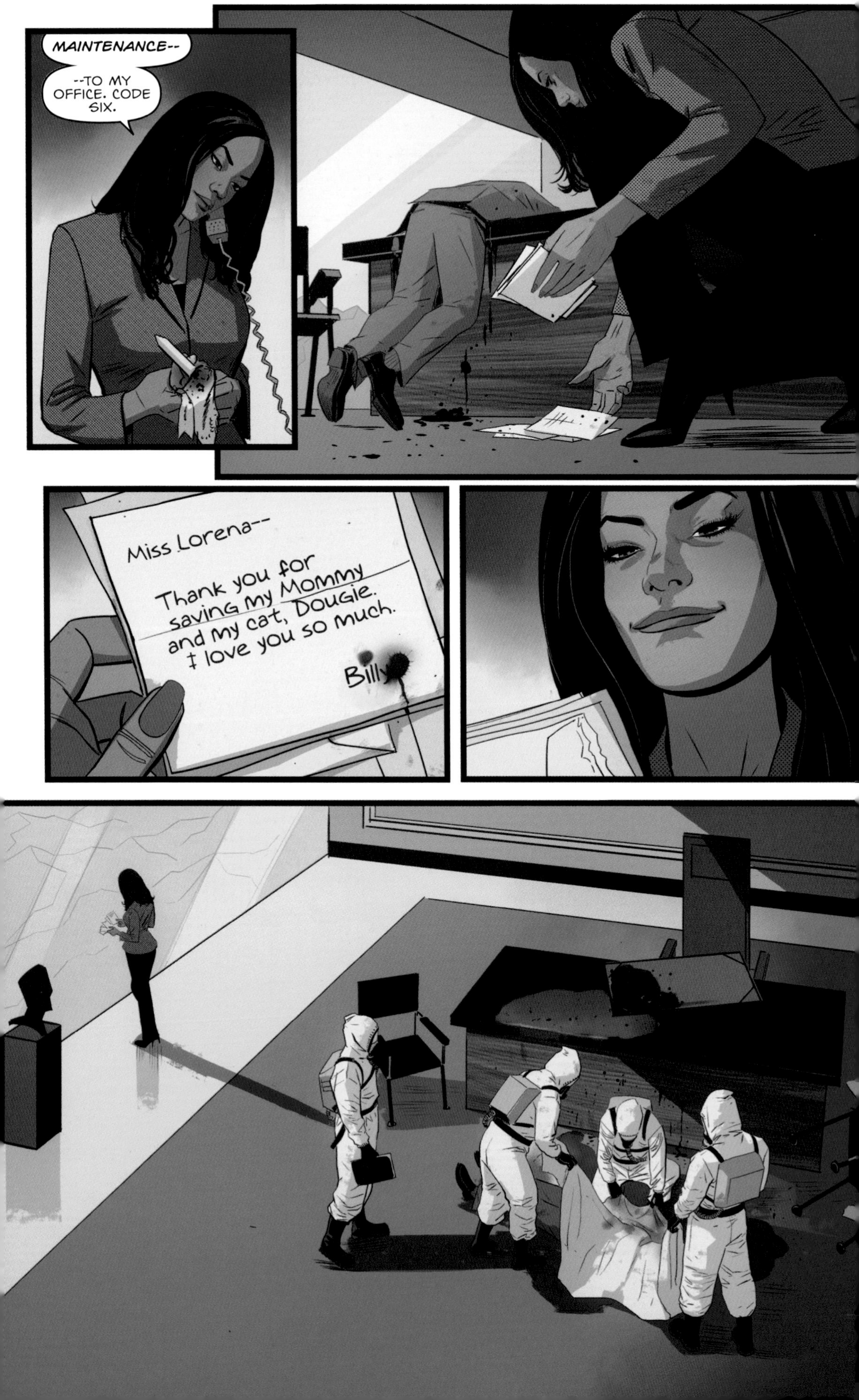
MAINTENANCE--
--TO MY OFFICE. CODE SIX.
Miss Lorena--
Thank you for saving my Mommy and my cat, Dougie. I love you so much.
Billy

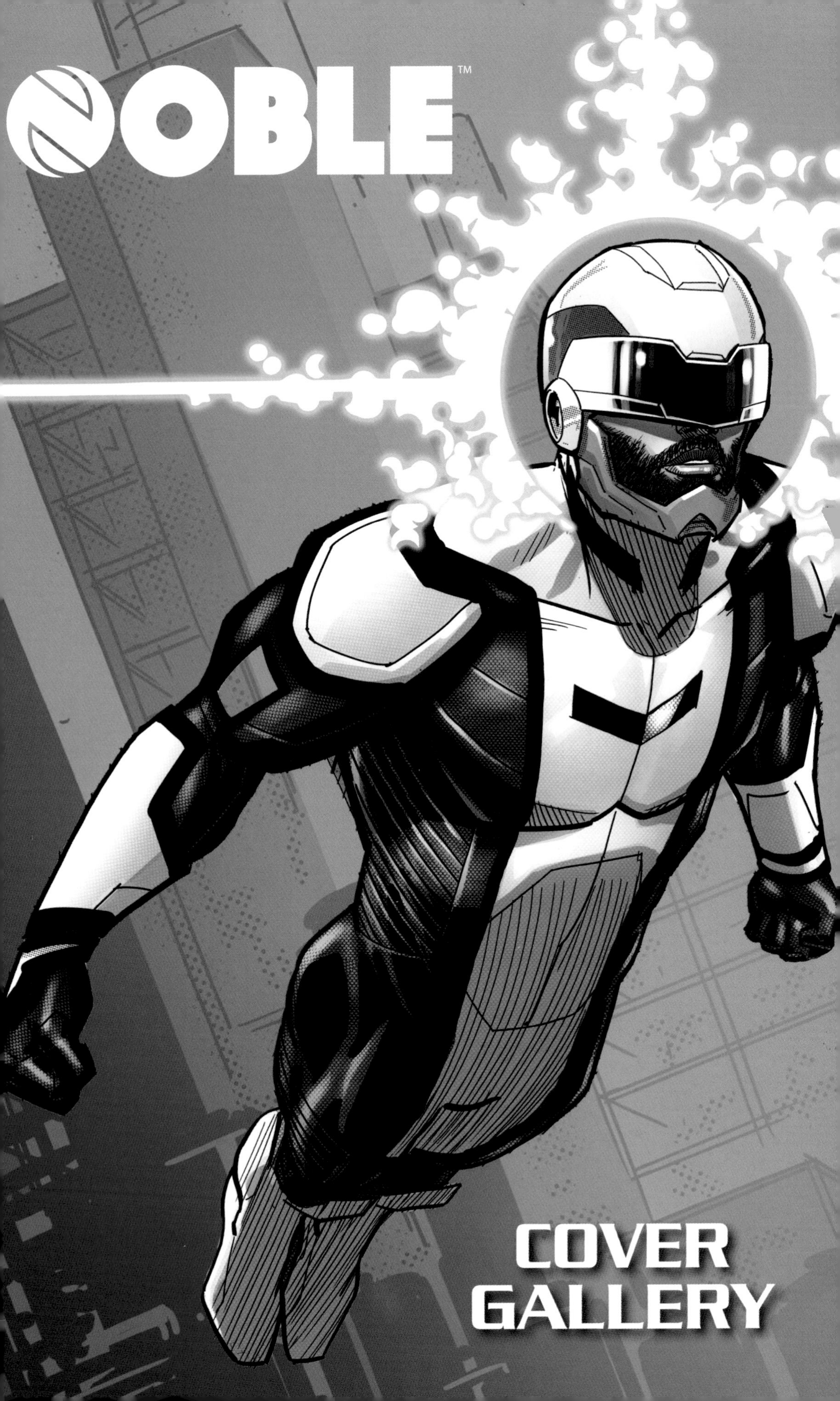
NOBLE™
COVER
GALLERY

Art by Roger Robinson and Juan Fernandez

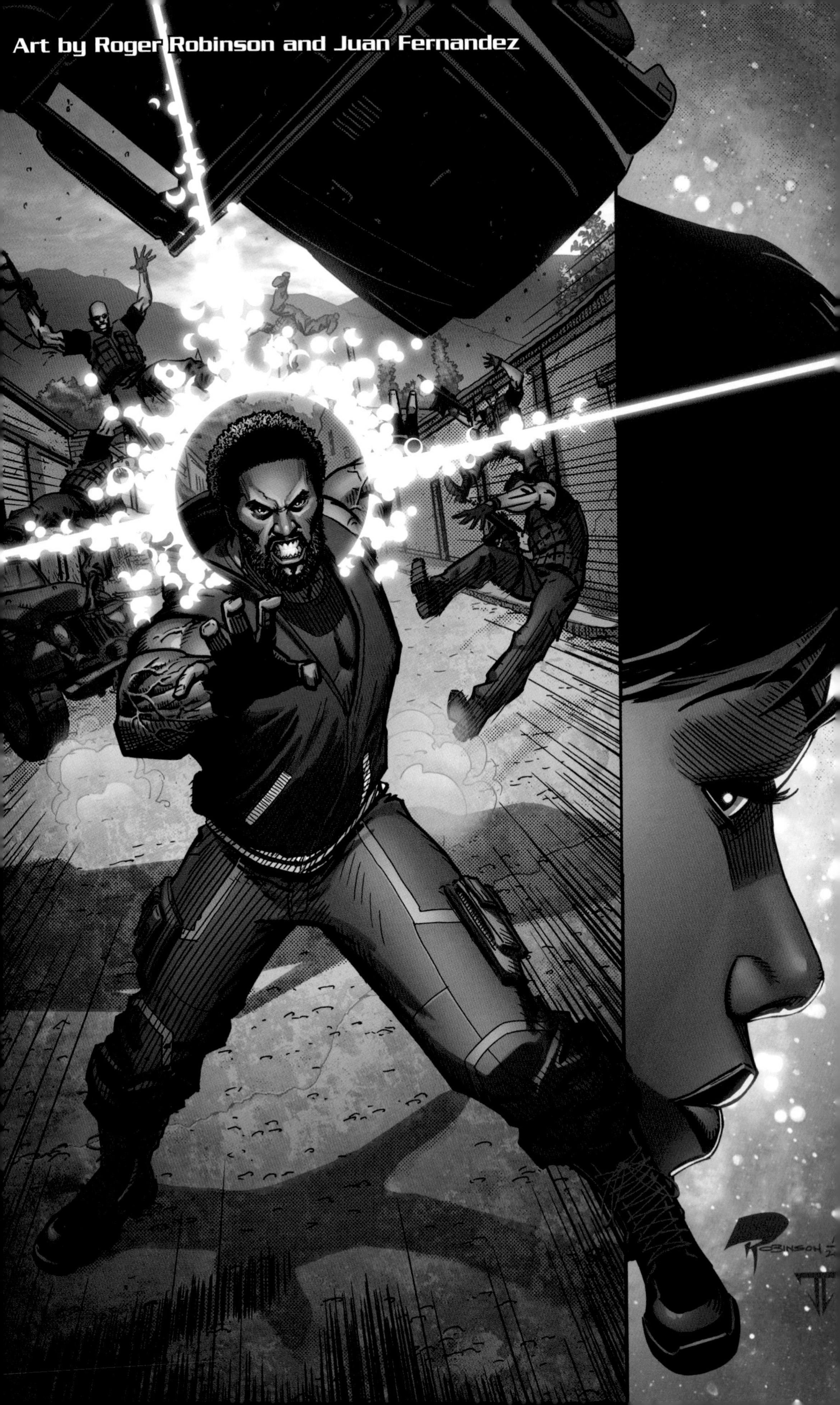

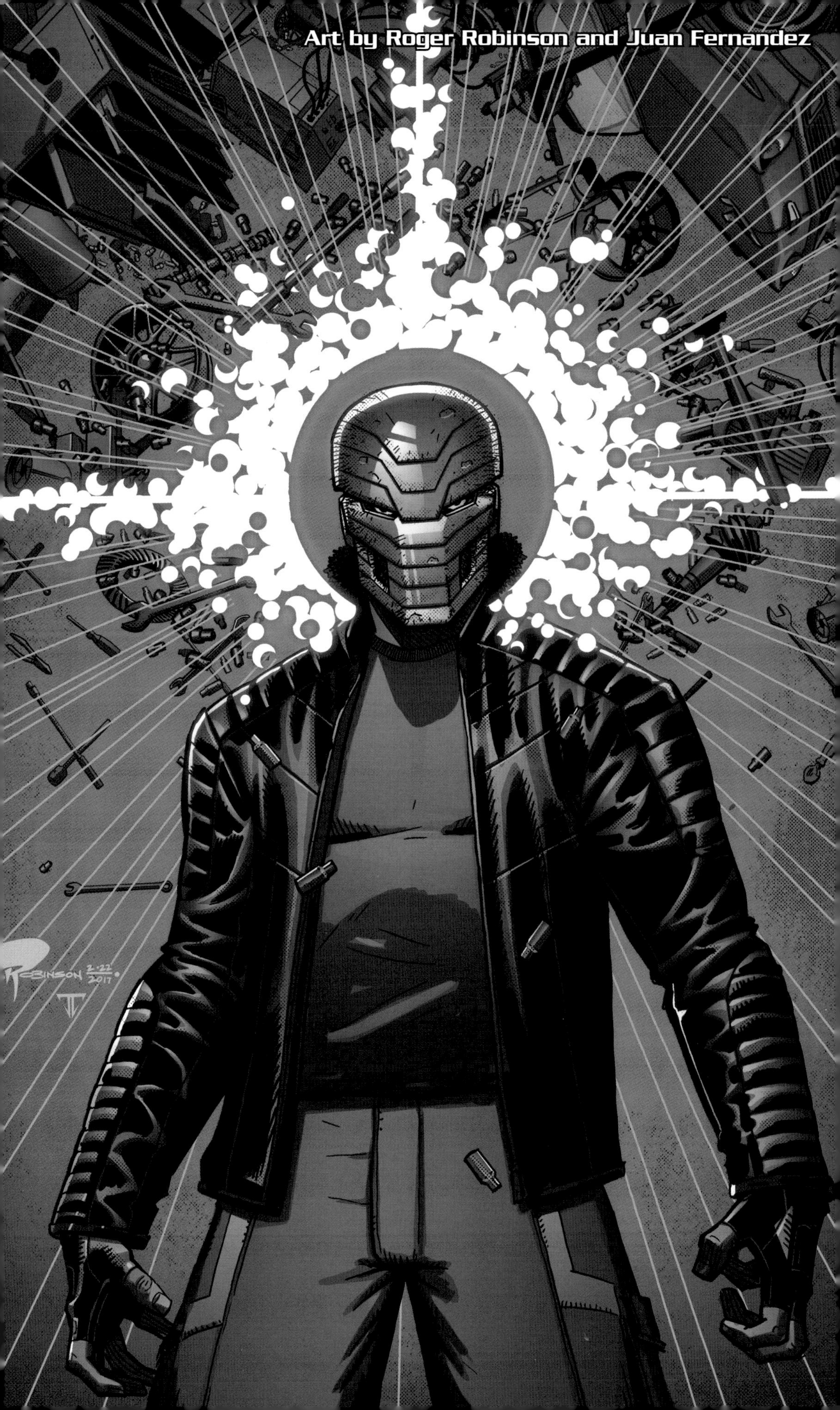
ROBINSON 2·22 2017
Art by Roger Robinson and Juan Fernandez

Art by Roger Robinson and Juan Fernandez

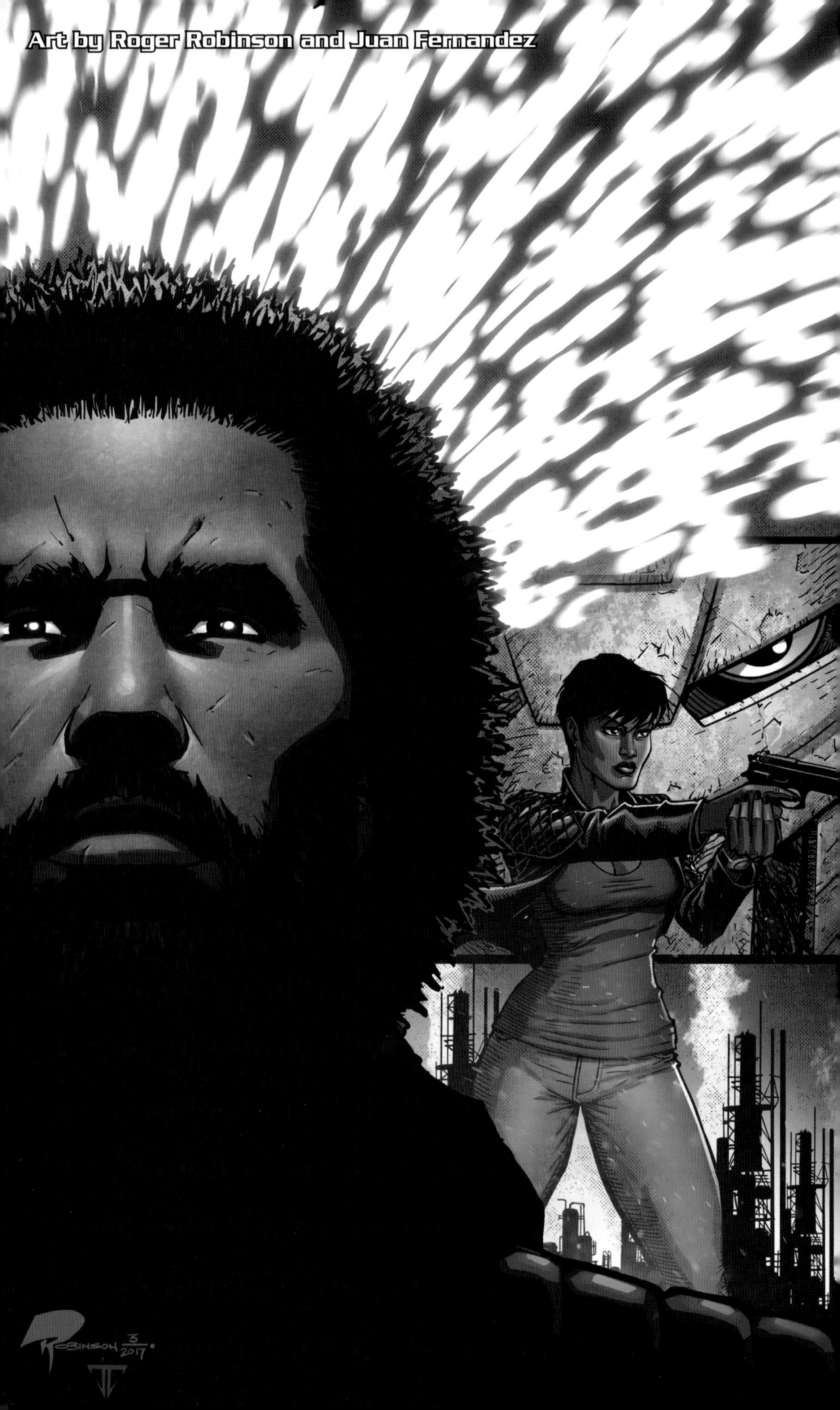
ROBINSON 3/2017

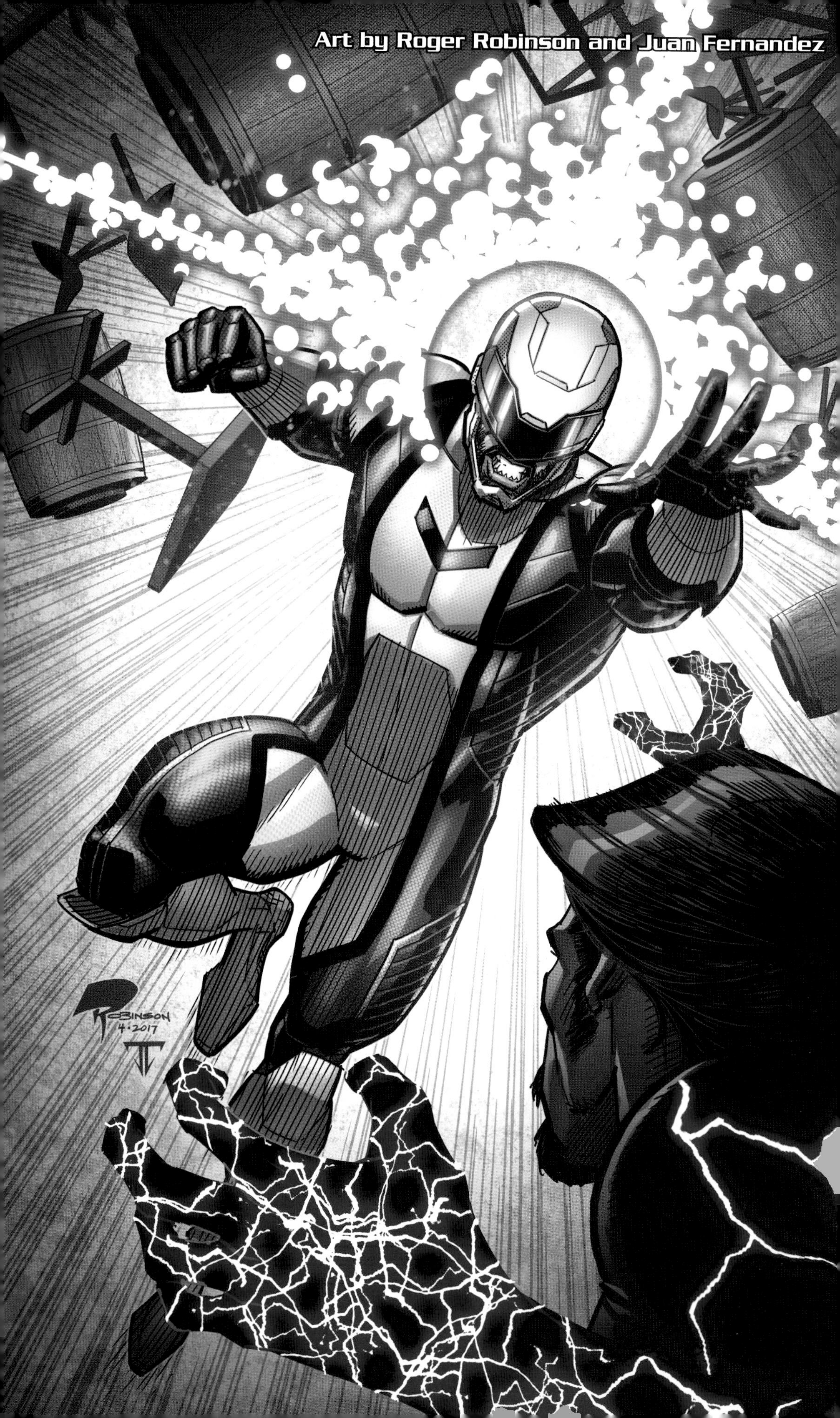
ROBINSON
4·2017
Art by Roger Robinson and Juan Fernandez

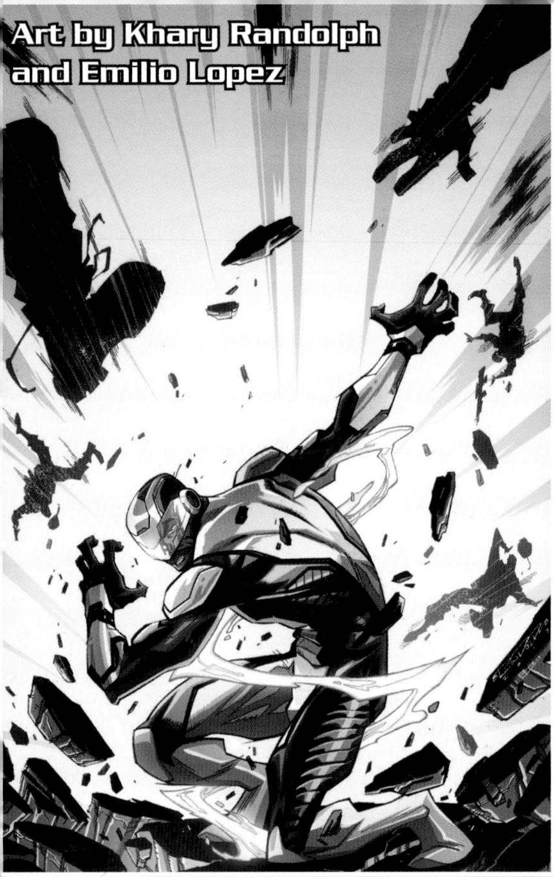
Art by Khary Randolph and Emilio Lopez

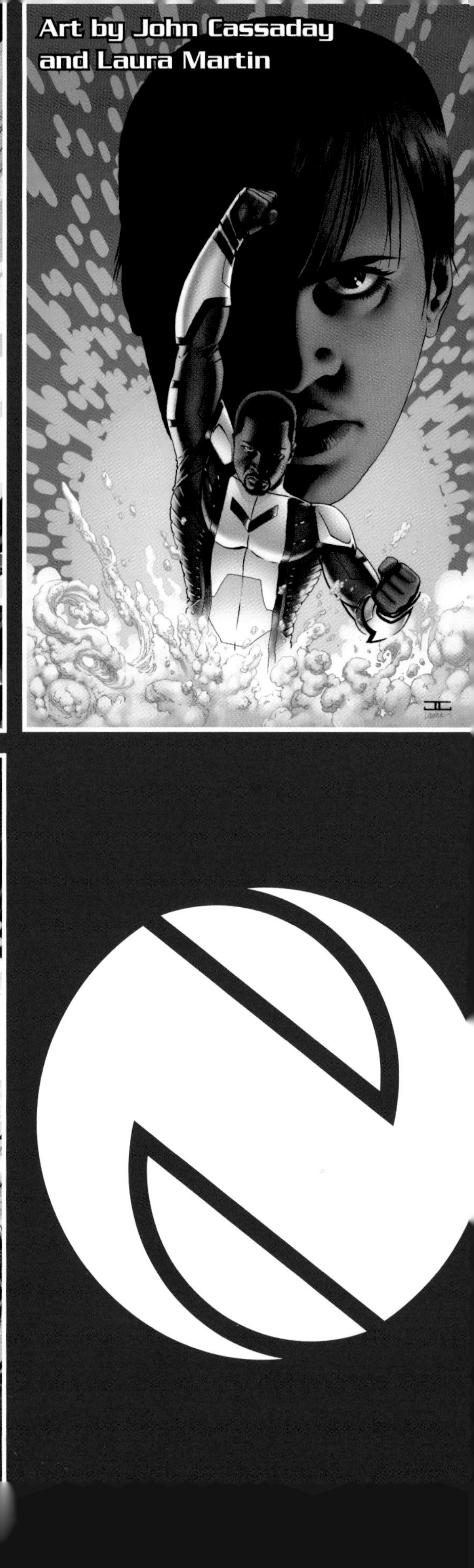
Art by John Cassaday and Laura Martin

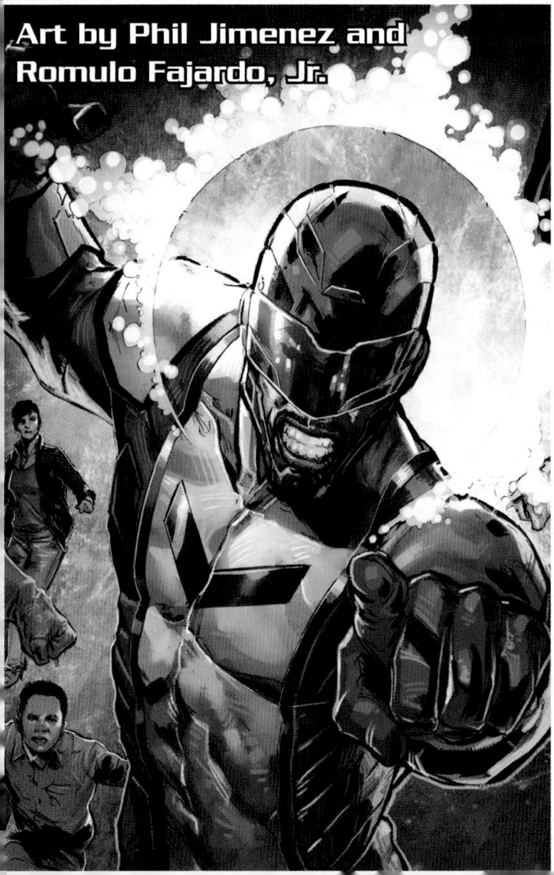
Art by Phil Jimenez and Romulo Fajardo, Jr.

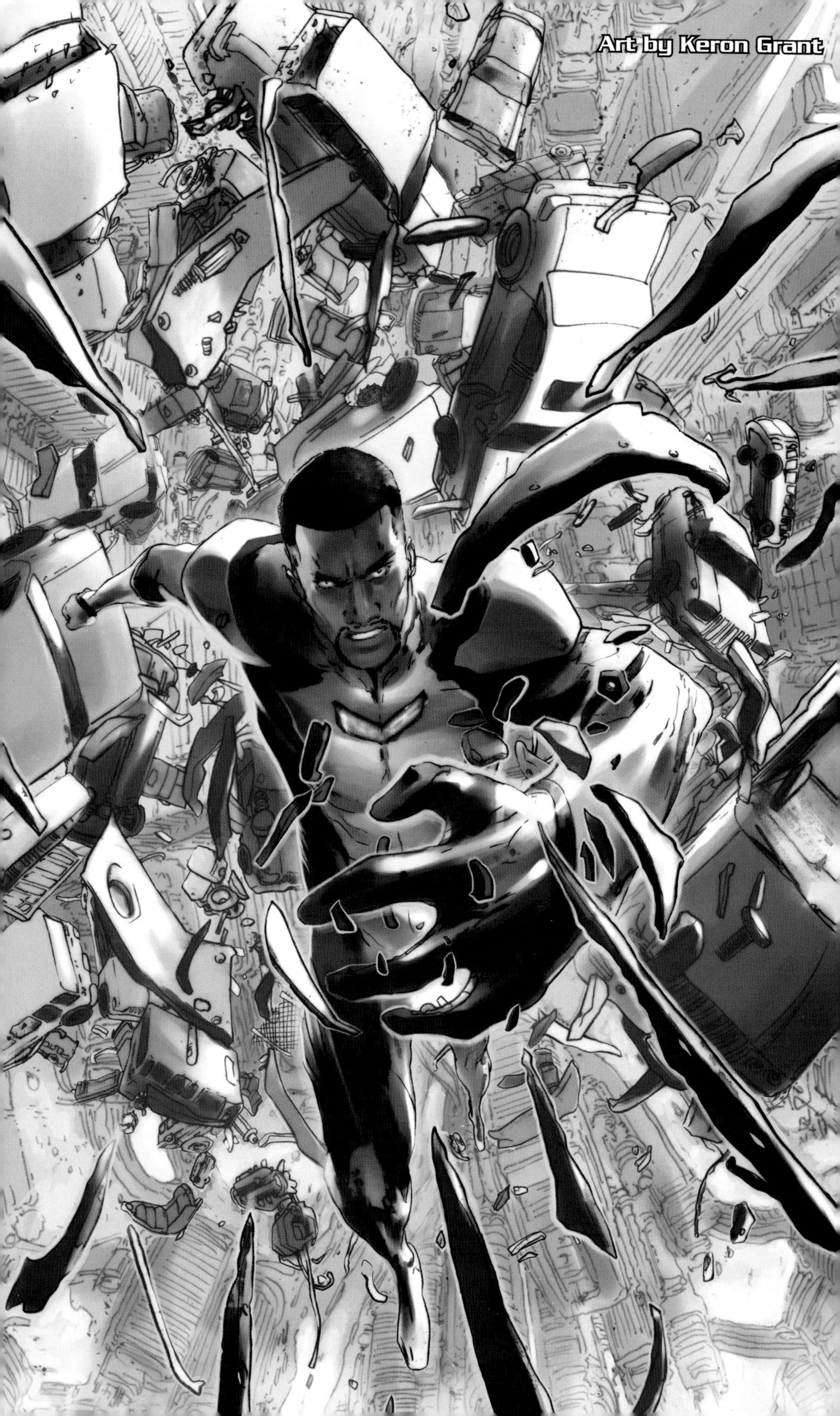
Art by Keron Grant

Art by Patrick Zircher and Paul Mounts

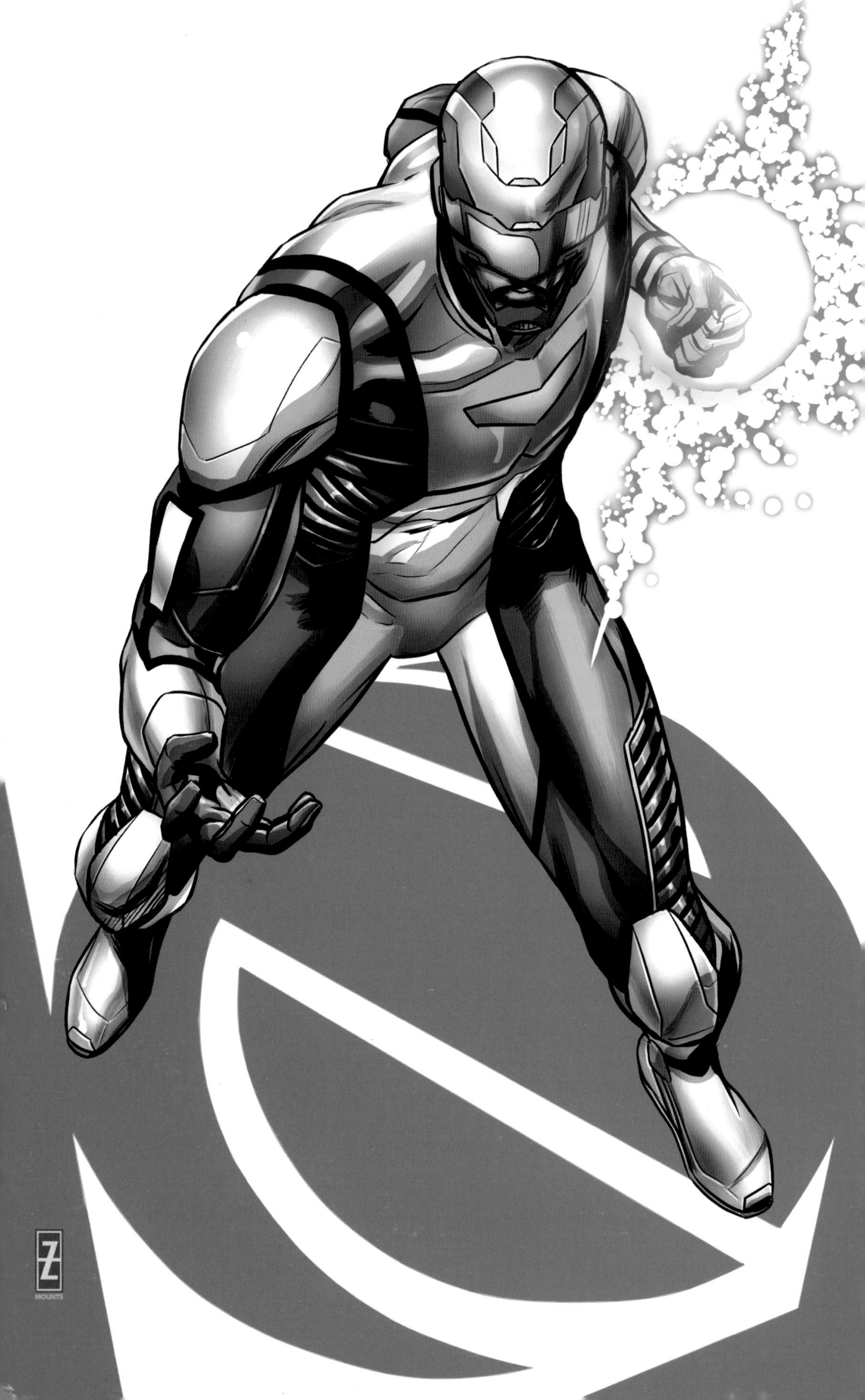